In Search of
the True Political Position
of the 'Ulama

LARS BJØRNEBOE

In Search of the True Political Position of the 'Ulama

An Analysis of the Aims and Perspectives of the Chronicles of Abd al-Rahman al-Jabarti (1753–1825)

AARHUS UNIVERSITY PRESS
THE DANISH INSTITUTE IN DAMASCUS

In Search of the True Political Position of the 'Ulama
© Lars Bjørneboe, The Danish Institute in Damascus
and Aarhus University Press 2007
ISBN 978 87 7934 281 1

Design, typesetting & cover: 2Krogh AS, Århus
Typeface: 10½ / 12½ New Baskerville
Paper: PhoeniXmotion Xantur 115 g
Printed by: Narayana Press, Gylling

Aarhus University Press
Langelandsgade 177
DK-8200 Aarhus N
WWW.UNIPRESS.DK

White Cross Mills,
Hightown, Lancaster, LA1 4XS
United Kingdom
WWW.GAZELLEBOOKS.CO.UK

Box 511
Oakville, CT 06779
USA
WWW.DAVIDBROWNBOOKCO.COM

Published with financial support from
The Danish Institute in Damascus,
C. L. David's Foundation,
C. L. Davids legat for slægt og Venner
and G. E. C. Gads Foundation

To Karin

Contents

ACKNOWLEDGEMENTS

This study on the chronicles of al-Jabarti has been in progress for many years. Many people have been involved, and I would like to express my gratitude for their patience and valuable assistance.

Lektor Søren Mørch and lektor Lars Erslev, Centre for Middle Eastern Studies at the University of Southern Denmark, Odense, and professor Thomas Philipp, University of Erlangen, Germany, have supervised my work within the framework of the Ph.D. programme. I would like to thank them for their patience and generous support and advice throughout my work. By making his translation of the MS Mazhar available to me, Thomas Philipp stepped up the speed of my undertaking enormously!

Mustafa Khaled Mohammad and his wife Grethe Bjorholm-Petersen have generously assisted me in the hard and difficult work of learning the Arabic language and provided me with valuable guidance in translating crucial passages of the chronicles. Lektor Dan E. Sørensen, University of Aarhus, kindly advised and examined me in the intricacies of Arabic grammar.

Lektor Jacob Skovgård-Petersen, who introduced me to the pattern of the medieval and Ottoman cities of Cairo and Damascus, and lektor Jørgen Bæk Simonsen, Carsten Niebuhr Institute, University of Copenhagen, have provided me with valuable support.

I would also like to thank the County of Vejle and especially the directors of education Sv. Aa. Petersen and Søren Kjær for kindly allowing me to take leave of absence from my work as headmaster at Horsens Statsskole and supporting me financially. Lektor Niels Thomsen, deputy headmaster at Horsens Statsskole, lektor Bente Laursen, adjunkt Gitte Barkholt and adjunkt Gert Bergstein cheerfully deputized for me. Gert Bergstein also helped me out with the printing, while his wife adjunkt Helle Bergstein corrected the first proofs.

A special thanks to Dronning Margrethe and Prins Henriks Fond who in 1994 offered me financial support. Not only did it enable me to spend two weeks in the Bibliothèque Nationale in Paris in 1995 in order to collect valuable documentation and information, but this being the first external manifestation of interest in my project, it cheered me up enormously and so really got it going!

I would also like to thank Institutionen San Cataldo for allowing me to spend a month in happy seclusion in November 1994 in order to prepare the project. The County of Vejle, Sven Riskær and C. L. Davids legat for slægt og Venner generously provided me with the necessary financial support to go there and to attend the International Language Institute in Cairo for five weeks in 1996.

The work would never have been accomplished, though, if it had not been for generous grants from the Danish Institute in Damascus and the Danish Ministry of Education, which allowed me to spend six months in Damascus in 1998 and a month in Paris in 2000. This support and the generous help and hospitality provided by Peder Mortensen, the director of the Institute in Damascus, and his wife, Inge Demant Mortensen, enabled me to find the necessary time to get to grips with al-Jabarti in earnest. Ludvig Preetsmann-Aggerholm og Hustrus Stiftelse kindly allowed me to stay in their flat in Rue de la Perle in Paris in February 2000.

In the last phase of the work professor Jane Hathaway, Ohio State University, lektor Jørgen Bæk Simonsen and the chairman of the committee, lektor Knud V. Jensen, Odense, provided me with additional and valuable guidance.

I would like to express my gratitude to the local library in Horsens, whose staff patiently and without a murmur of protest has supported my efforts throughout. As a student I was told that a local library being part of a worldwide network meant they could provide a student with all necessary material anywhere. This has proved to be very true!

Helle Bergstein, Olaf Bayer, Rebecca Spencer and Lucy Michaels helped me to prepare the English text for the dissertation.

Finally I would like to thank The Danish Institute in Damascus, C. L. Davids Fond, G. E. C. Gads Fond and Sven Riskær and C. L. Davids Fond for Slægt og Venner for their decision to publish the text and support it financially. Mary Starkey, Johannesburg, S.A. prepared the final text. Without her care and understanding it would have been nearly imposibble to get this far!

As these acknowledgements suggest, al-Jabarti has over the years become a well-known member of the Bjørneboe household. I would like to thank my wife Agnete Bjørneboe and my children Per, Thor and Karin for kindly letting him into the family, for their willingness to listen to what he had to say and cheerfully put up with the strain and stress this new acquaintance entailed!

Horsens 2006

Acknowledgements

ABBREVIATIONS

BSOAS   Bulletin of the School of Oriental and African Studies
IJMES   International Journal of Middle East Studies
JAH   Journal of Asian History
JESHO   Journal of the Economic and Social History of the Orient
JSAI   Jerusalem Studies in Arabic and Islam
MEJ   Middle East Journal
SI   Studia Islamica

INTRODUCTION

The Egyptian historian 'Abdal-Rahman al-Jabarti (1753–1825) has left several chronicles. Together they form an account of events in Egypt from 1688 to 1821 with the emphasis on the period from 1786 to 1815: the last phase of Ottoman rule; the French occupation from 1798 to 1801; the attempt by the Ottoman government, with British assistance, to restore its authority in Egypt; Muhammad 'Ali's rise to power; and the first ten years of his reign. In other words, al-Jabarti's historical writings cover the crucial final period of Ottoman Egypt.

The present study intends to add some new details to our understanding of developments in Egypt in the years around 1800 by means of an analysis of the opinions, values and outlook expressed in al-Jabarti's chronicles, and the way he expressed them and changed them in his writings.

It assumes that al-Jabarti's chronicles represent views and opinions current – explicitly or implicitly – in Egypt in these years and that it is possible, through an analysis of the textual form and content of the chronicles, to describe these views and opinions as part of a debate among the 'ulama. As al-Jabarti has left several editions of his work, it is possible to trace and describe the changes in these opinions and values and, in this way, to point out controversial areas subject to discussion and debate at the time. As such views and opinions are based on a more general set of values – a world-view or a mental universe, so to speak – the analysis should enable us to reveal how these values were affected. In this way it intends to present a modest empirical contribution to a description of the intellectual development in the Middle East, especially in Egypt around 1800, based on limited but primary sources.

As the title indicates, it is the thesis of this study that the chronicles of al-Jabarti represent a search for the true political position of the 'ulama. In the quickly shifting political environment of Egypt after the French invasion in 1798, the 'ulama – and especially their leading shaykhs – had to decide how to handle the new challenges, and the new possibilities, both intellectually and in practice. The different versions of the chronicles should be seen as a series of attempts to define the true political position of the 'ulama in specific situations, on the basis of different interpretations of past events. Not surprisingly, the main issue seems to have been the relationship between the 'ulama and the ruler. That the 'ulama should act as advisers to the ruler seems never to have been in doubt. The real issue was the degree of formal attachment between the ruler and his 'ulama counsellors. On this question, the author and his patron, the shaykh al-Sadat, seem to have adhered to the ideal of the humble, secluded *'alim*, living by the tenets of his faith and relying on his reputation for the ruler to seek his advice. But it is equally evident that this position met with some – occasionally vehement – opposition among the 'ulama. The chronicles of al-Jabarti indicate that the 'ulama were getting to grips, both intellectually and in practice, with a more specific political position in Egyptian society. But they also suggest that this development came to an end with the rise of Muhammad 'Ali.

The present study has been developed on the basis of an analysis of the chronicles of al-Jabarti alone, but al-Jabarti is not the only Arab-speaking person from these years whose writings have survived. The writings of al-'Attar, al-Khashshab and Nicolas Turc should also be mentioned. Written evidence of the positions of the shaykh of the mosque of al-Azhar in Cairo of this period, al-Sharqawi, and of the Ottoman government also seems to have survived. I have explored these other texts in order to see whether and how they may contribute to this interpretation.

For practical reasons the analysis is confined to the MS Mudda version, and the changes in the way the author presents his material, from the MS Mudda version, over the MS Mazhar to the MS Aja'ib, within the period covered by the MS Mudda , i.e. from June to December 1798. As this part of the text only constitutes a very limited part of the MS Mazhar, and especially of the MS Aja'ib, an analysis within these limits runs the risk of missing important features, essential for our understanding of the purposes of the texts. For this reason the analysis also includes a survey of the general compositional structure and new features of these two versions. Methodologically I have taken a textual approach to al-Jabarti's chronicles in combination with an analysis of his direct or indirect comments on the French and other participants.

It follows that the textual basis will be the works of al-Jabarti in their Arabic editions (Mudda 1975; Mazhar 1969; Aja'ib 1879) and, especially in connection with the surveys of the MS Mazhar and the MS Aja'ib, the English translations. For practical reasons the translations have been the primary tool in the analysis of the MS Mudda and the corresponding parts of the MSS Mazhar and Aja'ib. This, I know, is risky, but I have tried to verify all important points in the Arabic originals and in the case of the MS Mudda in the original manuscript at the University Library in Leiden as well.

I

THE 'ULAMA

1 The Ottoman Empire

The world of the chronicles of al-Jabarti is defined by the city of Cairo and its immediate surroundings: Bulaq, Old Cairo, and the Muqattam Hills. Only on rare occasions does al-Jabarti allow the reader to understand that this world was part of a wider entity, the Ottoman Empire, and that what was thought, said and done in Cairo was influenced and shaped by this framework. But the narrow geographical focus of his chronicles does not imply that their aims and perspectives were unrelated to what happened in the Ottoman Empire. As we shall see, there is reason to believe that they were quite intimately connected with developments in this wider area.

By 1600 the Ottoman Empire was a major world power ruled by the sultan in Istanbul. It encompassed the Balkan peninsula, most of Hungary, present-day Turkey, Cyprus, Greece (but not Crete, which was only conquered in 1669), Syria, Iraq, Lebanon, Palestine, Arabia, Yemen, Egypt, present-day Libya, Tunis and Algeria. Three hundred years later, on the eve of the First World War, some of the outlying provinces, the vassal states on the northern shore of the Black Sea, Hungary, Greece, and the North African provinces – including Egypt – had been lost. The end of the First World War signified the end of the empire itself. Like the Russian, Austrian and German empires it did not survive the vicissitudes of nationalism and world war.

The history of the Ottoman Empire from 1600 to 1918 has been presented as a period of decay. From the beginning of the eighteenth century the empire experienced mounting difficulties when trying to contain the Austrian and Russian attacks on its northern borders. The rapidly developing trade with Europe eroded the wealth of its lands. The ruling classes of the empire were faced with a demand to adapt to or apply European solutions to these problems. In the eighteenth century the military defeats in the Balkans and the growing European economic expansion in the Middle East eroded the foundations of the traditional view of the world, and mounting interest in the military and technical knowledge of the West could be detected. The change in attitude constituted the background of a series of modest reforms during the eighteenth and nineteenth centuries under Sultan Selim III (1789–1807), and especially under Mahmud II (1808–39) and his successors during the Tanzimat era.

In the 1980s, however, it became apparent that the idea of Ottoman decline was based on the writings of dissatisfied Ottoman bureaucrats in the sixteenth and seventeenth centuries. European historians of the Ottoman Empire had adopted the idea of decline in the eighteenth century when a need for some historical background arose among European decision makers in order to handle the so-called Eastern Question and relate to the problems in the area of the Balkans and the Middle East.[1] The uncovering of this connection suggested a new approach to the history of the Ottoman Empire from 1600 to 1918.[2] The Ottoman Empire had started out as a Balkan–Anatolian empire with a predominantly Christian population. The defeat of the Mamluk sultanate in 1517 and the conquest of Syria, Egypt and the Holy Cities turned it into a predominantly Muslim realm with new responsibilities to the heartlands of Sunni Islam and the Arab provinces. From this perspective the late sixteenth, the seventeenth and eighteenth centuries of Ottoman history can be seen not as the dark, oppressive 'pre-modern' prelude to the period of reform in the nineteenth century, but as a period in which the empire began to come to terms with these responsibilities.

In this reorientation of Ottoman history two features have come to the fore: decentralization and the formation of households as a vehicle of power. The search for ways to handle the problems of government brought about a diffusion of power at the centre, at the court of the sultan, while matters that did not affect the entire empire directly would increasingly be left to the local elites. This was supported by an expansion and professionalization of the bureaucracy. Larger corps of functionaries would be making the rounds of the provinces, with all the opportunities that this mobility entailed for forging ties with local elements and for becoming localized themselves. In this process of diffusion of imperial power, the main socio-political vehicle seems to have been the household. This can be defined as a highly fluid and dynamic conglomerate of kinship and clientele ties, covering the empire in a network of personal obligations, horizontally and vertically, socially and geographically, between social groups as well as between centre and the provinces. The household as the germ of a socio-political structure will be present in any society, but in the Ottoman Empire the discrepancy between the theoretical demand for sultan-centred order and the actual absence of such order in the seventeenth and eighteenth centuries led to attempts to replicate the patrimonial role of the sultan. The sultans were incapable of performing their duties as before, and their deputies were unable to hold the empire together on their behalf. The selection, training, rewards and ultimate survival of the sultan's servants and soldiers no longer rested with the sultan in any real sense, and imperial officials now directed their loyalties to intermediaries. In general, loyalties were career-based, but within each area – as scribe, soldier or 'alim – constellations of patron–client relationships animated the basic

The 'Ulama

structure of careers. In the Ottoman Empire households became an effective vehicle of power and influence for a considerable part of three hundred years. They replicated the essential sovereign–servitor relationship, now lacking in the empire. The attempt to fill that void accounted for the mounting strength of intermediary ties and household building in seventeenth- and eighteenth-century Ottoman society outside the political centre, especially among provincial governors and high palace officials.[3]

Seen from this perspective, administrative changes do not necessarily signify collapse and decay, but may be viewed as convenient adaptations. In the early days of the empire there had been more economic manoeuvrability. Foreign campaigns had occupied the military and brought new income to the treasury. Now the sultans had to balance rival interests. They had to purchase peace in the countryside or provinces, or trade the needs of the countryside and provinces for peace in Istanbul, a city dangerously dependent on the well-being of the imperial court and its garrisons.[4] Changes in the agricultural administration of the empire reflect this development. The *timar* system of land tenure, whereby provincial administrators received an assignment of usufruct from the proceeds of which they would equip cavalry troops, had been developed in the central Anatolian and European provinces of the Ottoman Empire, but was not introduced in many of the Arab provinces. The governors of Egypt, Iraq and North Africa remitted an annual tribute derived from taxes. By at least the seventeenth century tax-farming had taken root throughout the empire. Ottoman officials and local grandees distributed tax-farms (*iltizam*) purchased at auction among their clients in an extensive patronage network. The introduction of the life-tenure tax-farm, or *malikane*, at the end of the seventeenth century allowed provincial elites to forge heritable estates and so contributed to the entrenchment of those elites.

Seen from Istanbul the merits of decentralization would be measured by the degree to which it enabled the central government to fulfil its basic functions: the defence and/or expansion of the empire; and the protection of the faith, including the upkeep of the Holy Cities and the annual Pilgrimage. Decentralization meant that the practical realization of these aims should be left to the local elites. Only when they proved too weak or became too independent to maintain the basic interest of the empire in the various provinces did the Ottoman state interfere.[5] Reform or attempts at reform would concentrate on reining in powerful elites, curbing corruption in the allocation of revenues and ensuring efficient tax collection for these purposes. The attempts on the part of Selim III and Mahmud II to introduce European military organization and technology were part of this trend.[6]

The relations of the Ottoman government in Istanbul with Egypt may illustrate the central government's basic strategic and spiritual interests in this area and the way these responsibilities were handled in the decentralized Ottoman state. In 1517 Sultan Selim I (1512–20) eliminated the weaker of his two remaining rivals for the supremacy in the western part of the Muslim world, the Mamluk sultanate, and prevented the other, the Safavid Empire of Iran, from taking possession of the rich financial and military resources of Egypt. At the same time he appropriated the religious prestige connected to the protection of the Holy Cities, the Pilgrimage and the religious institutions of Cairo, including the shadow-caliphate, which the Mamluk sultans had maintained. From 1517 the Ottoman state was concerned to prevent any other power, local (Egyptian) or foreign (the Safavids of Iran; the Portugese; the French; the British), from having at its disposal the vast resources, the spiritual prestige and the commanding strategic position of Egypt vis-à-vis Syria and the Ottoman heartland of Anatolia to the north and the Red Sea to the south. The Ottoman state took pains to put at least some of these resources at the disposal of the central government in the form of a yearly tribute, contingents of soldiers for campaigns in other theatres and the prestige of being protector of the Pilgrimage and the Holy Cities.

At the end of the seventeenth century the threat from rival powers to the Ottoman province of Egypt had disappeared with the dwindling imperial might of the Safavids, Venetians and Portuguese. Egypt ceased to be the staging area for military engagements in the Red Sea and the eastern Mediterranean. Demobilization of forces on the European front in the wake of the peace of Karlowitz in 1699 reduced the role of Egyptian soldiers in European campaigns. Thenceforward, Egypt's importance to the Ottoman Empire would mainly hinge on the province's ability to deliver revenue and grains, and to provide for the Holy Cities.

As the process of decentralization progressed, the central government would leave the practical organization and execution of these tasks to the local elites and rely on the manipulation of the local balance of power among the web of patron–client ties to maintain its interests.[7] As long as a reasonable amount of grain and tribute reached its destination in Istanbul or elsewhere and the Pilgrimage caravan arrived safely back in Cairo, the central government would have no reason to interfere directly. Correspondingly, the appointment of Ottoman governors of Egypt shifted from veteran soldiers to bureaucrats and palace favourites.[8]

The 'Ulama

After a period of peace and relative prosperity in the middle years of the eighteenth century, the Ottoman government experienced new problems from the 1760s. The preceding years had seen wise policies concerning the economy, international peace and provincial discipline. But in the three wars with Russia in 1768–74, 1787–92 and 1809–12 decentralization proved to be a double-edged sword. Local grandees (*a'yan*), from the ranks of the tax-farming elite, turned into provincial warlords and attacked the Ottomans from within. Whole provinces defected or tried to defect until peace was restored.[9] In Egypt 'AliBey al-Kabir openly defied the central government – not only by discontinuing the tribute, but by minting coins with his own name, replacing the name of the sultan at the *khutba* with his own, and negotiating with the Russians, the enemy of the empire.[10]

But decentralization did not mean a helpless central government. The *a'yan* themselves were vulnerable. The patron–client relationships of their households, which were often precarious alliances in the first place, could be manipulated or broken. In the case of Egypt the Ottoman government countered the rebellious acts of 'AliBey by supporting a rebellion by his most trusted retainer, Muhammad Abu 'l-Dhahab, and had 'AliBey killed (1773). Muhammad Abu 'l-Dhahab for his part took care to acknowledge the sultan as his formal sovereign, but died suddenly in suspicious circumstances in the middle of a campaign in Syria (1774). In times of peace even more drastic measures might be employed. When Muhammad's two retainers, Ibrahim Bey and Murad Bey, who succeeded him as the leading emirs in Egypt, tried to appropriate the tribute for themselves, the central government in 1786 mounted a full-fledged military expedition to restore the flow of revenue. Hasan Pasha was dispatched with a fleet and an army that succeeded in occupying Lower Egypt and Cairo. But war broke out with Russia in 1787 and Hasan Pasha had to be recalled. The leaders of the rival households which he had brought to power to protect the interests of Istanbul were swept away by the plague. In 1791 Ibrahim and Murad returned to power.

International developments in the late eighteenth century placed the central government and the system of decentralization under such heavy pressure that it nearly broke the dynasty of Osman itself, or, as Bruce MacGowan has put it: 'having taken the first draught of *a'yan* assistance in the war of 1768–74, the Porte took a near fatal dose in 1788–92'.[11] Sultan Selim III had supported an attempt to create a new-style army and navy, but did not have a firm commitment to reform and the ability to crush the resistance of the

Janissary corps. In the complicated diplomatic and military manoeuvrings following the French invasion of Egypt in 1798 he proved unable to control the local elites and warlords. Arabia and the Holy Cities were lost to the Wahhabis, a religious sect led by the Saudi family of the Nejd. Egypt fell into the lap of a talented Albanian mercenary, Muhammad 'Ali, in 1805. In 1806, as the war in Europe entered the process leading up to reversal of coalitions culminating in the treaty of Tilsit in 1807, the army in Edirne rebelled against the central government. A combination of Janissaries, high 'ulama and opponents of reform deposed the sultan in May 1807. In a counter-coup by a coalition of reformers and warlords from Rumelia in July 1808 the imprisoned Selim and his successor Mustafa IV were murdered. The successor, the young Mahmud II, proved a more capable politician. He survived the coup in November 1808 which brought back the conservative coalition of Janissaries and 'ulama with the support of the Bulgarian clients of the warlord in power. Seriously weakened, the new government in Istanbul fell back on a policy of cooperation and manipulation. In the case of Egypt the government still held the power to legitimize the rule of Muhammad 'Ali as governor, and for this a price could be asked in the form of tribute and/or military support. Muhammad 'Ali took care to acknowledge his sovereign and consented to participate in his wars against the Wahhabis in Arabia (1811–19) and the rebels in Greece from 1822. From the point of view of the government such assistance could not go wrong: if victorious, it held out the hope of restoring its prestige; and if defeated, it would weaken or, even better, break the power of the assisting warlord.[12]

From this short summary of relations between the Ottoman central government and its Egyptian province it becomes apparent that even though the Ottoman Empire had long since become a participant in the European concert of powers and its shifting international alignments, this alone does not explain the pattern of Ottoman history. As might be expected in a state the size of the Ottoman Empire, the network of and balance between patron–client relationships in the decentralized state constitute a major key to Ottoman politics. But such networks are not easily identified, verified and described.

The family of the leader was central to the household. The more intimate group of officials, servants, officers and soldiers often entered into a more formalized relationship with their master.[13] But clientele ties would often be loose, dynamic and fluid, and for this reason difficult to define. They would encompass not only the powerful members of the ruling elite in Istanbul or provincial *a'yan* but also the weak and humble citizen, be he an *'alim*, a merchant or a village shaykh, in stronger or weaker connections, from family ties to short-lived alliances.[14] They would connect men from different parts of the empire in a criss-cross web ranging from Istanbul to Cairo to Bulgaria and Erzurum. But even if such ties are hard to document and only rarely visible, they should still be kept in mind as possible explanations of the actions of men and of the aims and perspectives of their writings.

These developments in the empire apparently did not involve major changes in established political theory. By the fourteenth century political thinking in the Muslim world was centred around security and the ability of the ruler to maintain law and order, rather than on justice and piety. An unjust ruler was better than none, because thanks to him 'highways are kept secure, canonical penalties are applied, holy war is fought against the enemy, and spoils are collected' (Ibn Taymiyyah, d. 1328). This position became the ruling political doctrine among the majority of Muslims of all sects until the nineteenth century. It was based on a belief in the unquestionable duty of Muslims to obey their rulers, and the inherent sinfulness of any rebellion against the established order.[15] This was still the generally accepted position in the eighteenth century, at the time of the scholar Sayyid Murtada al-Zabidi (1732–91), the master and friend of al-Jabarti. To Zabidi, al-Ghazali's position that authority follows power was still valid.[16]

It should be noted, however, that in the same centuries a body of literature, of Persian and Arab origin, counselling kings on the execution of their duties, was produced. This presents a theory of government clearly influenced by other, un-Islamic, traditions. The emphasis is on justice as a precondition of political power, on the dire consequences of injustice, and on service to the cause of religion and welfare of the people as the only legitimizing aspect of acts of despotism on the part of the ruler.[17] It should also be kept in mind that the theory of submission included a strong obligation on the part of the ruler to take advice from the community, from the 'ulama, the leaders of opinion and those qualified to give an opinion of value on the matters in hand.[18] In the Ottoman period this took the form of diwans, consultative bodies attached to the central government of the sultan and to the offices of the provincial governors, consisting of the chief officials and military commanders, the leaders of the local notables (a'yan), 'ulama, merchants, guilds and sufi orders.[19]

In Ottoman society there was a place for everyone, and it was one of the sultan and his grand vizier's fundamental functions to keep everyone in his place and to maintain the equilibrium among the classes of society. The shared beliefs of the members of the ruling elite in the late seventeenth-century Ottoman Empire as set down in the advisory and morality literature of the age stressed the importance of order. Social mobility continued to be of value, but only in narrow streams, closely watched by those into whose ranks the new men would flow. Those who overstepped the limits of their position destroyed this order.[20]

The use of the title of caliph in the Ottoman Empire in the late eighteenth century has been interpreted as a sign of change in this idea of sultan-centred order. At this time the claim was made that the Ottoman sultan was the caliph in the sense in which the successors of the Prophet Muhammad had been caliphs.[21] In 1774 in connection with the treaty of Küçük Kaynarca the Ottoman sultan assumed the title of caliph, with spiritual powers over all Muslims, as a counter to the Russian right to guide and protect the Orthodox Christian subjects of the Ottoman Empire. But this did not signify a return to traditional Islamic political thinking on the part of the central government in Istanbul. Traditionally the 'ulama had denied the caliph any spiritual function. He was supposed to implement the *shari'a* as developed and interpreted by the 'ulama. It should be kept in mind, however, that the idea of the sultan as caliph could strengthen Muslim unity in the face of Western expansionism by creating a new focus of loyalty for the Muslims both inside and outside the boundaries of the Ottoman Empire.[22] Seen in this context, the revival of the title of caliph and its implications of authority in the Muslim world in general and the learned class, the 'ulama in particular, on the part of the Ottoman government in the late eighteenth century may be interpreted as part of a conscious reformulation of Islamic political thinking in the face of the problems of authority affecting the central government in this period.[23]

[1] Douglas A. Howard, 'Ottoman Historiography and the Literature of "Decline" of the Sixteenth and Seventeenth Centuries', *JAH* 22 (1988).

[2] Jane Hathaway, 'Problems of Periodization in Ottoman History: The Fifteenth through Eighteenth Centuries', *Turkish Studies Association Bulletin* 20, 2 (1996), p. 27.

[3] Madeline C. Zilfi, *The Politics of Piety. The Ottoman 'Ulema in the Post-Classical Age*, Minneapolis 1988, p. 201; G. Pieterberg, 'The Formation of an Ottoman Egyptian Elite in the Eighteenth Century', *IJMES* 22 (1990).

[4] Hathaway, 'Problems in the Periodization'; Zilfi, *The Politics of Piety*, p. 87; S. Faroqhi, B. McGowan and D. Quartaert, *An Economic and Social History of the Ottoman Empire*, vol. II, Cambridge 1994, pp. 639ff.

[5] In Egypt such efforts were made in 1660, 1670, 1675, 1761, 1767 and

1786. See S. Shaw, *Ottoman Egypt in the Eighteenth Century*, Cambridge, MA 1962, p. 5.

[6] Hathaway, 'Problems in the Periodization', p. 31.

[7] J. Hathaway, *The Politics of Households in Ottoman Egypt: The Rise of the Qazdağlis*, Cambridge 1997, p. 166.

[8] Ibid., p. 7.

[9] Faroqhi et al., *An Economic and Social History of the Ottoman Empire*, vol. II, pp. 643–5.

[10] D. Crecelius, 'Russia's Relations with the Mamluk Beys of Egypt in the late Eighteenth Century', in Farhad Kazemi (ed.), *A Way Prepared, Essays in Honour of Bayley Winder*, New York 1988, pp. 56–67.

[11] Faroqhi et al., *An Economic and Social History of the Ottoman Empire*, p. 663.

[12] Ibid., p. 645; S. Shaw, *Between Old and New, the Ottoman Empire under Sultan Selim III*, 1789–1807, Cambridge, MA 1971, pp. 367ff.; S. Shaw and Ezel Kural Shaw, *History of the Ottoman Empire and Modern Turkey*, vol. II: *Reform, Revolution and Republic*, 1808–1975, Cambridge 1977, pp. 1ff.

[13] In the case of soldiers, of slave (*mamluk*) or freeborn descent, the term *tabi'* (follower) seems to designate the member of a household. See Hathaway, *The Politics of Households*, p. 23.

[14] Hathaway sees the household in Ottoman Egypt as a feature of the Ottoman Empire as a whole and not as a simple continuation of similar institutions of the Mamluk Empire. See ibid., p. 18. This position has been questioned. See Fay, in *MEJ* 52 (1998), p. 282; Pierce, in *American History Review* 104 (1999), pp. 286–7; Behrens-Abouseif, in *BSOAS* (1988), pp. 342–3. Hathaway has restated her position, in '"Mamluk Households" and "Mamluk Factions" in Ottoman Egypt: A Reconsideration', in T. Philipp and U. Haarmann (eds.), *The Mamluks in Egyptian Politics and Society*, Cambridge 1998, p. 116: 'The military society that had evolved in Ottoman Egypt by the seventeenth century was a provincial variation of a household based elite culture that spanned the entire empire. The political culture that this society cultivated was richly evocative, drawing on a number of traditions – Ottoman, Mamluk, Arab and others.' But, as Behrens-Abouseif points out, it is important to keep in mind that 'Ali Bey al-Kabir is reported by al-Jabarti to have identified himself and his companions with the Mamluks of the past. It is not a question of whether this parallel is justified or not, but that it did exist in the *Zeitgeist* of eighteenth-century Egypt.

[15] Hamid Enayat, *Modern Islamic Political Thought*, Austin 1982, p. 12. Shahrough Akhavi notes that in spite of the fact that in Islam religion and state are merged in a theoretical sense, practically speaking the overweening power of the governmental authority was, from the time of Umayyad period, the constantly operating factor which resulted in centralization, absolutism and autocratic behaviour: S. Akhavi, *Religion and Politics in Con-*

temporary Iran: Clergy–State Relations in the Pahlavi Period, Albany, NY 1980, p. 5.

[16] Albert Hourani, *Arab Thought in the Liberal Age*, Cambridge 1983, p. 27.

[17] Enayat, *Modern Islamic Political Thought*, p. 13.

[18] Hourani, *Arab Thought*, p. 20.

[19] Ibid., p. 31; S. Shaw, *The Financial and Administrative Organization and Development of Ottoman Egypt*, Princeton 1962, p. 2; Shaw, *Ottoman Egypt in the Eighteenth Century*, p. 4; Doris Behrens-Abouseif, *Egypt's Adjustment to Ottoman Rule: Institutions, Waqf, and Architecture in Cairo (Sixteenth and Seventeenth Centuries)*, Leiden 1994, p. 60.

[20] Norman Itzkowitz, 'Men and Ideas in the Eighteenth-Century Ottoman Empire', in Thomas Naff and Roger Owen (eds.), *Studies in Eighteenth Century Islamic History*, Carbondale and Edwardsville, IL 1977, pp. 23ff.; Zilfi, *The Politics of Piety*, p. 197.

[21] Hourani, *Arabic Thought*, p. 27.

[22] Enayat, *Modern Islamic Political Thought*, p. 52; Thomas W. Arnold, *The Caliphate*, Oxford 1965, p. 165ff.; H.A.R. Gibb (ed.), *Whither Islam?*, London 1932, p. 36. Gibb suggests (p. 38) that the story that the last shadowy representative of the ancient caliphate had transferred his rights to the Ottoman sultan in 1517, in connection with the Ottoman conquest of the Mamluk sultanate, was put into circulation about the same time.

[23] Norman Itzkowitz, on the other hand, suggests ('Men and Ideas') that the intent, spirit and vocabulary of the agreement between the sultan and the *a'yan* in 1808 signifies a departure from the Islamic traditions of government and society. To him, the need for equilibrium and the notion of justice was gone. The agreement of 1808 was an arrangement between the notables and the weak central government, couched in the language used and understood by men of action. But Shaw (*History of the Ottoman Empire and Modern Turkey*, vol. II, p. 3) finds that this document had only a limited effect and significance, and considering the circumstances (it was not signed by the sultan and a majority of the *a'yan*) it seems doubtful whether the vocabulary can be used as evidence of political thought.

The 'Ulama

2 Ottoman Egypt in the eighteenth century

Although Cairo was the centre of al-Jabarti's attention, he was well aware that his beloved city was an integral part of the Ottoman province of Egypt. The Ottoman period in Egypt is often presented as the sad and unproductive gap between the glories of the Mamluk sultanate and the reign of Muhammad 'Ali. This tendency has been compounded by the fact that what might be termed the Ottoman period proper from 1517 to 1805 is framed by two defeats. In 1517 the Ottoman conquest did away with the splendour of the Mamluk sultanate and transformed it into an Ottoman province. The French invasion in 1798 and the political chaos in the wake of their subsequent evacuation in 1801 are usually presented as the absolute nadir of Egyptian fortunes, only relieved by the fact that it prepared the way for Muhammad 'Ali's spectacular reforms, military adventures and de facto independence. In keeping with this the Ottoman period has been looked upon as a period of overall decline.

Recent studies suggest a different picture. Economically the first century of Ottoman rule in Egypt witnessed a recovery from the epidemics and turmoil of the late Mamluk sultanate. Commerce and agriculture expanded. This economic expansion appears to have petered out before the beginning of the eighteenth century, but from 1730 to 1770 Egypt again witnessed a period of prosperity. Only towards the end of the eighteenth century, especially from 1777 to 1812, did both the urban and rural economics experience a serious setback in economic activity through a combination of political turmoil, natural disasters and adverse movements in international trade.[1] France had been Egypt's main foreign trading partner throughout the eighteenth century. The re-export of Mocha coffee via Egypt completely dominated the trade until the 1740s, when the French began to draw upon the Antilles as a new source. But coffee still accounted for two-thirds of Egypt's imports from the Red Sea in the late eighteenth century, mostly re-exported to other Ottoman provinces or abroad. French exports into Egypt between the 1740s and 1780s increased seven-fold; only in 1783 did trade barriers to imports in France tilt the balance against Egypt. In addition to the inter-regional and European trade, the old pattern of imports – spices from South Asia and slaves, gold and ivory from East Africa – still persisted.[2] The population of Egypt increased until the natural disasters and political turmoil of the late eighteenth century began to reverse the trend. Although Cairo was reduced from an imperial capital to a provincial capital in 1517 it grew from 150,000 inhabitants at the time of the Ottoman conquest to 250,000 in 1800. Upper Egypt became better integrated into the provincial economy as grain from more and more southern villages was commandeered for the growing number of imperial pious foundations supporting the Holy Cities.

After the Ottoman conquest Egypt was gradually integrated into the empire. The Ottomans removed many Egyptian artisans and 'ulama to Istanbul, while large numbers of Ottoman troops and officials were left to garrison and administer the province. Later, as Egypt's role within the empire began to change in the seventeenth century, eunuchs of the imperial harem were often exiled to Egypt, where they amassed wealth and attracted large followings. In the second half of the eighteenth century Syrian Christians were installed as the leading minority in finance, and increasingly brokered Egypt's exports to Europe. Socially, this integration was especially pronounced between Ottoman officials and soldiers garrisoned in Egypt, and Egyptians. The soldiers sought entry into the crafts as a means of supplementing their unreliable government pay. As for the Egyptians, it was not only possible but desirable to have themselves placed on the rolls of one of the regiments. In this way, the Egyptian became, as it were, an honorary soldier and drew his regiment's monthly payment while enjoying the military's tax-exempt status. By the eighteenth century, some 14,000 residents of Cairo, or between 5 and 6 per cent of the city's population, were inscribed on the rolls of the Ottoman regiments. Only a fraction of these would be actual combatants.[3]

From the time of Süleyman I (1520–66) a *vali* or pasha governed the Ottoman province of Egypt. From the seventeenth century the government in Istanbul appointed him annually. He held the rank of either *beylerbey* or vizier. A council, a diwan, assisted him where the governors of sub-provinces, beys, the heads (*agha*) of the regiments (*ojak*s), the bureaucrats, the chief judge (*qadi 'askar*) and the religious dignitaries were represented. In addition to paying tribute to the capital (in cash and kind), the pasha was responsible for maintaining the Holy Cities, for the military and administrative expenses and for pensions paid to 'ulama, widows and orphans. He also had the right to deal in diplomatic matters with the consuls of European countries in Egypt. In the eighteenth century a governor's term of office was usually one year.[4]

The institutions of Ottoman rule in Egypt seem to have been neither a continuation of the late Mamluk system nor a new imposition of the classical Ottoman system. They came to represent a new

The 'Ulama

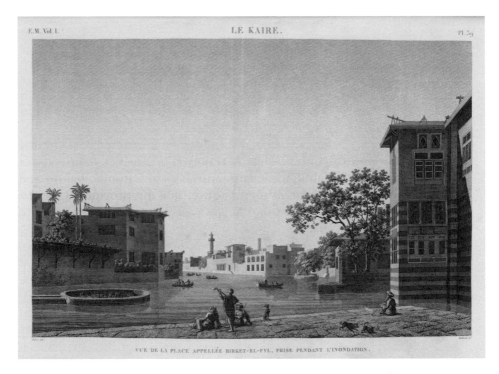

VUE DE LA PLACE APPELLÉE BIRKET-EL-FYL, PRISE PENDANT L'INONDATION.

View of the Birkat al-Fīl during the inundation of the Nile (Description de l'Egypte, Etat Moderne, vol. I, pl. 39). In 1798 the Nile at Cairo was still subject to annual inundations. In the low-lying areas west of the city the floods turned places like Birkat al-Fīl and al-Azbakkiyya into lakes on which pleasure boats and transports could float. On the banks of these lakes the rich and the powerful built their spacious houses and gardens. Some of these gardens were open to the general public. Photo: The Royal Library, Copenhagen.

administrative strategy that attempted to accommodate both Ottoman soldiers and former *mamluk*s. The governors of the thirteen sub-provinces were expected to hold the rank of *sancak beyi*, and there seems to have been some expectation that regimental commanders (*agha*s) would be promoted to this rank. But by the latter half of the sixteenth century a new group of beys had emerged, apart from the military. The gap between beys and officers engendered intense struggles over influence and revenues between the two groups. These conflicts were compounded by the prevalence of the *iltizam* (tax-farm), which gave beys and soldiers two objects of competition: the grant of tax-farms and the imperial favour that allowed one to hold them undisturbed. The *iltizam*s themselves grew more desirable at the end of the seventeenth century, when the Ottoman Empire adopted life-tenure hereditary tax-farms, known as *malikane.*

In the first half of the eighteenth century the beys came to dominate the institutions of Ottoman Egypt through the evolution of the Qazdagli household from a military household to a beylical one under Ibrahim Kahya (d. 1754). Important positions, such as those of beys and their leader, the *shaykh al-balad*, and other key of-fices – such as that of the governor of the sub-province of Jirja in Upper Egypt, the *vali* of Cairo who was responsible for policing the city together with the Janissary *agha*, and especially the important (and profitable!) post of commander of the Pilgrimage (*amir al-hajj*) – tended to be occupied by members of this household. At the same time the ruling elite in Ottoman Egypt, formerly a mixed society whose households combined freeborn Muslims with predominantly Anatolian antecedents and *mamluk*s of various origins, became a body dominated by Georgian *mamluk*s and other Caucasians.

Except for a short period after 1786 the Qazdagli household came to dominate the local political scene in Ottoman Egypt until the French invasion in 1798. 'Ali Bey al-Kabir (d. 1773), already mentioned above, one of the Georgian *mamluk*s of Ibrahim Kahya, continued his master's policies of household building and domina-tion of political and economic life by keeping a large retinue of mer-cenaries, attempting to monopolize significant areas of economic life to pay them (especially the sub-provincial tax-farms, the urban tax-farms of Cairo and the customs of Bulaq and the Mediterranean ports) and to guarantee internal security favourable to trade. In ad-dition he launched a programme of territorial expansion into Upper Egypt, the Hijaz and Syria, when the war of 1768–74 provided an opportunity. At his death his most trusted retainer, Muhammad Abu 'l-Dhahab, took over. At the death of Muhammad in 1774 the leader-ship was split between two of his retainers, Ibrahim Bey and Murad Bey, who, although unable to control the province to the degree ac-complished by 'Ali and Muhammad, nevertheless dominated politi-cal life in Ottoman Egypt until the arrival of the French in 1798.[5]

No household (*bayt*) could survive or attain elite status with-out a relatively stable source of revenue as the basis for further ex-pansion and influence. Such revenue could derive from tax-collect-ing rights in both city and countryside, from property rentals, from investment in trade or a combination of all these. In pre-Ottoman times successive Egyptian rulers had administered urban and rural revenues, especially the land tax (*kharaj*), in three ways: by appoint-ing officials under central state supervision to collect them; con-tracting them to tax-farmers; or assigning them directly to the military. Systems of tax-farming and military assignment often resulted in officials and/or soldiers taking up an intermediary position between the central government or its local representatives and the producers. In the history of Egypt, as elsewhere, such intermediary groups arose periodically, enlarging their share of revenues at the expense of the central treasury.

An important vehicle for this, used equally by the central government and individuals, was the *waqf* (pl. *awqaf*), an endowment of property in support of some charitable or pious activity (the upkeep of mosques, fountains, schools, colleges or the Holy Cities). The endowment was permanent, and the property exempt from taxation. Before the late Fatimid period most Egyptian *awqaf* consisted of urban land and buildings. After this time significant amounts of rural land were converted into *awqaf*. The income of a pious foundation could also be assigned to the heirs of its maker and transferred to a designated charitable or pious activity only upon the extinction of the family line. This could be a useful legal device for protecting a family's property.[6]

Egypt's new Ottoman masters re-established central control of the agrarian administration and expanded the area of state-owned land. A new cadastral survey was completed in 1609. After a brief period in which taxes were collected directly by treasury agents, the Ottomans revived the practice of tax-farming. A tax-farm (*iltizam*) was sold at a public auction. A tax-farmer (*multazim*) was responsible not only for delivering the tax assessed on his village, but also for seeing to the maintenance of local irrigation works. He was expected to advance seed or livestock for cultivation if his villagers needed it. In addition to the basic tax due to the treasury, the tax-farmer was permitted to collect an additional amount as his profit. He usually resided in the town, while agents performed the actual collection of revenue in the countryside. The treasury soon lost control of the relation of the price of a tax-farm to productivity, and simply accepted the highest bid. The establishment of life tenure of tax-farms (*malikane*) and inheritance of *iltizam*s at the end of the seventeenth century allowed the children of *multazim*s to inherit their holdings for a payment equal to only three-eighths of the normal purchase price.[7] Official sanction for the inheritance of *iltizam*s favoured the transformation of their holders into a semi-hereditary rentier stratum as well as the fragmentation of *iltizam*s into smaller and smaller holdings. These changes reflected the transformation of the *iltizam*s from what was originally a state office into a form of pseudo-property.[8]

The shift in the composition and strategy of the military elite of the province by the mid-eighteenth century seems to have coincided with other important changes. As the leading military households in the first half of the century coalesced with the beylicate and combined their urban tax-farms and trading enterprise with the sub-provincial tax-farms the market of rural tax-farms was opened up to a composite class of land-owners in which women, 'ulama and wealthy merchants played a significant part. To the military elite these groups would represent valuable additional assets. The aims and political weight of households would depend on the ambition of its founder and the resources he was able to lay his hands on or muster through alliances or intermarriage with other, lesser or bigger, households. They would include a variety of people – family, *mamluk* retainers, soldiers and artisans – as well as ties with 'ulama and merchants. In the highly competitive and dynamic process of household building household leaders would constantly be on the watch for profitable connections, and not only among rivals in Egypt's military society and in the Ottoman state apparatus.

1 K. Cuno, *The Pasha's Peasants: Land, Society, and Economy in Lower Egypt,* 1740–1858, Cambridge 1992, p. 27; André Raymond, *Le Caire de Janissaries: l'apogée de la ville ottomane sous 'Abd al-Rahman Katkuda*, Paris 1995, p. 66.

2 Faroqhi et al., *Economic and Social History*, vol. II, p. 731.

3 Hathaway, *The Politics of Households*, pp. 7–14; Faroqhi et al., *Economic and Social History*, vol. II, p. 732.

4 Behrens-Abouseif, *Egypt's Adjustment*, pp. 49ff.

5 Hathaway, *The Politics of Households*, pp. 27, 50, 173; Faroqhi et al., *Economic and Social History*, vol. II, pp. 675–6; Raymond, *Le Caire des Janissaries*, pp. 17ff.; Pieterberg, 'Formation' p. 275-89.

6 Cuno, *The Pasha's Peasants*, p. 19.

7 Ibid., pp. 26ff.

8 Ibid., p. 33; Faroqhi et al., *Economic and Social History*, vol. II, p. 675.

3   The 'ulama

By birth and training al-Jabarti was an *'alim* (pl. *'ulama*), a Muslim
scribe. In Sunnism – and in the Ottoman Empire the majority of
the believers were Sunnis – the 'ulama were regarded as the guardians, transmitters and interpreters of religious knowledge, of Islamic
doctrine and law. The term also embraces those who fulfil religious
functions in the community that require a certain level of expertise
in religious and judicial issues, such as judges and preachers, the im-
ams of mosques etc., if they had received the required education and
training. Although the 'ulama were progressively constituted as such
by the study of *fiqh* (jurisprudence, i.e. the science which deals with
the observance of rituals, the principles of the Five Pillars and social
legislation), their essential characteristic was the knowledge of *hadith* (traditions relating to the deeds and utterances of the Prophet
as recounted by his Companions). Over the centuries the 'ulama
evolved as a distinct group of educated religious leaders. The practice of wandering in search of knowledge facilitated contacts among
students of the diverse regions of the Muslim world and contributed
to a consciousness of identity among scholars and to the standardiza-
tion of knowledge and of its transmission. Numerous major scholars
were also engaged in the composition of poetry, or produced works
of *adab*. In addition, universal and local histories, on classes or generations of scholars – vital aids to the study of tradition – were often
written by 'ulama.

Socially, the 'ulama occupied a middle position between the
ruling elite and its subjects. They had firm roots among the common
people, by descent and through their position as leaders in the sufi
orders. For this reason there was a tendency by the people to look to
them – and for the 'ulama to look upon themselves – as the people's
spokesmen and agents in relation to the rulers, especially if these
were of foreign descent. On the other hand, their social position
and relations with the rulers often gave them the status of a wealthy,
privileged elite. This duality in their position often caused a division
along class lines within the 'ulama itself.

A ruler's policy towards the religious leaders was largely determined by his own interests and objectives. In theory, church and
state in Islam were one. In practice, the two spheres of politics and
the religious establishment each had their own functions and areas
of competence, but since they needed each other, they formed an
uneasy partnership, with the politicians holding the upper hand, to
preside over Islamic society. Vulnerable regimes invariably protected

their flanks by conciliating the religious leaders in order to secure the necessary legitimacy. The 'ulama also interacted with subsidiary movements. The weaker these movements were, the more they favoured support by the traditional intellectual elite.[1]

It has been suggested that the reform and *jihad* movements in the periphery of the Muslim world – in India, South East Asia and West Africa – in the late eighteenth century should be seen as political manifestations of religious change and renewal in the centres of Islam connected with a revival and renewal of sufi tradition. No doubt such intellectual networks existed, but unfortunately it has been impossible to give them a more specific intellectual content. The idea of an eighteenth-century revivalist movement, based on or inspired by *hadith* studies and a reformulation of sufi tradition, has met with general opposition among scholars.[2] However, even if the existence of such a general movement in the Muslim world of the eighteenth century, however vague, still has to be substantiated,[3] it should be kept in mind that tensions and movements of this character are well known throughout the history of Islam. The puritanical Kadizadeli movement in the seventeenth-century Ottoman Empire had faded, but it was far from dead in the eighteenth century.[4]

But the existence of such networks calls attention to the fact that to the 'ulama of the eighteenth century, Mecca and Medina were more than the symbolic heartland of Islam, they were centres of religious study and intellectual interchange. Many scholars came to the Holy Cities from all parts of the Muslim world, not only to perform the Pilgrimage, but also to study and teach. The gateways to the Holy Cities were Zabid in Yemen, Damascus and Cairo, ancient centres of religious learning in their own right. Together they formed an inner circle of the Muslim world where significant intellectual interchange could take place between scholars of the Ottoman Empire and those from India, Kurdistan, Arabia and other areas that together may be designated as an intermediate region within the intellectual Islamic world. The frontier regions – South East Asia, Bengal and West Africa – represent a third circle. Pilgrims from these areas studied in the Holy Cities, in Cairo, Damascus or in Zabid, and had an opportunity to interact with the scholars of the cosmopolitan core of the global Muslim community.

Through these channels the 'ulama would become aware of new trends in the Muslim world, both in the frontier regions and elsewhere. They would be informed of significant spiritual developments within the Sunni and Shi'a communities, and would be acquainted with the shifting fortunes of the 'ulama inside and outside the Ottoman Empire. They would also learn of such movements of

Islamic reform in the late eighteenth and early nineteenth centuries as the puritanical Wahhabis in Arabia.[5] The Wahhabi movement, by virtue of the threat it posed to the Holy Cities and the Pilgrimage and to the prestige of the Ottoman state, clearly constituted a challenge to established thinking, especially in Egypt with its close spiritual and commercial connections to the Ottoman province of Hijaz.

In the capital of the Ottoman Empire a system of hierarchy within the religious establishment had been formalized by successive sultans, beginning with Mehmet II (1451–81). In the eighteenth century the higher positions within this system were more or less monopolized by certain 'ulama families. By the beginning of the eighteenth century the Ottoman religious establishment had become heavily Istanbul- and medrese-centred. If members of the wider Ottoman religious hierarchy aspired to high status, regular subsidies and influence in the empire, they were well advised to cultivate this establishment.[6]

The sultan had to take care to appease the 'ulama. Sultan Ahmad III (1703–30) and his successors recognized that the state could best survive by seeking some kind of accommodation with the multiplicity of family and patron–client networks behind the official careers of contemporary 'ulama. In the eighteenth century pensions, ranks and lectures in the presence of the sultan were regular and permanent features of a system of rewards and rituals that put the 'ulama as a group closer to the sultan and the centre of official political life.[7] The support of the state added to the Ottoman 'ulama's near-monopoly of Ottoman education and assured their pre-eminence in the ritual life of the empire.

The 'ulama's unrivalled official status automatically meant the consistent subordination of other religious expressions, however popular.[8] As in other parts of the Muslim world, the Ottoman 'ulama were intimately connected with the sufi orders. In the seventeenth century the sufis had been more popular than ever. With the doors open to the lay population, the mystical–intellectual component of the orders increasingly gave way to appealingly simplistic and lively rituals. To the orthodox the most troublesome mystics were those who encouraged disdain for the holy law's living and written guides. For this reason the moderate Khalwati order was generally favoured in 'ulama circles, while orders such as the Bektashi, favoured by the Janissaries, were considered of dubious orthodoxy.[9]

In the late eighteenth century war and military reform presented the Ottoman 'ulama with problems of a different nature, and the tensions created by these problems seriously upset the cohesion and stability of the religious institution.

A number of prominent 'ulama not only supported the reforms of Selim III and Mahmud II, but actually worked to carry
them through. The fact that many of the leading Ottoman 'ulama
had close relatives who had served or were serving in the highest
administrative offices of the state was bound to influence their outlook. It brought them into contact with the political and military
leaders of their time and helped them to gain a clearer insight into
the major problems of the empire. This insight convinced them
that the *shari'a* could be accommodated to the circumstances of the
state whenever this would yield an advantage. To these high 'ulama
the *shari'a* had been laid down to help the propagation of Islam,
not to place obstacles in its way. With this attitude they joined forces
with certain sufi orders, especially the Mevlevi order, which enjoyed
the favour of both Selim III and Mahmud II and therefore of high
society. Enmity towards the Janissary corps and the Bektashi sufi
order, which was closely associated with it, also seem to have played
a part. The higher 'ulama took a most hostile attitude to the unorthodox behaviour of the Bektashi order, in which uneducated men
could rise to the highest ranks.[10]

Other 'ulama joined the coalition of Janissaries and other
opponents of reform to depose Selim III in 1807. To some of the
reforming 'ulama these opponents were uncultured provincials, una-
ware of the customs of government and careless of the established usages of social intercourse. Nevertheless, in 1807 the *seyh ül-Islam*, Mehmet 'Ata'ulla, the *qadi* of Istanbul and high-ranking *mollah*s (judges)
played a prominent part in the opposition while many 'ulama of
lower rank – and especially the numerous students of the religious
colleges (*medreses*) – seem to have joined the opposition out of envy
towards the leading 'ulama families. In addition, many members of
the popular sufi orders and unattached dervishes objected violently
to the policy of reform.

---

[1] A. H. Green, *The Tunisian 'Ulama* 1873–1915, Leiden 1978.

[2] Peter Gran, *The Islamic Roots of Capitalism: Egypt*, 1760–1840, Austin 1979,
has suggested this, but has found scant support: see G. Baer in *JESHO* 25, [2]
(1982), pp. 217ff. and F.de Jong in *IJMES* 14 (1982), pp. 381ff. (with Gran's
reply). N. Levtzion and John O. Voll (eds.), *EighteenthCentury Renewal and
Reform in Islam*, New York 1987, pp. 8ff., still claim that such a change took
place, but Frederick de Jong, 'Mustafa Kamal al-Din al-Bakri (1688–1749),
Revival and Reform in the Khalwatiyya Tradition?', in Levtzion and Voll
(eds.), *Renewal and Reform*, pp. 117ff., finds no evidence for it in the Khalwatiyya.

[3] R.S. O'Fahey and B. Radtke, 'Neo-Sufism Reconsidered', *Der Islam* (1993).

[4] Zilfi, *The Politics of Piety*, p. 234.

[5] Apart from the Wahhabis in Arabia there were the Padri movement in Central Sumatra 1784–1847, the Fara'idi movement in East Bengal, launched by Hajji Shariat Allah in 1821 and the Fulani Jihad in the Hausa region of West Africa from 1804. In all these movements Islamic precepts seem to have played a major – sometimes determinative – part. Although they took place on the fringes of the Muslim world, there are indications that the leaders of these movements may have been acquainted with each other's ideas through the network created by the Pilgrimage and the Holy Cities. They all seem to contain an element of religious puritanism, which was transformed into a more direct and militant expression of economic and social discontent. See W. Roff (ed.), *Islam and the Political Economy of Meaning, Los Angeles* 1987, *pp.* 4, 31–52.

[6] In 1715 this situation had been officially sanctioned by the legislation of Sultan Ahmad III (1703–30). From 1703 to 1839, eleven families accounted for twenty-nine of the fifty-eight *seyh ül-Islam*s. The entire judicial half of the Ottoman religious institution was dominated by men whose fathers were judges rather than simply 'ulama of random grade. See Itzkowitz, 'Men and Ideas', p. 19; Zilfi, *The Politics of Piety*, pp. 47ff., 56.

[7] Zilfi, *The Politics of Piety*, p. 228.

[8] Ibid., pp. 232–4.

[9] Ibid., p. 166.

[10] Ibid., p. 233; Uriel Heyd, 'The Ottoman 'Ulema and Westernisation in the Time of Selim III and Mahmud II' [1961], repr. in A. Hourani et al. (eds.), *The Modern Middle East: A Reader*, London 1993, pp. 31, 41, 47.

4 The 'ulama in eighteenth-century Ottoman Egypt

As shaykh of the Jabarti riwaq (college) at the mosque of al-Azhar in Cairo, al-Jabarti was a member of the 'ulama of Ottoman Egypt. However, when considering their position in Egypt, it is important to keep in mind that the status of the Egyptian 'ulama has been at the centre of the historical debate ever since al-Jabarti wrote his chronicles. Contributions to this field have come about in the light of shifting perspectives: orientalism; modernization; nationalism; Islamic revivalism; and what might be termed the anthropological perspective. In addition, it should be remembered that the 'ulama were the main producers of the sources for their own history. The fact that the sources were written by the very persons under study makes it hard to keep the correct perspectives and proportions. A group of intellectuals writing the history of the society in which they live and work will, consciously or not, emphasize the importance of the theoretical and practical contributions of their own group.

The contributions to our understanding of the social and political position of the Egyptian 'ulama in the eighteenth century provided by Stanford Shaw,[1] André Raymond,[2] Afaf Lutfi al-Sayyid Marsot[3] and Daniel Crecelius[4] rely on information provided by al-Jabarti and 'Ali Basha Mubarak, supplemented by some primary contemporary sources. These contributions concentrate on the social status of this group and its relation to power.[5] Marsot tends to evaluate the position of the 'ulama from a nationalist perspective, seeing its leading members as a native Egyptian religious elite (as opposed to the Ottoman dignitaries dispatched from Istanbul), while Shaw, Raymond and Crecelius view the position and actions of 'ulama in the light of their responses to the process of modernization. The studies by de Jong[6] and Michael Winter,[7] although working within a different periodization, but on the basis of the same type of sources, still seem to adhere to the idea of the 'ulama in Ottoman Egypt operating as intermediaries between the rulers and the common people in order to maintain their worldly position. The problems created by this approach will be discussed below.

For the Ottomans, who had to govern Egypt from a distance, it was a matter of vital interest to satisfy the local religious establishment, and they seem to have demonstrated great flexibility in their dealings with this aspect of life in the province. Apart from the introduction of the office of *qadi 'askar* (chief judge), whose great administrative–judicial authority had no parallel in the Mamluk past, no radical changes were instituted. Despite the official priority of the Hanafi *madhhab* (rite or school of jurisprudence), the Ottomans respected the traditional pluralism of rites in Egypt, even at the mosque of al-Azhar. In the courts Egyptian deputy qadis continued to judge according to the four rites, and leadership in the religious establishment, represented by the scholars of al-Azhar and the leaders of the Bakriyya and Wafa'iyya sufi orders, remained in the hands of Egyptians.

But Ottoman influence was felt in more subtle ways. New centres of authority came to the fore. The Ottomans aimed at gaining the support of a long-established class of 'ulama and at 'ottomanizing', as far as possible, the pious deeds of the Mamluks. After the conquest the Ottomans made an extensive investigation of all the pious foundations (*awqaf*). Those supported by proper documentation were confirmed, the rest were confiscated. A register was established and supervision of the *awqaf* was assigned to the *qadi 'askar*. New awqaf were established, either on the basis of revenues from former Mamluk foundations or by diverting state revenues to new *awqaf*. *Awqaf* established by the sultans were mainly for the maintenance of the Holy Cities.

Under Mamluk rule the religious foundations of the Mamluk sultans and their great emirs had offered the most privileged positions. Under the Ottomans these foundations lost a great deal of their former prestige to al-Azhar, which was supported by a multitude of sponsors from various groups in society and by the Ottoman rulers. Furthermore, the institutions of the Mamluk sultanate were often converted to other types of religious institutions in compliance with Ottoman interests, without regard to their original stipulations. The eminent position of the mosque-college of al-Azhar in Cairo, already a famous centre of learning before the Ottoman conquest, as the heart of the 'ulama institution in Egypt could be said to be part of the new Ottoman setting in which Egypt developed from the sixteenth to the nineteenth centuries. But the foundations not only served to uphold the prestige of the new regime. The Ottomans also gained a share in the economic enterprises of the area. A superintendent was appointed directly from Istanbul for the great *awqaf* of the Mamluk sultans, as well as those established later by the Ottoman sultans. In Cairo, because of its important trade connections and large markets, the Ottoman governors were active, not only on behalf of their masters, the sultans, but also in their own rights and interests.[8]

The 'ulama of Ottoman Egypt did not constitute a clearly defined group. As elsewhere in the Muslim world in this period they included all those considered experts in the shari'a. Some (*qudat,* sg. *qadi*) would be in charge of its enforcement in the religious courts, while others (*fuqaha*; sg. *faqih*) holding positions as teachers in mosques and schools, assisting at its acquisition and repetition in schools and other places, or its study and interpretation (*muftis*). But it also included the much more numerous group of persons of pious intent or vocation who were not formally affiliated to religious or educational institutions, together with the *ashraf* or *sayyids*, claimants of descent from the Prophet and his Companions, if they had the necessary education.

Socially the situation of the 'ulama in eighteenth-century Ottoman Egypt seems to have shared the familiar trends of the decentralized Ottoman state. On one hand, the 'ulama were being co-opted into the patron-client network of the households of the ruling elite. From their point of view such ties provided a measure of security against the emirs' practice of seizing and distributing the revenues of villages of vanquished enemies as political spoils. They also propped up their position as *multazims* in a situation of mounting fragmentation of the individual *iltizams*. But patronage also meant access to profitable positions such as superintendent (*nazir*) and other positions in public or private *awqaf* controlled by the households of the ruling elite.[9] To the leaders of these households the 'ulama as the guardians and interpreters of religion and the legitimizers of human action would be important partners, not only in the political game, but also as a natural and necessary part of the symbolic wealth and power of the household, lending prestige to gatherings in the mansions or palaces of its leading men. The mounting number of non-Ottoman qadis in Egypt in the last quarter of the eighteenth century observed by Shaw[10] can be seen as an aspect of this trend and as part of the more general process of decentralization, in which important and/or profitable positions were left to be filled by local *a'yan* in order to conciliate them and win their support. Such grants of favour allowed the emirs to strengthen their ties with the 'ulama by holding out the prospect not only of financial security, but also of profitable careers.

The Ottoman government, although not averse to the idea of accommodating the local elite in this as in other ways, would be equally aware of the importance of forging its own links with the 'ulama in Egypt. As the sultan developed his image as protector of the faith and courted the 'ulama in the capital, he and his deputy, the pasha, were doing the same in Cairo. Visiting the tomb of Imam al-Shafi'i became part of the itinerary of the new pasha's entry procession when taking up office in Cairo in the eighteenth century.[11]

Important Mamluk *awqaf* were entrusted to the al-Bakri and al-Sadat families by order of the sultan. Salvation prayers for the sultans were said in the *zawiya* of the al-Sadat family.[12] Even more important was the regular dispatch of the annual Pilgrimage caravan from Cairo, which brought the new *kiswa* (the covering of the Ka'ba) to the Holy Cities, as well as cash, grain and a multitude of other supplies needed by the citizens of Mecca and Medina. Large funds had been set aside for this purpose. From the late seventeenth century the prestigious and profitable position of *amir al-hajj* had been monopolized by the military elite. But the sultan still had the moral responsibility, and the blame for any mismanagement in this respect fell on him. Such mismanagement was used as an argument for the dispatch of Hasan Pasha in 1786 and the attempt to restore the revenue due to the imperial treasury.[13]

This competition may account for the fact that although sons of 'ulama often followed in the footsteps of their fathers there seems to have been no aristocratic hereditary caste of 'ulama in Egypt. Such social fluidity would leave the field open to both Ottomans and the local elite to promote their own men. According to Marsot, most of the prominent 'ulama were of *fellah* (peasant) origin. Although other lesser 'ulama came from all social levels, and some were sons of 'ulama, and some sons of merchants, she finds no evidence that the 'ulama families exclusively dominated the learned institutions as they did in Istanbul. Marsot notes that the profession of 'ulama in Egypt, in contradistinction to the capital, seemed to be a powerful vehicle of social mobility for the lower classes, and especially for the peasants.[14] Ottoman influence seems to have been especially prominent in the organization of *ashraf*. The descendants of the Prophet were respected for religious reasons, and enjoyed high social status and economic privileges. They were distinguished by their green turbans, and always appeared as a group in religious processions, especially during saints' birthdays (*mawalid*). *Ashraf* were generally noted for their religiosity. They came from all walks of life, but many were 'ulama and al-Azhar graduates and held positions as qadis and muftis. Some were distinguished by their wealth and influence.[15]

The status of the *ashraf* was considerably enhanced under the Ottomans, whatever their social class. After the conquest their leader, the *naqib al-ashraf*, had been nominated from Istanbul, but from at least the middle of the eighteenth century onward he was usually a member of the al-Bakri or al-Sadat families. This very much enhanced the influence and importance of the shaykhs of the Bakriyya and Wafa'iyya sufi orders. By the eighteenth century they ranked as the most important members of the religious elite. The shaykh al-

The 'Ulama

Bakri appears routinely as the addressee of imperial decrees issued in the name of the sultan in Istanbul.[16] This imperial favour was obviously meant to connect the Ottomans directly not only to the *ashraf* but to the Egyptian sufi orders over which these shaykhs had a certain authority.[17]

Al-Jabarti's necrology of Husayn al-Maqdisi al-Hanafi, a prominent *sharif* from Jerusalem, who died in 1780, suggests the nature of these connections between the Ottomans and the *ashraf* and between the *ashraf* and the Wafa'iyya. Husayn acquired his basic education in Jerusalem and proceeded to Damascus, where he studied and practised calligraphy. Then he went to Cairo, took up residence in the riwaq of the Syrians at al-Azhar and attended lectures of the shaykhs al-Shubrawi, al-Hifni and al-Jawhari. After that, he travelled to the Holy Cities for further studies. He returned to Cairo and proceeded to Istanbul where he 'realized some of his wishes, associated on intimate terms with the great, learned the language and gained the attention of leading men'. In 1758/9 he came to Cairo 'with one of the amirs of the empire' (al-Jabarti does not say whom). He then attached himself to the sayyid Muhammad Abu Hadi ibn Wafa, the shaykh al-Sadat. When Muhammad became *naqib al-ashraf*, Husayn became his trusted deputy. At the death of Muhammad, Husayn became unhappy with Cairo and left for Istanbul. In the capital he turned to teaching and wrote a commentary on the compendia of the Hanafi school of law.[18]

The career of Sayyid Husayn is interesting not only because it demonstrates the ties existing between the capital, the *naqib al-ashraf* in Egypt and the shaykh al-Sadat. These ties would explain the attraction of the position of the naqib to both the Ottomans and to Egyptians as a vehicle for influence in the capital and visa versa, but it also helps to understand the fact that the incumbent of the position of naqib in the eighteenth century did not always come from the same family. Husayn's departure at the death of sayyid Muhammad in 1762/3 coincided with the transfer of the position of the naqib al-ashraf to the al-Bakri family. Although we do not know the exact circumstances of this shift, it would be reasonable to suggest that 'Ali Bey al-Kabir had a hand in it: in 1781 his retainer Murad Bey invested his successor as shaykh al-Bakri and naqib al-ashraf.[19] The Ottomans and the emirs had been competing for control of this important and influential position, but in the late eighteenth century the emirs seem to have gained the upper hand, backing the al-Bakri family in the process.

The education of a prospective 'alim was mainly provided at the mosque of al-Azhar. During the period of direct Ottoman rule the shaykh al-Azhar was either a Maliki or a Shafi'i, and never a Turk.[20] Apart from al-Azhar, teaching was performed at twenty other colleges in Cairo and in about eighteen or twenty provincial towns with college-mosques as well. In all these colleges the teachers, although usually of local origin, had been trained at al-Azhar.[21] While the activities of the provincial college-mosques were limited to local needs, those of Cairo were considerably wider, as they admitted students not only from Egypt, but from other Islamic countries as well. At al-Azhar each province, country or *madhhab* (Hanafi, Maliki, Shafi'i) had its own riwaq where the students were lodged, fed and taught. Although many nationalities were gathered in al-Azhar, it appears that it was the teachers, not the students, who moved between the *riwaqs*. The number of students there in the eighteenth century is unknown, but is generally believed to have been well above the figure of 1,300–3,000 of the 1830s. The number of teachers/shaykhs at al-Azhar at the time of the French occupation seems to have been somewhere between forty and sixty.[22] In addition, the institution included a riwaq for blind students and more than 1,500 beggars and destitute people who received their daily rations from pious foundations attached to the mosque. In times of tension both groups could be relied upon to support the 'ulama.[23]

The 'ulama studied and worked within the framework of the *madhhab*, each of which had its own scholarly and legal tradition with textbooks and authorities. The *madhahib* were social units, and tensions between students and 'ulama belonging to different ones were not uncommon. The students' affiliation to a rite usually depended on family tradition and place of origin.[24] In the eighteenth century Cairo was predominantly Shafi'i, although it also had sizeable Hanafi and Maliki communities. The former drew much of its strength from the fact that it was the official rite of the Ottoman rulers and the Turkish community. The Malikis were intimately connected with North Africa, where the rite was dominant. In the provinces of Egypt, the province of Sharqiyya in the eastern Delta was Shafi'i, Gharbiyya in the western Delta was a mixture of Shafi'i and Maliki, while Buhayra in the westernmost part of the Delta on the Cyrenaican border was entirely Maliki. Likewise the region of Upper Egypt, al-Sa'id, was mostly Maliki. The Hanbali rite all but disappeared in Egypt during the Ottoman period.[25]

When a student had completed the study of any one work, his teacher granted him an *ijaza*, which gave him permission to teach that work to others. In the ordinary course of events, when a student felt that he was qualified to teach he would begin to do so to a small circle of students. This circle would gradually increase. If he succeeded in answering the pertinent questions of his opponents he was recognized as an 'alim and would take up his post at some vacant pillar in the hall of the mosque, as tradition prescribed.

This did not mean that he ceased to study. Shaykhs still followed courses and received *ijazas*, and many travelled for the sake of study and for the acquisition of *ijazas* from famous teachers. These journeys brought the travelling 'alim into contact with the wider intellectual network of the Muslim world, as we have seen in the case of sayyid Husayn mentioned above. Journeys to the Holy Cities for this purpose were very frequent, and study was often combined with the Pilgrimage. Other destinations would be Damascus and Zabid[26] in Yemen. But travel to Cairo by non-Egyptians seems to have been more common than that of Egyptians to other countries.[27]

The most important destination for Sunni 'ulama in the Ottoman Empire would be the capital, Istanbul, with its many colleges and possibilities of patronage. This was certainly the case with Syrians. Apparently a considerable number of Syrian scholars, especially the more ambitious, went to Istanbul to seek enlistment in the Ottoman cadres. The habits of Egyptian scholars in this regard have not been studied, however. Shaw mentions Egyptians who went to Istanbul to study, and Marsot says that the Egyptian 'ulama were used as emissaries of the Egyptian emirs to the capital, as virtual 'plenipotentiaries', but does not pursue this fact with the obvious suggestion that they had already been there as students and/or shaykhs.[28] The predominance of the Shafi'i rite among Egyptian shaykhs, in contradistinction to the often Hanafite Syrian scholars, may explain their reluctance to go to the mainly Hanafite capital.

Training as an 'alim did not involve membership of a sufi order, but in the eighteenth century few people would call themselves Muslim without belonging to one or more of these religious orders, and the 'ulama seem to have been no exception. Religious life was no longer governed by the simple tenets of Islam, but rather by the various sufi interpretations of religious law and texts. The 'ulama devoted much time and energy to the reading of sufi literature, and by far the greatest proportion of their literary output consisted of this kind of writing and of sufi poetry.[29] It is interesting to note that the Khalwatiyya order and its branches, the favourite order of the 'ulama in Istanbul in the seventeenth century, seems to have been dominated by 'ulama, and even al-Azhar-based ever since Kamal al-Din al-Bakri's (d. 1749) principal khalifa in Egypt, Muhammad b. Salim al-Hifni, had been shaykh al-Azhar from 1757 to 1767.[30]

Quite a few sufi orders (*turuq*) seem to have been active in Egypt at the end of the eighteenth century.[31] In the sixteenth century corporations of *ashraf* (descendants of the Prophet and his family) had transformed themselves from family groups into mystical sufi associations such as al-Bakriyya (descendants of Abu Bakri), al-Inaniyya (descendants of 'Umar), al Khudayriyya (descendants of al-Zubayr) and al Wafa'iyya (descendants of 'Ali b. Abu Talib). The al-Bakriyya can be traced as a prominent sufi family in Cairo from the sixteenth century. In the early Ottoman period they were associated with the Shadhiliyya, while in the first half of the eighteenth century they became attached to the Khalwatiyya by Shaykh Mustafa al-Bakri (d. 1749), a member of the Damascene branch of the family active in Egypt.[32] The family of al-Sadat al-Wafa'iyya claimed descent from the Idrisi royal dynasty of the Maghreb. According to family tradition they came to Egypt from Tunis and Sfax at the beginning of the fourteenth century. They established a sufi family order which was a branch of the Shadhiliyya.[33] The Wafa'iyya continued to have connections with the Maghreb and like most Maghribis belonged to the Maliki *madhhab* while the Bakriyya were Shafi'ites.[34] Both orders shared the characteristics of the Shadhili order: few outward signs of belonging to the order, but a keen interest in spiritual matters and good deeds, sobriety and a certain elegance. For this reason they attracted the intellectual elite, although actual membership of the orders, in contradistinction to other sufi orders, was a question of birth, but as the leadership became hereditary they slowly lost their innovative spirit.[35] The Wafa'iyya was famous for wealth, poets and meetings where sufis played musical instruments, in spite of the displeasure of the more orthodox.[36]

The Ahmadiyya order, founded by Ahmad al-Badawi in Tanta, was apparently considered culturally inferior to the Shadhiliyya. The shrine of its founder in Tanta was the object of strong popular veneration and fashionable among the ruling class, and for this reason was probably more influential socially.[37] The order divided into several sub-sections with some degree of autonomy. The supreme leaders of all the Ahmadiyya orders, like the leaders of the *ashraf* corporations, were referred to as shaykh al sajjada. They controlled shrines, were beneficiaries of *awqaf* revenues and the administrators of *awqaf* which had become virtually hereditary within their respective families.

The Khalwatiyya order takes its name from its central principle, the concept of the khalwa (solitary retreat). Members were obliged to retreat for long periods to their cells for prayer and contemplation and for the austere discipline demanded by fasting and silence. In the sixteenth century it was an unorthodox order, and as most of the Khalwatis came from a Turkish milieu it was extremely popular with the Turkish soldiers and rulers, both in Istanbul and in Cairo. In the eighteenth century, as noted above, it retained its connections with the ruling Ottoman elite, but had become a bastion of orthodoxy, with an unrivalled supremacy among the 'ulama of al-Azhar. From its inception the order offered a well-developed mystical system and a Way that demanded a strict novitiate under a master.[38] Leadership in the order was still open and non-hereditary in the eighteenth century.

The Mawlawiyya (Mevlevi) and Bektashiyya (Bektashi) orders both paid allegiance to the mother *takiya* in Turkey, and the al-Sa'diyya. The Naqshbandiyya is known to have had representatives in Egypt from the beginning of the eighteenth century, but no self-perpetuating group seems to have come into being. Under the Ottomans little fusion took place between these orders and local sufism, and their influence remained confined to the Turkish ruling establishment.[39]

No doubt initiation into one or more of these orders signalled the spiritual and social leanings and affiliation of the young 'alim. Unfortunately we do not have sufficiently accurate information about the spiritual implications of membership of the various turuq to understand what such membership implied, but not all of them were considered suitable for orthodox 'ulama. Al-Jabarti viewed some of them with strong disfavour or condemned their practices outright as *bid'a* (blameworthy innovations),[40] but other 'ulama obviously thought otherwise.[41] It is equally evident that membership implied not only spiritual but also social obligations – and perhaps economic ties – towards the shaykh of the order and vice versa. Some sort of patron–client relationship seems to have existed, but the exact nature of the obligations of the aspirant to his master is not easy to ascertain, probably because it was considered so commonplace a feature that it was unnecessary to enlarge upon it. Generally the aspirant was expected to obey his shaykh in all things, even those that he found suspect, and this obedience extended beyond the grave. How far these obligations went in practice would probably vary in time and from person to person.[42] It should be remembered that being initiated into several orders was the norm, despite the fact that the vow of allegiance given by the novice to his shaykh bound them together and existed alongside the rivalry between orders. This apparent paradox may be explained by the distinction between full membership in an order as a social organization, entailing obedience to a shaykh and regular participation in the rituals and ceremonies, and learning the formulas of the orders for itself or for gaining a blessing. It would seem that such superficial affiliation with more than one order was tolerated in the case of more mature educated and independent persons, but not for the common people.[43]

The worldly fortunes of an 'alim would depend on such connections as well as on his ability as a teacher. Although schools were not organized in any salaried hierarchy as they were in other parts of the Ottoman world, some kind of payment was nevertheless given.[44] If the lectures and classes of a young 'alim were conducted with eloquence, quality and coherence, and if he had a distinguished appearance and the necessary ability to handle people, his reputation grew. He would be invited to the houses of important and influential people to read and expound on religious texts. Marriage into the right circles was another possibility. Raymond notes the existence of numerous family ties between artisans and 'ulama, especially the merchant families of Cairo.[45]

The accumulation of any kind of capital was based on social relationships, such as finding patrons among the wealthy merchants – and especially among the ruling elite and the Ottomans, who controlled careers and sources of wealth.[46] As a prospective ally, the up-and-coming 'alim would be offered gifts. This required a certain standing, of course, but if he had attained this, several possibilities were open to him. The Ottoman government and the emirs were constantly on the watch for such luminaries, and would be eager to prove their appreciation publicly by handing out pensions and gifts from the imperial revenues of the province.[47]

The major source of income derived from the religious endowments (*awqaf*). The position of *nazir* (superintendent of a waqf) entitled the holder to a fee, but even more importantly, it allowed him to dispose of the revenues of the waqf at his discretion, provided he kept within the general terms of the provisions of the *waqf*. Where the waqf was an old one or where the legitimate heirs had died or were unable to protest, the superintendent had carte blanche to dispose of the revenues. Some awqaf were attached to a position, such as the shaykh al-Azhar or shaykh of a *riwaq*, but as an incumbent would often gather additional *awqaf* during his tenure, it would often be difficult to distinguish between what belonged to the office and what to the person.[48] Positions such as *nazirs* of *awqaf* involved the 'ulama in business and demanded some business acumen, as the proceeds of the revenues were to be managed to cover the expenses. *Awqaf* involved the employment of significant numbers of people – as Qur'an reciters, prayer-leaders, teachers, overseers, clerks and guards – and gave their administrators the power of admittance to the benefits of the *awqaf* (to students, orphans etc.). In this way the 'ulama acquired important responsibilities towards the spiritual and secular well-being of the Muslim community.[49]

The second major source of wealth was the tax-farm (*iltizam*). The function of a tax-farmer (*multazim*) was not only to collect the taxes for the government: as part of every *iltizam* he received a grant

The 'Ulama

of land (*usya*), which was tilled for him by corvée labour; he was also able to impose extraordinary taxes on the peasants. A further source of wealth came in the form of allowances from public grants for services. Daily salaries were bestowed on people and paid out of the head-tax paid by non-Muslims or from the receipts of the customs of Bulaq or the *awqaf* supporting the Holy Cities. Once these salaries were allotted they became semi-permanent and were passed on to a man's heirs. Allowances from the revenues of the local regiments were also paid to the 'ulama in the form of monthly dues. Likewise assignments in kind were paid out of the imperial granary.

Once an *'alim* had acquired a little capital, he usually invested it in real estate or small urban businesses such as shops, caravanserais, baths or coffee-houses. The more ambitious also invested in trade and commerce, both national and international.[50] The diversified capital investments of the 'ulama show not only their economic acumen (and that of their wives, who, like the wives of the emirs, because of the protected status of women often played an important part in the management of the estates of their husbands),[51] but also their links with the suq (bazaar), the countryside and the ruling class.

These connections, in combination with their origin and standing as guardians of religious tradition, explain the support and veneration that the 'ulama commanded from the population. To the rulers, on the other hand, this made them an important tool of government, not only as a source of advice and consultation, but also as mediators and spokesmen when the demands of the elite were enforced on the population.[52] This intermediary position, as broker between competing social groups and power centres in a fluid, dynamic world, naturally offered great possibilities for spiritual and political influence as well as wealth. However, there were also dangers and temptations, which called for caution and circumspection, as they had to navigate between the Ottoman rulers, the emirs and the common people in order to protect and enhance their spiritual and worldly responsibilities towards the people in their care.

This was especially so in the case of leaders of the religious establishment in Ottoman Egypt in the late eighteenth century. These dignitaries were drawn from both the learned 'ulama hierarchy and the religious orders of the sufis. The most influential positions of this elite – apart from the chief qadi, who was appointed annually from Istanbul – were the shaykh al-Bakri, the shaykh al-Sadat, the muftis of the three *madhahib* (Hanafi, Maliki and Shafi'i), the *naqib al-ashraf* and the shaykh al-Azhar.[53]

The shaykh al-Bakri was the titular head of a family of ashraf which in the course of time had turned itself into a sufi order, the al-Bakriyya. The exact nature of his position is not certain. Crecelius and Marsot are of the opinion that the shaykh al-Bakri was the recognized head of the sufi orders in Egypt and presided over all the Egyptian religious festivals at which the dervishes performed, and as such enjoyed enormous prestige and influence, including a role in the selection of 'ulama to high office. De Jong and Winter agree that the shaykh al-Bakri was responsible for the festival of the Prophet in which all the sufi orders took part, but find no evidence for a coordinating role until the 1870s. According to de Jong the shaykh al-Bakri from 1802 to 1812, Muhammad Abu 'l-Su'ud, exercised a certain, unofficial, authority over other orders. In 1812 the new shaykh al-Bakri was given authority by Muhammad 'Ali over the sufi orders and sufi-linked institutions, which had not previously been subject to a central authority.[54] The shaykh al-Sadat was the titular head of the *ashraf* family of Wafa'iyya, which like the Bakriyya had turned itself into a sufi order.

Both Crecelius and Shaw rank these two shaykhs as the foremost leaders in the religious establishment. In the opinion of Crecelius, both derived their power from their leadership of widespread sufi organizations which were completely independent of the regime and embraced every level in society. Crecelius and Shaw remark that the sufi orders had, by the end of the eighteenth century, attained an impressive position of influence and power among the people. According to Crecelius the shaykh al-Sadat was slightly inferior in status and power to the shaykh al-Bakri, but nevertheless remained the second most powerful native religious leader. This evaluation is based on the 1785 report of the Ottoman governor in Syria, Ahmad Jazzar Pasha, to the Ottoman government, in which Ahmad Jazzar presents the two shaykhs as strong opponents of the ruling emirs and potential supporters of an able Ottoman governor in Egypt. According to Ahmad Jazzar, their power derived from the support they commanded from the 'ulama of al-Azhar, mosque leaders and preachers, the Qur'an reciters, the poor of the city and people from Anatolia and Europe who had come to join the Pilgrimage caravan as soldiers, as well as from the North African merchants. Accordingly, both these shaykhs would be able to assemble great numbers of armed men to support them.[55]

It should be kept in mind, however, that this report was part of the preparations for the military expedition of 1786, which Ahmad strongly supported. His suggestion that the two shaykhs were pro-Ottoman and ready to support an able governor to restore Ottoman authority should be seen as part of the attempt to persuade the government of the feasibility of a campaign from which Jazzar himself stood to gain. For this reason his evaluation of the power of the shaykhs should be viewed with caution. It supports the suggestion of intimate ties between the shaykh al-Sadat and the government in Istanbul suggested above. But when Hasan Pasha arrived in Egypt in 1786, only the Bakri family joined the Ottomans, while al-Sadat, according to al-Jabarti, proved to be no more than a lukewarm supporter. Actually, al-Sadat helped the emirs, which proved to be a turning point in his career. When Ibrahim and Murad returned to Cairo, they fined al-Bakri and transferred the Husayni shrine, the supervision of which (as well as the administration of its *waqf*) had been in the Bakri family for a long time, to the shaykh al-Sadat.[56]

The relative positions of these two religious offices and their occupants seem to be in some doubt. Crecelius, again quoting Jazzar Pasha's report, disagrees with Shaw, who sees the shaykh al-Sadat as the most powerful of all these dignitaries, while Marsot views the relation between the shaykh al-Bakri and shaykh al-Sadat as a rivalry between two families, both ashraf and contenders for the title naqib al-ashraf and the *shaykh mashayikha al-turuq al-sufiyya*, essentially the coordinator of all the mystical orders in the country: 'The two families formed a virtual hereditary aristocracy even if their orders, the Bakriyya and Wafa'iyya, were not the most numerous or even the most popular in the country. The titular heads of these two families, that is, the shaykh al-sijada, were without doubt the two richest 'ulama in Egypt and the two most powerful.' Marsot adds that each of the two most important religious festivals in Cairo was arranged by one of the families: that of the Prophet by al-Bakri, that of Husayn by al-Sadat. She notes that al-Sadat – and to a lesser extent al-Bakri – were very influential in every major political event under the emirs, under the French and even under Muhammad 'Ali.[57] Apart from the doubtful existence of the *mashayikha al-turuq*, this evaluation, which suggests that the 'ulama of Egypt were divided in two camps around the families/orders of al-Bakri and al-Wafa'iyya, is supported by Winter.[58] But the existence and nature of this rivalry is based on information provided by al-Jabarti, especially in his necrology of al-Sadat in the MS Aja'ib. For this reason it should be treated with caution.[59] As we shall see, there is reason to believe that the real rivals were the shaykh al-Sadat on one side and Shaykh al-Sharqawi, the shayhk al-Azhar, on the other, and that the shaykh al-Bakri usually sided with the latter.

The *muftis* of the Hanafi, Maliki and Shafi'i rites came second. Due to the fact that he represented the official rite of the Ottoman government, the Hanafi mufti assumed slightly greater importance than the other two, but in terms of political influence, all three ranked behind the chief qadi and only slightly above the shaykh al-Azhar.[60]

The importance of the position of the *naqib al-ashraf* in Ottoman Egypt has already been touched upon above. From 1754 to 1762 the office belonged to the al-Sadat family. From this date until 1793 it was in the possession of the al-Bakris. In 1793 another Egyptian, 'Umar Efendi Makram al-Asyuti, obtained the office at the hands of Murad Bey. His appointment was extraordinary, since he was a stranger without social or family contacts in Cairo and was neither a sufi nor an 'alim. From September 1798 until 1802 it reverted, at the instigation of the French, to the al-Bakri family. With the return of the Ottomans, Khalil al-Bakri was dismissed from his position as *naqib*. A Turkish sufi and preacher, Yusuf Efendi, appeared in Cairo with a letter of confirmation from the government in Istanbul naming him *naqib*. The chief *ashraf* refused to accept him and persuaded the Ottomans to dismiss him two-and-a-half months after his appointment, and from 1802 to 1809 'Umar Makram was back in office.[61] When 'Umar Makram was exiled in 1809, the shaykh al-Sadat held the post until his death in 1813. From 1813 until his dismissal in 1816 Shaykh Muhammad al-Dawakhili held the office. From 1816 to the end of the nineteenth century the al-Bakri family again held it.[62] In other Ottoman provinces the naqib usually exercised a most powerful influence in political affairs. His duties included the obligation to keep the registers that formed the basis of the distribution of pensions awarded by the government and the exclusive right to punish *ashraf* and to execute punishment demanded by others; but in Egypt his influence was circumscribed by the division of the Egyptian *ashraf* into the two great families of the Bakriyya and the Wafa'iyya. During the French occupation and the rise of Muhammad 'Ali the *naqib* emerged as the most powerful native leader in Egypt.[63] De Jong considers the reversion of the office of *naqib al-ashraf* to the al-Bakri family in 1816 as part of Muhammad 'Ali's general policy, initiated in 1812, of restricting the independent power and influence of the 'ulama.[64]

The origins of the position of shaykh al-Azhar are obscure. Shaykh Muhammad 'Abdallah Khurashi (d. 1690) appears to be the first to have carried the title. The *mashayikha* of al-Azhar had attached to it extensive *awqaf*, and for this reason it constituted one of the most coveted of all the religious offices; but despite the great revenues connected to it, the position appears to have been inferior in importance and influence to the other local religious leaders. With respect to governmental or ceremonial functions, the shaykh al-Azhar ranked as the least important, and the al-Azhar administrative system further compromised his leadership. The muftis were responsible for the affairs concerning their respective rites. The students attending the mosque registered with one of the *riwaqs* and were thus subject to its shaykh. In addition, although al-Azhar was the most renowned, well-endowed and well-attended religious institution in the country, there were other important *madrasas* and the shaykh al-Azhar had no authority to interfere in their affairs. At the end of the eighteenth century the transformation of the office of shaykh al-Azhar into the supreme authority in Egyptian Islamic education that it was to become in the early twentieth century had not yet begun.[65]

As Nelly Hanna has pointed out, the Ottomans do not seem to have had a policy of 'ottomanizing' culture. They did not try to impose their language, which never became the language of culture and learning, nor did they attempt to interfere directly with the education system. They did encourage cultural expressions that enhanced their rule, but the process of decentralization meant that the ruling classes did not find clear-cut models to follow. By the eighteenth century the focal points for culture had moved from the courts of the rulers or their local representatives to the households of prominent emirs. As the real centre of power was transferred from the pasha's headquarters in the Citadel to the private residences of the rival contenders for political power, the households of the leading emirs became cultural centres through which they tried to support and enhance their social positions towards the 'ulama and the population.

Equally important for our understanding of the cultural environment of Egypt and Cairo at the time of al-Jabarti is the fact that the kind of knowledge associated with the 'ulama was not the only kind of socially accepted knowledge, and that the scholars of al-Azhar did not confine their activities to that institution, but operated on a wider basis and forged links with many social groups. The 'ulama involved themselves in a variety of activities that were independent of al-Azhar, but which at the same time widened the horizons of the shaykhs and their followers with regard to subjects or approaches to knowledge that were not within the domains of this learned institution.[66] To al-Jabarti these activities and informal channels for the diffusion of knowledge formed the great attraction of the intellectual milieu of the city of Cairo. The house in Azbakiyya of the merchant family of Sharaybi with its extensive library facilities; the magnificent, but slightly decadent, gatherings in the house of the emir Ridwan Katkhuda al-Jalfi (d. 1754); the intense and multi-faceted intellectual intercourse in the house of his father, Hasan al-Jabarti (d. 1774); and his teachers and friends al-Sayyid Murtada al-Zabidi and Isma'il al-Khashshab are contrasted to the house of the shaykh al Sadat, Abu Anwar Shams al-Din (d. 1813). Previously, during the time of al-Murtada al-Zabidi, who was a member of the salon of al-Sadat,[67] the family residence had been the seat of correct guidance, of authority and faith, but in Abu Anwar's time it became 'something like the house of a police magistrate'.[68] Some fields of knowledge, especially the sciences, were much more developed outside institutions of learning. Astronomy seems to have been particularly in vogue in the eighteenth century. To al-Jabarti, though, this was a thing of the past. Times had changed![69]

This kind of informal and educational activity included literary salons, scholarly evenings (*majlis 'ilm*) or literary evenings (*majlis adab*) in the houses of the rich and influential families of Cairo which were attended by numerous 'ulama and sufi shaykhs, as well as students and travelling scholars and artists. These activities were facilitated by the fact that private libraries were numerous and literacy was widespread among the higher and middle classes as well as some of those of the lower orders. Nelly Hanna, on whose observations on the culture of Ottoman Egypt in the eighteenth century these remarks are based, suggests that the informal channels of information and knowledge, and the level of literacy among the urban population, may serve to explain many features of the cultural production in this period. The literary population formed a fairly wide readership whose tastes would be taken into account by writers, thus giving a certain direction to the work produced. The literature written during the Ottoman period included many works in popular fields such as the lives of the saints and their virtues, embellished with miracles and wondrous stories. Many theological works were written, not to explain theological matters, but to set down the rules for good conduct for good Muslims. Much oral literature passed into writing. Some of this learned cultural production was actually created by people who did not form part of the educated elite.

On the more popular level, the Ottoman period witnessed the expansion of coffee-houses. In the eighteenth century more than 1,200 such establishments existed in Cairo, not counting those of Bulaq and Old Cairo. The coffee-house, being frequented by men of different socio-economic strata, became an important feature in the lives of the urban population. Coffee-houses also became the centre for various kinds of performance.[70] Artists and entertainers probably gained in economic security from this and developed certain kinds of verse and prose that were in keeping with the tastes and level of the audience and the informality of the premises. The techniques of popular art and entertainment were felt in the way historians narrated events. Hanna notes that Mustafa al-Qinali, in his chronicle ending in 1739, seems to use the methods of the storyteller to create dramatic effect and applies repetition of certain passages, which in oral literature would have reminded the audience of a message that might be lost in the course of the narrative.[71]

The 'Ulama

Unfortunately, we know very few details about discussions on political affairs, even in elite society. Where and how was news of a political nature received and discussed at the different levels of society? Where was past experience formulated and put into circulation, and in what material form? Did something approximating public opinion exist? The existence of chronicles such as those of al-Shadhili, al-Qinali, al-Hallaq and al-Damurdashi in the eighteenth century attests to a need to put the past into some order. Such histories are usually a sign of the existence of a political debate, but the exact nature of such a debate and its participants eludes us. More formal forums existed, such as the Diwan of the Ottoman governor, the weekly council held in the Citadel to conduct the business of government of the province.[72] Similar more or less formalized diwans probably existed in the households of the leading emirs. But it would be natural to suppose that subjects of a political nature would be part of the discussions in the literary salons and the coffee-houses, too.

The questions raised above also suggest the need for a reconsideration of the role played by the written manuscript in a society such as Ottoman Egypt. Who were these chroniclers writing for? The authors themselves, or an audience; and if they wrote for an audience, then for whom? Moreh, in his evaluation of the purposes of the chronicles of al-Jabarti, seems to take it for granted that handwritten manuscripts and the copies made of them played the same role in the creation of opinion as the printed book. But this, of course, cannot be the case, considering the scarcity of copies. A proper evaluation of the purpose of chronicles such as al-Jabarti's demands a firmer knowledge of the role played by the handwritten manuscript in the intellectual discourse and the formation of opinion in a society without printing presses. What was the function of the written word in the communication of knowledge and ideas? How was it used in practice? How was it put into circulation? As Hanna points out, authors such as al-Qinali (and, by implication, al-Jabarti) would surely be aware of these aspects and arrange their writing accordingly. The purpose of their chronicles, the message they contain, would be fashioned to suit this framework.

In the eighteenth and nineteenth centuries, before the introduction of printing rendered the flourishing industry of copying manuscripts obsolete, it was possible to make a living as a copyist and / or as a professional book dealer.[73] Authors also submitted manuscripts to important people in order to curry favour. It seems that such a present sometimes implied that the author read his work or passages from it aloud in the presence of this person,[74] but manu-

under Tahir Pasha and Muhammad 'Ali.

[16] Marsot, 'The 'Ulama of Cairo', p. 151; Behrens-Abouseif, Egypt's Adjustment, p. 61. De Jong, Turuq and Turuq-Linked Institutions, p. 12 dates the shift from Turk to Egyptian to about the middle of the eighteenth century. See also Winter, 'The Ashraf and Niqabat al-ashraf', pp. 22–3, 34–5 and Winter, Egyptian Society, p. 144.

[17] There seems to be some disagreement on the question of this authority. See below.

[18] MS Aja'ib, II, 71.

[19] Ibid., 71, 72; de Jong, Turuq and Turuq-Linked Institutions, pp. 219, 220; MS Aja'ib, I, 316; Winter, 'The Ashraf and Niqabat al-ashraf', p. 37 has a different interpretation of the sequence of events. As for the position of shaykh al-Sadat, it was passed on to Ahmad ibn Isma'il and not to Shams al-Din Abu 'l-Anwar, who nevertheless retained his ambitions. In 1768/9 Ahmad died and Shams al-Din got the position. But he had to wait until 1809 to become naqib al-ashraf: MS Aja'ib, IV, 186.

[20] Behrens-Abouseif, Egypt's Adjustment, pp. 94ff. Shaykh 'Abdallah al-Shubrawi (d. 1757) was the first Shafi'i shaykh al-Azhar. In 1778 al-Jabarti reports an abortive attempt to promote the Hanafi mufti and Khalwati sufi shaykh al-'Arishi to the post, with the support of the emirs, the shaykh al-Sadat and the Maghribis: MS Aja'ib, II, 52ff.; Winter, Egyptian Society, p. 122. It is interesting to note that shortly before, between 1774 and 1778, al-'Arishi had travelled to Istanbul, 'to transact some business'!

[21] H.A.R. Gibb and Harold Bowen, Islamic Society and the West, London 1950–7, vol. I, part 2, p. 155; J. Heyworth-Dunne, An Introduction to the History of Education in Modern Egypt, London 1938, pp. 15ff.; MS Aja'ib, II, 60.

[22] Heyworth-Dunne, Introduction, pp. 25ff.

[23] Raymond, Artisans et commerçants, vol. II, p. 419.

[24] A shift from one rite to another did happen, but was considered a major event in the life of an 'alim. See MS Aja'ib, II, 247, III, 354.

[25] Winter, Egyptian Society, pp. 113–14; MS Aja'ib, IV, 229.

[26] Al-Jabarti's master and friend Murtada al-Zabidi came from this town. For this reason al-Jabarti's chronicles contain a fair amount of information on Zabid as a centre of learning. See MS Aja'ib, II, 89–90, 196.

[27] Heyworth-Dunne, Introduction, pp. 68ff.; Gibb and Bowen, Islamic Society, p. 155.

[28] Shaw, Ottoman Egypt in the Age of the French Revolution, p. 98; Marsot, 'The 'Ulama' of Cairo', p. 152. Al-Jabarti in his necrologies mentions several such instances of 'ulama and sufi shaykhs, who in the second half of the eighteenth century journeyed to the capital to study and seek favour: MS Aja'ib, II, 32, 35, 71, 77, 99, 127, 237, 252.

²⁹ Heyworth-Dunne, Introduction, p. 10. De Jong seems to suggest a two-way traffic in his evaluation of the firman of 1816 which gave the shaykh al-Bakri authority over the sufi orders in Egypt: 'Its proclamation widened the gap between 'ilm and tasawwuf and contributed to the ossification of Islamic mysticism in Egypt, since the opportunity for the head of a tariqa to obtain official sanction from al-Bakri eliminated – at least partially – the need to prove himself a scholar' (Turuq and Turuq-Linked Institutions, p. 23). On the other hand, de Jong seems to be critical of the importance of the sufi orders in Ottoman Egypt prior to the nineteenth century (p. 13, n. 35).

³⁰ De Jong, Turuq and Turuq-Linked Institutions, pp. 21–2; Zilfi, The Politics of Piety, p. 97.

³¹ De Jong, Turuq and Turuq-Linked Institutions, pp. 9ff.

³² B.G. Martin, 'A Short History of the Khalwati Order of Dervishes', in Keddie (ed.), Scholars, Saints and Sufis, p. 298.

³³ Winter, 'The Ashraf and Niqabat al-ashraf', pp. 34–5; Martin, 'A Short History', pp. 297–8.

³⁴ Winter, Society and Religion, pp. 130, 224.

³⁵ E. Geoffroy, Le Soufisme en Egypte et en Syrie sous les derniers mamelouks et les premiers ottomans, Damascus 1995, pp. 208–9.

³⁶ Winter, 'The Ashraf and Niqabat al-ashraf', p. 35.

³⁷ Winter, Society and Religion, p. 101. Winter describes the situation in the sixteenth century, but from al-Jabarti's account of al-Sharqawi it appears that this was still so in the eighteenth century.

³⁸ Ibid., pp. 106, 105; Winter, Egyptian Society, pp. 138ff.

³⁹ Behrens-Abouseif, Egypt's Adjustment, p. 105. The famous Maliki mufti at al-Azhar, al-Dardir (d. 1786), is reported to have founded his own order which was supposed to reconcile the Khalwati and Naqshbandi orders. Al-Jabarti, however, describes him as a staunch Khalwati, one of al-Hifni's greatest lieutenants: MS Aja'ib, II, 147.

⁴⁰ MS Aja'ib, III, 39–40, IV, 120; de Jong, Turuq and Turuq-Linked Institutions, pp. 25, 27; Winter, Egyptian Society, p. 153.

⁴¹ In al-Jabarti's time one of the more important khulafa of the al-Arabiyya was the well-known Azhari scholar Muhammad al-Amir: de Jong, Turuq and Turuq-Linked Institutions, p. 28.

⁴² Winter, Egyptian Society, p. 146.

⁴³ Ibid., p. 152.

⁴⁴ A teacher at al-Azhar received between three and twenty loaves of bread per day, depending on his level of seniority and the riwaq to which he belonged. A village faqih might receive anything from ten to sixty loaves of bread a month, but 'ulama usually held more than one teaching position at a time and were paid from more than one source. More importantly, they were also paid for performing extracurricular activities, such as teaching

or holding mystical seances or Qur'anic recitations in private houses. In times of crisis the 'ulama were paid to read al-Bukhari's hadith collection, known as sahih, and all 'ulama at whatever level in society received gifts and fringe benefits that accrued to them by virtue of their function within Muslim society. Marsot, 'Wealth of the Ulama', p. 212; Winter, Egyptian Society, p. 116.

45 Raymond, Artisans et commerçants, vol. II, pp. 421ff. Al-Jabarti relates a story of how 'Ali Bey al-Daftardar appointed a certain Sharif al-Awadi to a teaching position at the al-Husayni mosque, because he had won a debating contest with Shaykh al-Khalifi: MS Aja'ib, III, 115.

46 Marsot, 'A Socio-economic Sketch', p. 314, uses al-Mahdi and al-Sharqawi as examples. To al-Jabarti, who was much taken up with this feature of 'ulama life, Shaykh Muhammad al-Mahdi al-Hifni (d. 1814) offered one of the more impressive examples of an 'alim who made his fortune on the basis of his intellectual and social abilities. See MS Aja'ib, IV, 233.

47 Murtada al-Zabidi received such favours: MS Aja'ib, II, 200

48 Al-Jabarti mentions a couple of such incidents: MS Aja'ib, IV, 161.

49 Al-Nahhal, Judicial Administration, pp. 68ff.

50 Marsot, 'Wealth of the Ulama', pp. 208–12; Raymond, Artisans et commerçants, vol. II, p. 428 adds further details. Even students took part, using connections in their place of origin: MS Aja'ib, II, 104; Winter, Egyptian Society, pp. 115ff.

51 According to al-Jabarti, al-Sharqawi's wife played such a role: MS Aja'ib, IV, 161.

52 Marsot, 'The Wealth of the Ulama', pp. 206–7; Winter, Egyptian Society, pp. 125–6.

53 Crecelius, 'The Emergence of the Shaykh al-Azhar', p. 110. Shaw and Marsot are more inclusive (Shaw, Ottoman Egypt in the Age of the French Revolution, p. 97; Marsot, 'The 'Ulama' of Cairo', pp. 152–3). All three concentrate on what Crecelius terms 'an unofficial hierarchy of native religious leaders'. Crecelius and Marsot note the existence of 'an official Ottoman hierarchy drawn almost exclusively from Istanbul' (Crecelius), but do not discuss the relationship between the two.

54 De Jong, Turuq and Turuq-Linked Institutions, p. 9 n. 9, p. 39; Winter, Egyptian Society, p. 143.

55 Crecelius, 'The Emergence of the Shaykh al-Azhar', p. 113; Shaw, Ottoman Egypt in the Eighteenth Century, p. 23. The dating of this important document has been questioned: see Pieterberg, 'Formation', p. 279.

56 MS Aja'ib, IV, 189.

57 Crecelius, 'The Emergence of the Shaykh al-Azhar', p. 114; Marsot, 'The 'Ulama' of Cairo', p. 151.

58 Winter, Egyptian Society, p. 144.

59 The same applies for Gran's statements (Islamic Roots of Capitalism, pp.

4, 42) that the Wafa'iyya was a basically quietistic order, based on upper-class/merchant patronage and that the followers of this order, as the continuators of ahl al-bayt (descendants of the Prophet's family), were making a certain claim to the right to rule. The shaykh al-Sadat in the 1790s, Shams al Din Muhammad, like other great sufi leaders at the time, thought that he had an assured social basis of support and could freely pursue the accumulation of wealth.

[60] Crecelius, 'The Emergence of the Shaykh al-Azhar', p. 113.

[61] Winter, 'The Ashraf and Niqabat al-ashraf', p. 38.

[62] De Jong, Turuq and Turuq-Linked Institutions, p. 220.

[63] Crecelius, 'The Emergence of the Shaykh al-Azhar', p. 113.

[64] De Jong, Turuq and Turuq-Linked Institutions, pp. 31, 220.

[65] Crecelius, 'The Emergence of the Shaykh al-Azhar', p. 110ff. The fact that the shaykh al-Azhar 'Abdallah al-Sharqawi played a leading, if not the most important, role in the period 1798–1811 can, according to Crecelius, be put down to a question of personality. As Crecelius sees it, in a period when political power was diffused and functions undifferentiated, the influence of any religious office might be temporarily expanded or reduced by the personality of the occupant. But al-Sharqawi's influence may also stem from the fact that he was an administrator of revenues from awqaf which supplied the bread-rations for students and the poor at al-Azhar: see MS Aja'ib, IV, 162.

[66] Nelly Hanna, 'Culture in Ottoman Egypt', in M.W. Daly (ed.), The Cambridge History of Egypt, vol. II, Cambridge 1998, pp. 88ff.

[67] MS Aja'ib, II, 206.

[68] MS Aja'ib, I, 204, 192, 385, II, 197, IV, 333, 186.

[69] MS Aja'ib, I, 5, 203, 332.

[70] Al-Jabarti relates how Qasim Bey Abu Seif (d. 1801–2) built a palace with a beautiful garden. This garden was opened to the public and a place to drink coffee was opened inside. Elite and rank and file could meet there: MS Aja'ib, III, 219.

[71] Hanna, 'Culture in Ottoman Egypt', p. 110.

[72] Shaw, Financial and Administrative Organization, pp. 1ff.

[73] Skovgaard- Petersen, Defining Islam, p. 54. Franz Rosenthal, A History of Muslim Historiography, Leiden 1968, p. 68 notes: 'As in classical antiquity, the publishing of a book in Islam required that the author's finished work was given to friends or pupils for the purpose of making copies of it, or it was turned over to the professional copyist and bookdealer, who made a number of copies of the particular work for sale.' But this picture only gives us an idea of how things were organized in the fourteenth and fifteenth centuries. I have not come across evidence as to how the production, distribution and function of the manuscript/book in the forming of public opinion were organized at the time of al-Jabarti. Further studies into

his chronicles should address this important question in order to gather whatever hints they contain on this issue.

74 P.M. Holt, 'Literary Offerings: A Genre of Courtly Literature', in Philipp and Haarmann (eds.), The Mamluks, pp. 3ff.

75 The following observations are based on Skovgaard-Petersen, Defining Islam, pp. 52ff.

The 'Ulama

5   Egypt's years of crisis and change

The political turmoil of the 1780s did not favour a quick recovery, but conditions in the countryside may have improved somewhat in the 1790s. After the death of Isma'il Bey, Murad and Ibrahim enjoyed uncontested rule until the arrival of the French. The famine caused by low floods in 1791 and 1792 was relieved, at least in Cairo, by grain from the Balkans. The flood in 1793 was again low, but an adequate amount of land was irrigated and a good harvest ensured by the extra care taken to repair village dikes and canals. Al-Jabarti's account suggests that once the fighting ended and a degree of security was restored, agricultural production was headed for recovery.[1] Modern historians, relying on al-Jabarti and French sources, have suggested that the tyranny of the Qazdagli emirs Murad and Ibrahim ruined the richest province of the eastern Mediterranean and paved the way for a French invasion. More recent studies show a more complicated picture. There is no clear proof that the net burden of taxes borne by the peasantry actually increased in the eighteenth century. The nominal rise in the value of taxes in the late eighteenth and early nineteenth centuries may have been more than offset by the devaluation of the coinage and inflation. It has been suggested that by 1793 conditions were improving, and this is supported by the fact that after the settlement between the emirs and the 'ulama in November 1794, al-Jabarti has nothing unusual to report until the arrival of the French in July 1798.[2]

This settlement in November 1794 appears to have put an end to much of the political turmoil. The retainers of Muhammad Bey al-Alfi, one of Murad Bey's *mamluks*, had levied contributions in a village in Bilbays, in which the shaykh al-Azhar, 'Abdallah al-Sharqawi, owned some land. Al-Sharqawi assembled the shaykhs in al-Azhar. The doors of the mosque were closed and people ordered to lock up the markets and stalls. The next day the shaykhs and a large crowd went to the house of the shaykh al-Sadat. Ibrahim Bey sent Ayyub Bey al-Daftardar to negotiate. The shaykhs demanded the abolition of new levies and duties. Ayyub Bey temporized and passed the matter on to Ibrahim Bey and Murad Bey. Eventually a settlement was agreed by the mediation of the Ottoman governor in which the emirs agreed to pay the shaykhs their salaries, send the grain to the Holy Cities using the grain in the storehouses and the money from their fiefs, and abolish new imposts and duties except for those of Bulaq. They also undertook to prevent their retainers from appropriating the people's property.

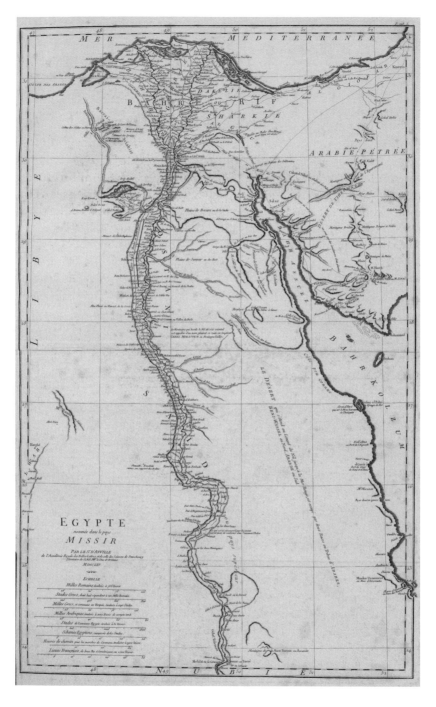

Map of Egypt by Bourginon d'Anville 1765. Reproduced from Description de l'Egypte (Etat Moderne, vol. 1). Photo: The Royal Library, Copenhagen.

Al-Jabarti's account of this settlement should be treated with caution. As we shall see, it was probably written ten years later, and with a specific purpose. But if we confine ourselves to the terms of the settlement, which are sufficiently precise to represent what was actually agreed upon at the time, they may illustrate two aspects of the situation in the mid-1790s.[3] In the first place, they highlight the plight of the emirs. The economic setback and inflation had weakened the power of the leading households. Less revenue meant less money to support or attract clients, buy *mamluk*s and pay for mercenaries to maintain power and peace. In this situation the emirs resorted to stricter collection of taxes or new levies to meet expenses. That would account for the forays of their retainers into the villages and the exception made for the customs in Bulaq, which was the port of Cairo and the centre of international trade for the city.[4] Economies in expenditure would be another measure. The provision of grain to support the Holy Cities would be an obvious place to start. Although this would be a short-term measure, impairing as it did the Red Sea trade in which the grain for the Holy Cities played an important part, it was attractive because the support of the Holy Cities was one of the ancient duties levied on the Egyptian province by the Ottoman government. The blame would fall on the sultan and the government in Istanbul. However, it did not enhance the religious prestige of the emirs, and offended the religious establishment by denying the shaykhs and their clients their salaries, but this apparently was a risk the emirs were prepared to take.

Second, the settlement may throw some additional light on the relation between the emirs and the 'ulama in the 1790s. Apparently the levies placed on the villages not only affected the income of the peasants but also that of the 'ulama. As the economic crisis reduced the attractiveness of *iltizam*s to most investors, the proportion of 'ulama among all *multazim*s increased further. Cuno, seeing things from the point of view of the peasants (and al-Jabarti), puts this down to the ability of the 'ulama to protect their peasants to some extent from the demands of the emirs;[5] and this is exactly the impression that al-Jabarti intended to convey.

An alternative interpretation may see it as an expression of a trend, already evident in the previous years, of the 'ulama being co-opted into the client–patron network of the dominant households and their allies to strengthen the political hand of the grandees in a critical period. The way al-Jabarti presents the story may illustrate the loose and dynamic character of this relationship. It indicates that the 'ulama were able to mobilize and control the people in support of their cause. The French historian André Raymond has

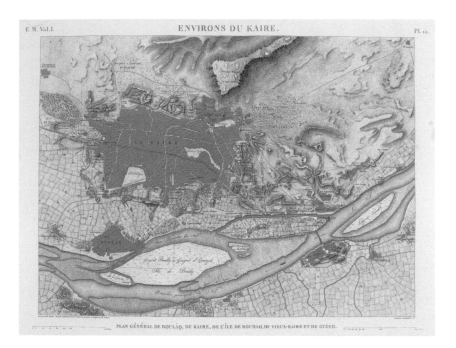

PLAN GÉNÉRAL DE BOULÂQ, DU KAIRE, DE L'ÎLE DE ROUDAH, DU VIEUX-KAIRE ET DE GYZEH.

Balzac del.

← *Plan of Cairo and its environs, published in Description de l'Egypte (Etat Moderne, vol. I, pl. 15). The city of Cairo had since Fatimid times in the late tenth century been situated between the Muqattam Hills to the east and the low-lying areas on the eastern bank of the Nile. Bulaq, the harbour of the city, is seen to the north (left on the map) on the eastern bank of the river. Gizeh, where Murad Bey and Bonaparte chose to stay, lies opposite the island of Rodah, on the western bank of the Nile and connected with the eastern bank by a pontoon bridge (constructed by the French). Opposite the southern tip of Rodah island lies Old Cairo, the site of Cairo in Roman and Byzantine times. Photo: The Royal Library, Copenhagen*

↓ *View of the house of al-Alfi on the bank of al-Azbakiyya (Description de l'Egypte, Etat Moderne, vol. I, pl. 52). This palace with its extensive gardens was taken over as the general headquarters of the French army from 1798 to 1801. Bonaparte himself preferred to stay on the western bank of the Nile in the palace of Murad Bey in Gizeh. Photo: The Royal Library, Copenhagen*

suggested that uprisings in Cairo, formerly simple and straightforward reactions on the part of the inhabitants to bad economic conditions, turned into open rebellions against the oppressive rule of the emirs after 1780, and from the 1790s became political movements in which the Egyptian middle class and the 'ulama took part in order to safeguard their interests.[6] The proceedings leading up to the settlement may indicate that it might have been the other way around, with the shaykhs orchestrating public demonstrations and protests while negotiating the conditions of their support with their patrons.

THE FRENCH OCCUPATION, 1798–1801

The French invasion threw the country back into turmoil. Bonaparte and his army landed in Alexandria on 1 July 1798, and marched overland to Cairo. The army of Ibrahim and Murad Bey was defeated on 21 July in the battle of Imbaba, the famous battle of the Pyramids to the French. Ibrahim fled eastwards to Gaza, and Murad to the south. The French proceeded to occupy the Delta, and sent an expedition to the south to establish French rule over the entire Egyptian province.

The Ottomans could not accept the occupation of Egypt by a foreign power, but the international situation was precarious. Only when news of the destruction of the main part of the French fleet in the battle of Aboukir on 1 August 1798 reached Istanbul did the Ottoman government feel safe to act. On 2 September it declared war on France. The pro-French ministers were arrested, and in their place Yusuf Zia Pasha, an ally of the 'ulama, was made grand vizier. Plans for joint military action by the Russian, British and Ottoman forces were agreed upon. Alliances were concluded with England and Russia in January 1799.[7]

In October the French were faced with rebellions in Damietta on the Mediterranean coast and in the city of Cairo itself. Both were put down with brute force. In February 1799 Bonaparte launched an attack up the Syrian coast to forestall a concentration of Ottoman forces in this quarter. An attempt to take the town of Acre (23 March–21 May) failed, and Bonaparte hastened back to meet another Ottoman army landing in Alexandria. This army was more or less annihilated. With these campaigns Bonaparte had secured French rule in Egypt. On 22 August 1799 he returned to France, which had become embroiled in a new war with Austria and Russia.

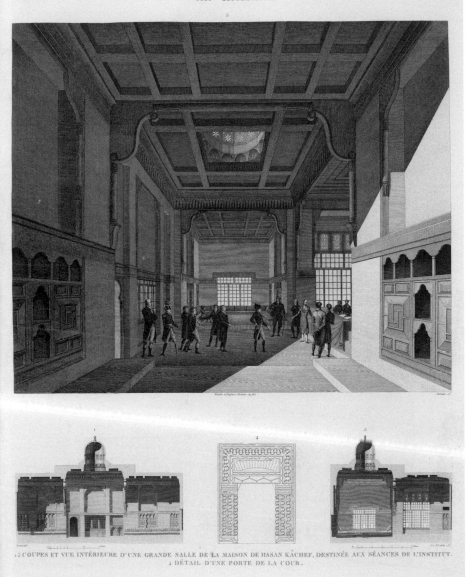

View of Bonaparte and his entourage visiting the Institut d'Egypte in the former palace of Hasan Kashif (Description de l'Egypte, Etat Moderne, vol. I, pl. 55). The Institut d'Egypte was inaugurated by Bonaparte in August 1798 as a centre for the scientists and artists accompanying the French expedition to Egypt. Photo: The Royal Library, Copenhagen

Portrait of General Jean-Baptiste Kléber (1753–1800). Drawing by André Dutertre. Kléber was wounded at Alexandria in 1798. He was French commander in Alexandria until General Bonaparte made him commander-in-chief when he left for France in august 1799. The Egyptians found Kléber a much less accommodating ruler than Bonaparte. But he won the respect of the French army by his energetic reaction to the failure of the convention of El Arish in January 1800. His murder in June 1800 was seen as a disaster. Chateaux de Versailles et de Trianon. Photo: Réunion des Musées Nationaux – Gerard Blot

On his departure, General Kléber took over the command of the French occupational forces in Egypt. On 24 January 1800 he concluded an agreement with the Ottoman government at El Arish, which allowed the French to leave Egypt and return to France. But the British, who were allies of the Ottomans, refused to acknowledge the agreement. General Kléber decided to face the Ottoman army, which was routed in the battle of Heliopolis outside Cairo on 20 March 1800. Part of this army, together with the returning emirs, was besieged in Cairo for several weeks, until an agreement with the French allowed them to leave the city and return to Syria. French rule was restored in Cairo and the Delta, while Murad Bey was allowed to take over Upper Egypt as the ally of the French. He died of the plague in April 1801. On 14 June 1800 General Kléber was murdered in his residence in Cairo, and command of the French forces was taken over by General Menou. The Ottoman government did nothing, and the situation created by General Kléber continued uncontested for another year. In Egypt the administration of Menou, a convert to Islam, created a more relaxed atmosphere.

In 1801 the Ottoman grand vizier, Yusuf Zia Pasha, and his army set out from Jaffa, this time in cooperation with a British expeditionary force landing in Alexandria. The French attempt to repel the British failed. General Menou and his army retreated into Alexandria, while the French in Cairo were defeated and capitulated to the Ottoman army of Yusuf Pasha, which was advancing on Cairo from the east. Menou held out in Alexandria until 31 August 1801, when the French were allowed to return to France under much the same conditions as at El Arish the year before. In the peace of Amiens concluded in 1802, which put an end to the war between the European powers, Egypt was returned to the Ottoman Empire.

The impact of the French conquest and occupation from 1798 to 1801 has been at the centre of a long debate on the origins of modern Egypt and the changes brought about by Muhammad 'Ali. A recent summary of the debate on the impact of the French occupation[8] suggests that it did change the international position of Egypt, which acquired a prominent position in the thinking of European diplomats and strategists and would remain important for generations. Control of Egypt would not be the whole of the 'Eastern Question', but it was part of it, and that would affect Egypt's history on many future occasions. Whether this consciousness was shared by Egyptians is still in doubt, however, and although the image of Egypt created by the descriptions brought back to Europe made a tremendous impact on the European mind, culturally and intellectually, it must be admitted that judging from the chronicles of al-Jabarti European culture seems to have had virtually no impact in Egypt. The economic conditions during the occupation are probably best understood as a continuation or extension of the crisis of the previous decades. From a broader perspective, therefore, the French occupation made little difference in basic patterns of production, exchange and consumption. The French did move in the direction of significant change in land tenure and taxation, with the elimination of the tax-farming system, but relied on the existing tax-collecting bureaucracy, staffed primarily by Copts, and following their evacuation there were efforts to re-establish the system.

After the occupation there were individual cases of condemnation, retribution or flight, but there does not seem to have been much change in the relationship between the Muslim majority and the Christian and other minorities. The most significant socio-political consequence of these years seems to have been the weakening of the ruling elite. Wartime deaths from battle and plague reduced the number of *mamluk* fighters from 10,000–12,000 to perhaps 1,200 in 1802.[9] The ruling households might have regenerated themselves relatively quickly if they had been left unchallenged and in full possession of their *iltizams*, but they were not – and perhaps it was no longer a question of recruits and resources. As already suggested by al-Jabarti, the old ruling order seems to have irretrievably squandered whatever legitimacy it once possessed through its ineffective performance against the French and through the destructiveness of its rivalries both before and after the occupation. But the British did not share this view at the time, as we shall see.[10]

The assertion that the 'ulama's participation in the French diwans created a new desire among them to become involved in government is doubtful. As we have seen, advisory councils did not constitute an innovation. The Ottoman governor of Egypt had made use of such bodies, consisting of Ottoman officials, officers, beys and leading shaykhs of the 'ulama.[11] Seen in this light the French diwans can only be said to contain any novelty because of the preponderance of 'ulama, important representatives of the merchants and the Christian communities. Considering the nature of Egyptian society in this period with its patron–client relationships, it may even be fair to suggest that this preponderance was new only to the French, who, having ousted the emirs, had no one else to turn to for local cooperation. The 'ulama for their part would still be connected to the emirs and the Ottomans by clientele ties and their experience during the preceding years would probably have suggested that they would be well advised not to forget their patrons, even in exile. Actually, a case can be made for the proposition that the 'ulama and merchants saw themselves as sitting on the French diwans as representatives of the emirs.

Portrait of General Bonaparte in Egypt. Drawing by André Dutertre, 1798. Bonaparte was 29 years old when the expedition to Egypt set out from Toulon. Chateaux de Malmaison et Bois-Preau. Photo: Réunion des Musées Nationaux – Daniel Arnaudet

Portrait of General Jacques-François Menou (1750–1810). Drawing by André Duter-tre. Menou was the French commander in Rosetta until he became commander-in-chief of the French forces in Egypt after the death of Kléber in June 1800. During his time in Rosetta, Menou converted to Islam and married an Egyptian woman. Al-Jabarti found him slightly comical (a view shared by many of the French officers), but had to admit that many of his decisions were quite reasonable. The senior French officers (especially General Reynier) found his handling of the military situation in 1801 a disaster, but his actions were in line with his instructions, which were to prolong the French occupation by a couple of months in order to support the French position at the negotiation of peace. Chateaux de Versailles et de Trianon. Photo: Réunion des Musées Nationaux – Franck Raux

The 'Ulama

Ottoman rule in Egypt had been restored by the treaty of Amiens, but only on the surface. The emirs under Ibrahim Bey and 'Uthman Bey al-Bardisi wanted to regain their former power and influence, and found a willing ally in the British army in Alexandria. The Ottoman vizier Yusuf Pasha and his troops, including a large contingent of Albanians commanded by Tahir Pasha, for their part favoured an attempt to turn Egypt and its rich resources into an Ottoman province in more than name.

The history of Egypt in the following years is the complicated story of how different groups manoeuvred against each other in order to get the upper hand. On one side there was the Ottoman grand vizier, Yusuf Pasha, and later the Ottoman governor in Cairo; on the other the emirs under Ibrahim and al-Bardisi. Soon the Albanians under Tahir Pasha became a separate force, while the British in Alexandria still had a hand in affairs, despite evacuating their army in March 1803. From 1801 to March 1803 developments were heavily influenced by the fact that the British commanded the most effective military force in the province, and their main objective was to prevent a return of the French by ensuring that a strong provincial government was established in Egypt. In their opinion it was the emirs rather than the Ottoman army who could perform this task. On the other hand, they did not want to disrupt the alliance with the Ottoman government, and so worked for reconciliation between the Ottomans and the emirs. In this task they were pressed for time. The preliminaries of peace concluded in October 1801 stipulated that the British should leave Egypt and return the province to the Ottoman government. The Ottoman government had no intention of restoring the emirs to power, and saw this as a golden opportunity to rid themselves of these rivals for the resources of Egypt. They found a willing ally in the French, who were working hard to restore their friendship with the Ottoman government and to disrupt the British designs. To the British the visit of the French agent, General Sebastiani, to Cairo in late 1802 appeared as a clear warning that the French still had designs on Egypt.[12] The people of Cairo, the 'ulama and their leading shaykhs joined the game on various occasions, either in open rebellion against or in alliance with one of these contestants. In February 1804 the emir Muhammad al-Alfi, who had left Egypt with the British army, returned after eleven months in England. The leading emirs, Ibrahim Bey and 'Uthman Bey al-Bardisi, joined Muhammad 'Ali in an attempt to eliminate this new rival. But al-Alfi evaded them and settled in Rosetta.

The story of how Muhammad 'Ali managed to overcome these dangers and establish himself as uncontested ruler need not be repeated here in detail. In May 1805 'Umar Makram and the shaykhs decided to back Muhammad 'Ali and had him appointed acting governor, deposing the incumbent, Ahmad Pasha. In June the government in Istanbul approved this, but it was not until the beginning of August that Ahmad Pasha was persuaded to leave the Citadel. The death of the emir al-Alfi in January 1807 proved crucial, as it eliminated the last serious opponent among the emirs. An abortive British occupation of Alexandria in that year added further to his prestige and resources. He gained control of the profitable export of grain to the British forces in Malta and Spain. In May 1807 Sultan Selim III was deposed. The new sultan found himself with little room to manoeuvre, and had no alternative but to leave Egypt in the hands of Muhammad 'Ali.[13] The final blow was struck in March 1811. Muhammad 'Ali, having invited all the remaining emirs and their retainers to a celebration of the inauguration of his campaign in the Hijaz against the Wahhabis, had them all – several hundred – massacred on their way from the Citadel. Those who had stayed away were hunted down and killed. Ibrahim Bey fled to Sudan, where he died in poverty in 1815.[14]

The consolidation of Muhammad 'Ali's power was accompanied by a slow and cautious move to gain total control of the agricultural administration and resources, including those of the 'ulama. In 1809 all beneficiaries of tax-free land set aside for religious purposes in *awqaf* as well as holders of *usya* land (land cultivated by tax-farmers on their own account) were ordered to present their title deeds. Those who failed had their land confiscated, and the rest was taxed. This attack on the privileges of the 'ulama triggered a revolt in July 1809 led by the *naqib al-ashraf,* 'Umar Makram. The revolt failed and 'Umar Makram was exiled to Damietta. In 1812 Muhammad 'Ali's son Ibrahim seized all land set aside for religious purposes in Upper Egypt. The ensuing complaints of the 'ulama were ignored.

By 1811 Muhammad 'Ali had succeeded not only in deposing his political rivals, but also in extending his control over the actual cultivators of land and ridding himself of the various intermediaries who stood between the state and the peasants: emirs, *multazims*, village shaykhs or religious scholars. However, in 1812 resumption of British trade with the Black Sea lowered demand for Egyptian grain. The military expedition to Arabia put a considerable strain on his finances. In order to counter this crisis Muhammad 'Ali ordered a general survey, a cadastre, of all agricultural land in Egypt. The survey was completed in May 1814. With this cadastre in hand his officials confiscated land for which the *multazims* were unable to produce title deeds. Land set aside for religious purposes was also required to produce title deeds and taxed as normal taxable state land. Owners of legal *awqaf* were paid a monthly pension in compensation and allowed to hold *usya* land on condition that the land could be sold only to the government.[15]

To historians of the older generation the revolutionary aspect of Muhammad 'Ali's long reign lies in his willingness to depart from traditional patterns and concepts of government;[16] but this would probably be overstating the case. In the key areas of urban–rural commerce, the peasant land regime and the rural social structure there was a greater degree of continuity between conditions in the eighteenth century and the time of Muhammad 'Ali's rule than has usually been thought. Even the Pasha's reform of the agrarian administration had certain precedents in the Ottoman and Fatimid past.[17] Actually, Muhammad 'Ali seems to have conformed to the old pattern of household building and manoeuvring to rid himself of potential rivals and intermediaries in the agricultural administration by surveys and confiscations. Even the dissolution of the partnership between the 'ulama and the ruling elite, which has been seen as the most dramatic and far-reaching consequence of his rule, takes on another aspect after closer inspection. The changes in the agricultural administration only deprived the 'ulama of profits which might accrue from their access to the surplus and income of the *awqaf* and *iltizam*s. This surplus could be traded or invested, and it was probably this right that Muhammad 'Ali wanted for himself. The 'ulama lost their status as commercial partners, but not their regular income. As already indicated, the emirs of the late eighteenth century probably used these possibilities to tie the 'ulama into the network of the ruling households. Muhammad 'Ali also wanted to control the 'ulama, but having eliminated his rivals in the ruling class, he could afford to use other and cheaper methods. The exile of the *naqib al-ashraf*, 'Umar Makram, in 1809 was arranged with the assistance and full cooperation of the leading shaykhs of the 'ulama: al-Mahdi, al Dawakhili, al-Sharqawi and al-Sadat. As the old religious leaders died their positions were changed in a way that enabled Muhammad 'Ali to control the religious institutions. When the incumbent shaykh al-Bakri died in 1812 his successor was invested with authority over all the sufi orders of Egypt, thus seriously limiting the authority of his rival, the shaykh al-Sadat. When the shaykh al-Sadat, 'Umar's successor as *naqib al-ashraf*, died in 1813 his wealth was confiscated and the offices of shaykh al-Sadat and *naqib* separated. When the new *naqib*, al-Dawakhili, was dismissed in 1816, the office was awarded to the shaykh al-Bakri, who thus gained control of all the Egyptian sufi orders. When the shaykh al-Azhar, al-Sharqawi, died in 1813, the Pasha backed an outsider from a poor background, al-Shanawani, instead of the influential al-Mahdi and in 1815, at the death of Shanawani, he backed the poet and grammarian al-'Attar, who had just returned to Egypt after spending many years in Istanbul and Damascus.[18]

1 Cuno, *The Pasha's Peasants*, p. 31; MS Aja'ib, II, 250–1, 258–9, 262, 268.

2 Cuno, *The Pasha's Peasants*, p. 29; Raymond, *Artisans et commerçants*, vol. II, p. 106; MS Aja'ib, II, 258–9. Raymond (p. 104) notes that although conditions were improving from the end of 1793, the price of grain stayed relatively high in the years 1795–8. Nevertheless, in 1795 it was only half the price of 1793.

3 The terms of the settlement are reproduced by al-Khashshab. See the discussion below on the connection between these two sources.

4 Gran, *Islamic Roots of Capitalism*, p. 10 suggests that the vexations endured by the French merchants stemmed from their inability to pay for the Egyptian grain exported to France, owing to the French embargos and the British blockade of France.

5 Cuno, *The Pasha's Peasants*, pp. 36, 45, 32.

6 André Raymond, 'Quartiers et movements populaires au Caire au XVII-Iième siècle', in Holt (ed.), *Political and Social Change*, p. 115; Raymond, *Artisans et commerçants*, vol. II, p. 808 notes the silence of al-Jabarti 1794–8.

7 Shaw, *Between Old and New*, pp. 264–5, 267.

8 Darrel Dykstra, 'The French Occupation of Egpt, 1798–1801', in Daly (ed.), *The Cambridge History of Egypt*, pp. 134ff.

9 This number is based on Afaf Lutfi al-Sayyid Marsot, *Egypt in the Reign of Muhammad 'Ali*, Cambridge 1984, p. 38, who mentions that the Ottomans had placed an embargo on the importation of *mamluk*s to Egypt in 1802. Marsot does not supply the source. Al-Jabarti, MS Aja'ib, IV, 34 in his necrology of al-Alfi alludes to such an embargo.

10 Karol Sorby, 'The Struggle between Great Britain and France to Influence the Character of Government in Egypt 1801–1803', *Asian and African Studies* 22 (1986), pp. 168ff.

11 Shaw, *Financial and Administrative Organization*, p. 2; Shaw, *Ottoman Egypt in the Eighteenth Century*, p. 15.

12 Sorby, 'The Struggle', pp. 174ff.

13 K. Fahmy, 'The Era of Muhammad 'Ali Pasha, 1805–1848', in Daly (ed.), *The Cambridge History of Egypt*, p. 145.

14 Ibid., *passim*; MS Aja'ib, IV, 263.

15 Fahmy, 'The Era of Muhammad 'Ali Pasha', p. 149; Marsot, *Egypt in the Reign of Muhammad 'Ali*, p. 143; MS Aja'ib, IV, 209–11.

16 Crecelius, 'Nonideological Responses', p. 180.

17 Cuno, *The Pasha's Peasants*, p. 200.

18 Crecelius, 'Nonideological Responses', p. 181; de Jong, *Turuq and Turuq-Linked Institutions*, pp. 12, 20, 31; MS Aja'ib, IV, 164.

6   The golden age of the 'ulama?

The decades around 1800 have been presented as a period of un-precedented political influence and power for the 'ulama in Ottoman Egypt, and especially for the leaders of the religious establishment. According to Marsot, the years from the death of 'Ali Bey al-Kabir in 1773 until the deposition and exile of the *naqib* 'Umar Makram in 1809 were a 'brief golden age' in which the 'ulama, having realized how much the ruling elite were dependent upon them in controlling the political situation and in giving a semblance of legitimacy to their deeds, ruthlessly exploited their advantage to gain political authority and wealth. They showed a spurt of independence which became even more pronounced in 1805, when they decided to back Muhammad 'Ali as governor of Egypt. They did so because he had promised to govern Egypt in consultation with them; however, they were not willing to take an active share in government, and abdicated whatever political influ-ence they had as soon as Muhammad 'Ali moved to curb their powers.[1] Crecelius states that the 'ulama in these years were provided with vari-ous opportunities to maximize their political influence and raise their social positions through the acquisition of extravagant wealth.[2]

This picture of a 'golden age' of the 'ulama around 1800 and their subsequent slide from power has been crucial to the fortunes of this group in the history and politics of modern Egypt. They are depicted as having retreated when Muhammad 'Ali moved to reduce their power, leaving the process of the modernization of Egypt in the hands of secular-orientated, European-trained Egyptians and for-eigners. They are accused of thereby having missed the chance to make Islam an integral part of the new age – which was not only a mistake, but an act of treason, and seriously impeded their ability to find a place for religion and themselves in the society of modern Egypt. In the eyes of modernizers they simply could not be trusted to back the modernization process wholeheartedly.

This scenario is based on the assumption that the wealth of the 'ulama constitutes a gauge for their political stock, which rose when they were powerful and fell when they were not.[3] So what is the basis for the assertion of the mounting wealth of the 'ulama in these years? It is mainly based on information provided by al-Jabarti, to whom, as we shall see, such wealth constituted a serious moral prob-lem for the 'ulama.[4] The *waqfiyya* documents of al-Sadat, al-Sharqawi, 'Umar Makram and al-Bakri quoted by scholars may illustrate the diversity of the economic interests of the 'ulama, but do not easily lend themselves to estimates of personal wealth.[5]

The wealth and influence of these shaykhs would have been circumscribed by their responsibilities as leaders of large spiritual organizations. They were responsible for the livelihood of large numbers of people and the maintenance of the mosques and institutions in their care. The revenues at their disposal were also supposed to meet the expenses needed to celebrate such great and costly events of the Muslim year as the different *mawalid* as well as other major and minor events.[6] Their influence and power would to a large extent depend on how these responsibilities were discharged, and would be further circumscribed by religious tradition and their own spiritual leanings. Unlike the emirs they were not free to act as they pleased. The responsibility of the spiritual and secular well-being of the Muslim community rested on their shoulders. As leaders they would have to take part in the political game, and as such they would have to compromise; but, unlike the emirs, they would be allowed little leeway to diverge from their basic responsibilities towards the Muslim community.

The personal wealth of these shaykhs does not seem to have lifted them above well-to-do land-owners and men of business, and surely was no match for that of the members of the military elite. To this it should be added that this period was one of nearly uninterrupted crisis. Along with the urban economy, the rural areas were under pressure, with diminishing economic activity – especially from 1777 to 1812 – partly because of natural disasters (droughts, floods and epidemics), and partly because of inflation, political instability and nearly incessant warfare.[7] The nature of the sources of income of the 'ulama – *awqaf* and rural tax-farms – must have made it difficult to acquire 'extravagant riches' under such circumstances. If the many instances of 'ulama being obsessed with their economic situation quoted by al-Jabarti are based on fact, they could easily be seen as the natural and necessary attention paid by men to economic affairs in a time of a depressed economy and mounting inflation in order to meet the responsibilities towards all the people depending on them for their livelihoods.

The notion of a high degree of political influence on the part of the 'ulama is also based on information provided by al-Jabarti, but it is significant that in another contemporary chronicle, that of Nicolas Turc, the 'ulama are, if not completely absent in the description of events, then at least inconspicuous in comparison to the role assigned them by al-Jabarti. This would suggest that al-Jabarti, being an *'alim* with a natural interest in these matters, may have exaggerated the influence of the members of his profession. However, if the information supplied by al-Jabarti is based on facts, the political activity of the leading shaykhs does not necessarily reflect a high degree of political influence, but perhaps rather the need to take an active part in government when the institutions of the province were in a state of flux, just to protect their interests and those of the people in their care.

Seen in this light, the idea of a 'golden age' of the 'ulama in the decades around 1800 should at least be re-examined. The perception seems not only to be the outcome of relying too heavily on the chronicles of al-Jabarti, but also part of the paradigm of modernization and nationalism and as the necessary point of departure for the sad story of the mounting social isolation of the 'ulama in Egyptian society in the following years. From these perspectives, the decades around 1800 stand out as the years in which the 'ulama acquired a position of influence. This influence could have made them the natural leaders in the modernization of Egyptian society that was begun by Muhammad 'Ali if they had been able to see this activity as a cultural and ideological challenge[8] and act upon it, but they did not.

Why not? To some the answer lies in the very function of the 'ulama in Islamic society, which made political involvement a matter of secondary interest, a by-product of their social standing. They saw themselves as preservers of tradition, not as political innovators. Tradition decreed that though they might become involved in the political process they should neither direct nor lead it, save indirectly. Perhaps there remained vestiges of the concept that power corrupts. The 'ulama could not destroy that image of themselves. 'To obey those in authority has been followed by the 'ulama to the present day and in return those in authority have depended on the 'ulama in many respects!'[9] Others see the unwillingness of the 'ulama to accept the responsibilities of decision making both as a reflection of their concept of the basic divisions of functions among the various elements of Islamic government and as an admission of their inability to perform these vital functions themselves. Direct rule was too revolutionary an idea![10]

However, if the notion of a 'golden age' of influence and power diminishes or turns out to be a mirage, the importance of the question why the 'ulama did not seize power themselves disappears. If they did not miss an opportunity to take the lead, they simply acted in accordance with their position as cultural brokers, interpreters of tradition, legitimizers in Muslim society and leaders of large institutions. This position would always imply participation in the political process; but it would be qualified by tradition, which implied submission to the rulers. To expect the 'ulama to take the lead, alone or in support of Muhammad 'Ali, would be an anachronism. Rather, they would act politically according to the nature and power of the government and its administration and the strength of competing pressure groups, but with the important qualification that they would be guided by their responsibility towards the spiritual and secular well-being of the Muslim community, including tradition and the cumulative experience of men in their position.

What seems to be lacking in the evaluation of the political role of the 'ulama is an idea of how they looked upon themselves and their duties. How did they perceive their social and political activity? Although questions of this nature cannot confidently be answered, it would be helpful to have some sort of documentation on how the 'ulama themselves described their position and activities. The 'ulama are, in the words of Patrick Gaffney, both the symbolic articulator of fixed and sacred ideas and, by virtue of their own mundane roles in society, models for ordinary conduct in a changing world. Their efficacy as leaders depends on their capacity to maintain the dialectic inherent in and crucial to this double role. The right publicly to define the meaning of shared symbols and to interpret the inter-subjective experience by means of them is not arbitrary. Rather, it is the privilege and the responsibility of a designated role – in this case, that of preacher – to conjoin and expound the relationship between categories and values that are at once public and private (or sectional). The person or party who controls the assignment of meaning to religious or political symbols can also control the mobilization efficiency their central position has traditionally assigned to them.[11]

Such documentation has apparently been difficult to find, probably because, as Rudolph Peters has put it, this is the natural result of the outcome of the historical process. The forces of modernization have been victorious. They have determined the dominant vision of history, and in this vision there is little room for the losers![12] The purpose of the present study is, among other things, to examine some such documentation.

---

[1] Marsot, 'The 'Ulama' of Cairo', pp. 161–3.

[2] Crecelius, 'Nonideological Responses', p. 173.

[3] Marsot, 'The 'Ulama' of Cairo', pp. 156, 159.

[4] Ibid., p. 152. Marsot is aware of a certain negative bias in the attitude of al-Jabarti towards the acquisition of riches and political involvement of the leading 'ulama'ulama, but does not take the argument any further.

[5] Marsot, 'Wealth of the Ulama', pp. 212ff.; Marsot, 'A Socio-economic Sketch', p. 317.

[6] Marsot, 'A Socio-economic Sketch', p. 316.

[7] Cuno, *The Pasha's Peasants.*

[8] Crecelius, 'Nonideological Responses', pp. 179, 186.

[9] Marsot, 'The 'Ulama' of Cairo', p. 165; Crecelius, 'Nonideological Responses', p. 186.

[10] Crecelius, 'Nonideological Responses', p. 174.

[11] Patrick Gaffney, 'Authority and the Mosque in Upper Egypt: The Islamic Preacher as Image and Actor', in Roff (ed.), *Islam and the Political Economy of Meaning*, pp. 8 (editor's comments), 199, 203.

[12] R. Peters, 'Religious Attitudes towards Modernization in the Ottoman Empire', *Die Welt des Islams* 26 (1986), p. 76.

II

REALISTS, ACTIVISTS AND LOYALISTS IN CAIRO, 1798

al-'Aydarus, 'Ali al-Sa'idi, the Maliki *mufti* who preceded Ahmad al-Dardir, and Abu 'l-Imdad Ahmad ibn Wafa as his teachers.[4]

Considering his social status and education as a scholar it seems natural that al-Jabarti became associated with the Khalwatiyya and the Wafa'iyya sufi orders, those favoured by the orthodox educated upper-class Sunni Muslims in Cairo at the time. He was apparently initiated into the Khalwatiyya order by Shaykh Yusuf al-Hifni, brother of Shaykh Muhammad al-Hifni, shaykh al-Azhar, and became a friend of Sayyid 'Ali al-Zabira al-Rashidi, deputy of the Khalwati order in Rosetta. He calls Shaykh Mahmud al-Kurdi (d. 1781), an important Khalwati shaykh at the time, his shaykh and master. As for his connection with the Wafa'iyya, he proudly relates that when he was a child (in 1763–4) the former *naqib al-ashraf* and incumbent shaykh al-Sadat, Sayyid Ahmad, gave him the nickname Abu 'l-Azm (man of determination). He further mentions Sayyid Abu Anwar Shams al-Din ibn Wafa, shaykh al Sadat (d. 1813), as his master. Shaykh Muhammad al-Sabban al-Shafi'i, who was the right-hand man of the shaykh al-Sadat and a leading member of the Wafa'iyya, became his friend until his death in the plague in 1791.[5]

But his network also seems to have included people outside the 'ulama community. He became a friend of Sayyid Isma'il al-Khashshab, one of the luminaries of his time, who served as clerk for the French and later for Muhammad 'Ali,[6] and with Shaykh Hasan al-'Attar, the poet and grammarian who became shaykh al-Azhar under Muhammad 'Ali.[7] Other friends connected him with the administration and the ruling class of the emirs. Among these were Muhammad Efendi, chief clerk (*bas shagird*) of the *ruznama* (the daily account book at the provincial treasury in the Citadel),[8] Ibrahim Celebi ibn Ahmad Agha al-Barudi, whose mother was the daughter of Ibrahim Katkhuda al-Qazdagli and later married Muhammad Agha, the treasurer of this powerful emir.[9] Al-Jabarti also seems to have taken part, apparently in the company of his master al-Murtada, in high society in the house of Emir 'Abd al-Rahman Bey 'Uthman.[10] He calls Ahmad Kashif Shra'rawi, a former *mamluk* of Emir Salim Kashif, a *mamluk* of 'Uthman Bey al-Jirjawi, 'our dear amir'.[11] His connections included the family of the beduin shaykh and emir Humam al-Hawwari in Upper Egypt and the shaykh Suwaylim ibn Habib, one of the principal chiefs of the beduin in the province of Qalyubiya.[12]

Concerning his personal life, we know that in 1777 he built a house at al-Sanadiqiya near al-Azhar.[13] In 1780 he married the step-daughter of 'Ali ibn 'Abdallah, a freed *mamluk* of Darwish Agha, *bash ikhtiyar* (chief officer) of the regiment of the Chavushan, and a calligrapher.[14]

Realist, activists and loyalists in Cairo 1798

A portrait of al-Jabarti? André Raymond (in Annales Islamologiques 35 (2001), pp. 385–8) argues that as al-Jabarti seems to be the only person in Cairo in the years from 1798 to 1801 with any serious claim to be called an astronomer, this portrait by Dutertre, entitled The Astronomer (Description de l'Egypte , Etat Moderne, vol. II, pl. B 1), represents al-Jabarti. Photo: The Royal Library, Copenhagen

Of his official career we know very little. He does not mention any students of his own, and apparently held no teaching positions. In October 1800 the French under General Menou made him a member of their new diwan.[15] He informs us that in 1815 he functioned as supervisor of the Qarafa cemetery.[16]

These few facts, derived from his chronicles, suggest nothing extraordinary. Al-Jabarti seems to have been the son of a family of some standing and apparently fairly well-off. He apparently shared many of the interests and connections of an ordinary 'alim, especially with the mosque of al-Azhar and the sufi orders of the Khalwatiyya and the Wafa'iyya. What singles him out among his contemporaries is the voluminous body of historical works connected with his name. Professor Samuel Moreh, at present the scholar most intimately acquainted with the chronicles of al-Jabarti, has summarized his work as a historian as follows:[17]

1. In 1798 al-Jabarti wrote the *Ta'rikh muddat al-Faransis bi-Misr min sanat 1213 iala sanat 1216* ('A history of the period of the French [occupation] in Egypt from the year 1213[/1798] to 1216 [/1801]', in the following: MS Mudda). In spite of the title, this work covers only the first six months of the French occupation. Moreh is of the opinion that the manuscript he calls MS Mudda Leiden is al-Jabarti's personal autograph and that the many notes in the margins of this manuscript represent al-Jabarti's work towards the next version. A later owner of the manuscript provided the title. The fact that the manuscript lacks the *basmalla*, the traditional invocation at the beginning, has led Moreh to conclude that al-Jabarti considered it a part of the other material that was in his possession;[18] in other words, a draft version. It is this manuscript that Moreh published and translated.

2. In December 1801 al-Jabarti finished a new version on the basis of the MS Mudda with the title *Mazhar al taqdis bi-zawal dawlat al-Faransis* ('The demonstration of piety in the demise of French society',[19] in the following: MS Mazhar). The manuscript is dedicated to the Ottoman commander-in-chief, the vizier Yusuf Pasha, who entered Egypt after the departure of the French in 1801.[20] Moreh is of the opinion that the manuscript called MS Maz.Cam is al-Jabarti's personal autograph, and sees this manuscript as the source of the existing copies of this version, among these the manuscript that has been the basis of the printed text from 1969.[21]

Realist, activists and loyalists in Cairo 1798

3. In 1805–6 al-Jabarti finished the first three volumes of a third version, *Aja'ib al-athar fi' l-tarajim wa'l-akhbar* ('The marvellous compositions of biographies and wondrous seeds of men and their deeds',[22] in the following: MS Aja'ib). In the two preceding versions he had confined himself to the history of the French occupation. This time he started in the year 1688 (i.e. the beginning of the twelfth century AH) and carried on until 1805–6. Moreh considers the manuscript MS Aj.Cam to be the personal autograph of the author. A revised version of this copy has been the basis for the printed version from 1879, the Bulaq edition.[23]

From this summary it appears that the chronicles of al-Jabarti came about in a more or less continuous process from 1798 to 1805–6. This process can be followed quite closely through the author's personal autographs. The MS Mudda is a first draft, later elaborated into a manuscript dedicated to the returning Ottoman masters in Egypt after the evacuation of the French. Soon afterwards he set out to turn it into a full-fledged history of Egypt covering the preceding century and a half. After the appearance of the three-volume edition in 1805–6, al-Jabarti carried on collecting and editing material for his chronicle until his eyes failed him. This material was included in the Bulaq edition as volume IV.

Why did al-Jabarti start recording events? Why did he turn them into these voluminous chronicles? The chronicles themselves only supply vague and inconsistent answers to these questions, so important to the evaluation of this, the main narrative source to our understanding of the birth of modern Egypt. The analysis of the different versions in the following chapters will attempt to provide a more definite answer. At this point a few preliminary observations on the character of his chronicles will be appropriate.

The chronicles follow an annalistic pattern. In principle this means that every piece of information is connected with a date. This was the normal, traditional way of writing history at the time. The annalistic character of the chronicles places al-Jabarti squarely in the Ottoman–Egyptian historical tradition.[24] To readers – especially European readers – steeped in the tradition of history created under the impact of Romanticism and nationalism in the nineteenth century, with its openly stated purposes and flowing narrative based on reasoned causality, the annalistic approach of these chronicles to the writing of history seems a strange – not to say primitive and unreadable – way of communicating the past.

But the annalistic pattern has some advantages. Al-Jabarti's chronicles have kept their interest, not only because of their subject, but also because of the wealth of detail he supplies, and this is directly related to the annalistic approach, which can sometimes be a most fitting way of presenting the past. It is a genre perfectly suited to keeping track of contemporary events, in the eighteenth century as well as today, and in fact constitutes a well-defined narrative strategy, with a set of conventions and rules. As such it had and has some definite merits in the eyes of its readers, and in order to evaluate them properly as a historical source it is important to have a clear understanding of these merits.

To readers in eighteenth-century Egypt, usually trained for years in careful interpretation of texts and having only very limited access to reading material, the annalistic chronicle had many advantages. What the reader wanted, and what he could get in the annalistic chronicle, were facts presented in order, i.e. chronologically, commented on and elucidated by the author. The rest was up to himself and his ability to form it into a general picture of the past. Accordingly, reading books was considered a demanding task, calling for much thinking and discussion. For a reader steeped in this tradition, the modern, European historical narrative may have seemed an insult to his intelligence!

The attraction, both for the author and the reader, of the annalistic chronicle is that it allows the inclusion of facts bearing on several different aspects of society at the same time. In addition – and this was not unimportant either in Egypt or in Europe in those days – it was impossible to control. The annalistic chronicle posed grave difficulties to any attempt at censorship![25] Keys to the interpretation of events could easily be inserted into the text. They could also be excluded altogether, in favour of more subtle meanings and hints, such as juxtaposition of material and comments which only covered part of the contents and left the reader to draw his own conclusions on the basis of the rest.

It should also be kept in mind that in a place such as Egypt, still without printing presses and totally relying on scarce, costly, handwritten manuscripts, the annalistic framework was the most reasonable and economical way of giving the reading public access to the past, and supplying the reader with basic information. Besides, this way of writing of history could also have the advantage of making the task of the reader not only demanding but entertaining. He had to be trained in seeing the hidden meaning behind facts with no apparent connection (which, in a country like Egypt, would point to members of the 'ulama, whose education aimed at just that, as intended readers of the text). But if the reader did have this ability and the necessary time on his hands, the act of reading and interpreting history would have all the entertainment value of doing crosswords or a jigsaw puzzle![26]

Al-Jabarti obviously attempted to create a history of this kind.[27] The implication of the observations made above would be that the annalistically arranged text, just like life in general, contains many different types of material, loose ends and odd digressions, but that this does not prevent the author from conveying his interpretation of events to the reader, or the reader from getting the message! Like the creation of, and solving of, crossword puzzles, it just calls for a bit of hard thinking, imagination and the faculty of combination.

In the Ottoman annalistic historical tradition the material is generally arranged within a chronological framework of the reigns of the sultans and/or the local governor/pasha, creating the so-called 'sultan–pasha chronicle'. In her paper on three eighteenth-century Egyptian historians and al-Jabarti, Jane Hathaway has investigated the narrative strategy of these chronicles in eighteenth-century Ottoman Egyptian historical writing.[28] She notes that the dated events, the *akhbar/waqa'i* material, usually falls in one of four categories:

- political events, often augmented by official letters and stories drawn from local lore;[29]
- natural phenomena;
- necrologies, which al-Jabarti places at the end of the year and in order of importance, not alphabetically, as used to be the custom;
- curious stories.

Al-Jabarti obviously tried to emulate this pattern, but as Hathaway points out, he seems to have broken out of the narrative strategy of the classic sultan–pasha chronicle by abandoning the 'new pasha' rubric and by separating events from obituaries. Apart from this his presentation of events and obituaries retains the characteristics of earlier eighteenth-century chronicles, although he does embellish his obituaries by borrowing from the biographical tradition of the Mamluk sultanate. To Hathaway 'there is no denying that al-Jabarti was an innovator. Yet his innovations occurred within a living and evolving historical tradition.'[30]

The varying standard material of the sultan–pasha chronicle provides a useful tool for the modern reader to enter the strange and fascinating world of the annalistic chronicle in general, and the chronicles of al-Jabarti in particular. In the case of al-Jabarti we are fortunate enough to have several versions of the same work. We are able to follow his handling of his material closely through his personal copies with their multitude of marginal notes, and through this to understand some of the ideas behind the composition of his chronicles. A preliminary look at the MS Mudda shows that although the annalistic approach is already present in this version, much material is concentrated around a series of stories. One of these, the story of Muhammad Kurayyim, the man in charge in Alexandria when the French arrived, reads like a short story with a clear moral. In the MS Mazhar this story has been cut in half and has lost most of its moral implications. In the MS Aja'ib the story has been moved to the biography section at the end of the year, a feature which seems to have been developed in the MS Mazhar. This suggests that al-Jabarti actually tried to conform to the conventions of the sultan–pasha chronicle and that differences between these and the MS Aja'ib are the conscious (or unconscious, of course!) outcome of his working process.[31]

As already noted, authors habitually turn to the annalistic pattern when dealing with contemporary history. Al-Jabarti's chronicles deal with events that have taken place in his own lifetime, and as such they are contemporary history. All history – especially contemporary history – is written with an eye to the present. The author will, consciously or unconsciously, feel that the developments he describes concern – or even, if he writes contemporary history, include – himself and his contemporaries. His interpretation of the past will assume the character of personal experience from which to draw conclusions for the future for himself and others. As such all histories have repercussions for, or are part of, a debate on how the future should be. Al-Jabarti's chronicles are no exception.[32]

However, they are more than that. They tell the story of how his country came to be occupied by the foreign, non-Islamic forces of France. It is well known from similar historical writings, especially from the age of nationalism in the nineteenth and twentieth centuries, that defeat and occupation constitute a shattering experience, especially to the local ruling elites, whose ability to govern will be put in doubt. The outcome of the ensuing debate on how the defeat of the local forces came about is crucial for the future of these elites. From one of the more recent examples, the historical literature on the fate of occupied countries during the Second World War such as Denmark, Norway, Holland, Belgium and France, this message is quite clear. It is equally apparent that the indigenous historians of these countries seem to be relatively uninterested in the foreign occupying power. Instead, they concentrate on three quite different questions:

Realist, activists and loyalists in Cairo 1798

- how and why the local power failed to prevent the defeat and subsequent occupation;
- how the locals, the occupied people, rose to the challenge posed by the occupation, to their social, cultural and political independence;
- the lessons to be learnt from the answers given to the first two, politically or otherwise, for the future of the occupied country.

It seems to be impossible, even if the historian wants to, to avoid influencing the current political debate. History in this phase, i.e. the first ten to fifteen years after the occupation, has a political message, or at least a political implication, whether the historian wants this or not!

This would imply that in the phase of history writing concerning al-Jabarti and his contemporaries, the generation of historians during and after the French occupation, the picture painted of the actions of the occupying power was intended to provide a suitable background for the points of real interest: the challenge to the traditional, local order of things and the political implications for the future of how the locals rose to this challenge. It follows from this that if or when the picture of the occupying power changed, it did so not necessarily because of any change of interest in the occupying power as such on the part of the historians, but because of a change in the way they saw the challenge and its future political implications. Contemporary history, usually quite unconsciously because it has to do with the experience of the still living, sees the past as a function of the present. When the focus of the present changes, so does the past.[33]

Al-Jabarti wrote in a different age. The revolutionary wars of the 1790s and the French expedition to Egypt in 1798 are not the Second World War, not even the wars of the age of nationalism in the nineteenth century. But the similarities between the two periods and the focus of their historians do suggest that it would be worth considering whether al-Jabarti's changing views of the French (and other participants) stem from a change in his opinion of their doings as such, or from a change in his opinion of how the Egyptian, Muslim, side handled the challenge. And it would certainly be worthwhile to consider the political implications of his opinions on the local Egyptian political scene. Did his writings have a political resonance in Egyptian society around 1800, and to what degree does his presentation of facts fit this implication/message? The dedication of the MS Mazhar to the Ottoman vizier Yusuf Pasha and the prominent role afforded to the 'ulama in the introduction of the MS Aja'ib both suggest that this was the case. Al-Jabarti wrote in Arabic for an Arabic-speaking audience of whose nature we are only insufficiently informed, and it is reasonable to suppose that his main focus was on the actions of this audience and its handling of the French challenge, and only secondarily on the French themselves.

Al-Jabarti's opinions of the French invaders have been thoroughly analysed, and the findings in this respect still stand. The intention of the argument presented above is not to challenge them but merely to suggest that al-Jabarti, as a contemporary historian, wrote to influence his contemporaries, and that his changing views of the French do not necessarily reflect his opinion of the French at the time, nor constitute a clue to the purpose of his historical works. They may simply represent the idea of the French most suitable to other purposes of the author in writing his works on the occupation.

In 1798 an ordinary, but well-educated and well-connected, *'alim* set about recording the momentous events taking place in Ottoman Egypt and, once started, he carried on in a more or less continuous process until his eyes failed him twenty years later. We have an idea of the kind of society he belonged to, and are acquainted with its social structure and history. His chronicles supply us with information about his family, friends and connections. And most importantly, we have his chronicles and the story he tries to tell in them, composed in the annalistic Ottoman historical tradition. The task will be to fit these pieces together in order to place al-Jabarti and his chronicles as firmly as possible in the contemporary context of Egypt in the years around 1800.

1 D. Ayalon, 'The Historian al-Jabarti and his Background', *BSOAS* 23, 2 (1960), p. 237. I have not been able to consult the biographical entry of Murtada al-Zabidi on al-Jabarti, but according to Stefan Reichmuth, the biography lists the texts and books that al-Jabarti studied with al-Murtada: S. Reichmuth, 'Notes on Murtada al-Zabidi's *Mu'jam* as a Source for al-Jabarti's History', *JSAI* 25 (2001), p. 377.

2 Hasan seems to have had Maliki as well as Shafi'i connections. His guardian as a minor was Shaykh Muhammad al-Nasharti al-Maliki (MS Aja'ib, I, 70), and he studied with Shaykh 'Abdallah al-Basri al-Makki al-Shafi'i and Shaykh 'Umar al-Makki al-Shafi'i (MS Aja'ib, I, 84, 261). His connections with these two indicate strong ties to the Holy Cities.

3 Ayalon, 'al-Jabarti and his Background'; see his necrology in MS Aja'ib, I, 385ff.

4 MS Aja'ib, IV, 258, II, 196ff., I, 287, 364, 375, II, 52, 167, 252, I, 404, II, 88, 97, II, 169, II, 262, II, 181.

5 MS Aja'ib, I, 301, 339, II, 61, I, 316, II, 197, II, 228.

6 MS Aja'ib, II, 84, necrology, IV, 238.

7 MS Aja'ib, III, 109, 307.

8 MS Aja'ib, III, 290.

9 MS Aja'ib, II, 214.

10 MS Aja'ib, II, 222.

11 MS Aja'ib, III, 176.

12 MS Aja'ib, I, 345, 349.

13 MS Aja'ib, III, 215.

14 MS Aja'ib, II, 96.

15 MS Aja'ib, III, 137.

16 MS Aja'ib, IV, 261.

17 Moreh, 'Introduction', p. 18. In a recent paper Moreh (S. Moreh, 'al-Jabarti's Method of Composing his Chronicle', *JSAI* 25 (2001)) has restated his positions on many of the questions touched upon in the following. I have attempted to include his findings in this book wherever relevant. I would like to thank Jørgen Bæk Simonsen of the Carsten Niebuhr Institute, Copenhagen, for calling my attention to this paper.

18 Moreh, 'Introduction', p. 1, n. 3, p. 12, n. 41.

19 Crabbs' translation, in Jack A. Crabbs, *The Writing of History in Nineteenth-Century Egypt*, Cairo 1984, p. 45.

20 According to a note in the manuscript a Shaykh Ibrahim bought it from al-Jabarti in 1232(/1816–17) and noted that 'al-Jabarti was one of the savants of the council which the French established in Egypt . . . As he used to associate with the French scientists during their stay in Cairo, he was worried about his safety after their evacuation, so he compiled this book in order to relieve his conscience and to demonstrate his allegiance to the Ottoman Empire' (Moreh, 'Introduction', p. 8).

21 'Abd al-Rahman al-Jabarti, *Mazhar al-taqdis bidhihab dawlat al faransis, ed. Hasan Muhammad Gawhari and 'Umar al-Dasuqi, Cairo* 1969. Professor Thomas Philipp has kindly provided me with a translation of this text, covering the first two years of the French occupation (1213 and 1214 AH).

22 Crabbs' translation, in Crabbs, *The Writing of History*, p. 43.

23 'Abd al-Rahman al-Jabarti, *Aja'ib al athar fi'l-tarajim wa'l-akhbar*, 4 vols., *Bulaq* 1879–80. An English translation of this edition was published in 1994: *'Abd al-Rahman al-Jabarti's History of Egypt, ed. and trans. Thomas Philipp and Moshe Perlman et al., 3 vols. (vols. I–II: text, vol. III: guide), Stuttgart* 1994.

24 Crabbs, *The Writing of History*, p. 55; J. Hathaway, 'Sultans, Pashas, Taqwims*, and Mühimmes: A Reconsideration of Chronicle-Writing in Eighteenth-century Egypt', in Crecelius (ed.), *Eighteenth-Century Egypt*, pp. 77, 78. Hathaway sees al-Jabarti as an innovator of this genre, but contends that his innovations took place within a living and evolving historical tradition.

8 Composition and purpose of the MS Mudda

In the MS Mudda al-Jabarti tells the story of the French invasion of Egypt from a few days before their landing in Alexandria on 1 July 1798 to some time in January 1799. But he does not tell us when and why he set out to write it. In this chapter we will analyse the manuscript for traces of composition and other textual devices in order to find an answer to this question.

The MS Mudda contains additions and emendations. This suggests that the author saw it as an entity, a small book. In his introduction Moreh notes that the published text (MS Mudda Leiden) is an autograph and probably the first work, written by al-Jabarti in 1798 under the strong influence of the events of the French occupation.[1] Moreh points out that the lack of introduction and ordinary Muslim invocation, the copious marginal emendations and additions and missing colophon from the end, in addition to the number of folios in the MS, all indicate that MS Mudda is a rough draft.[2] To Moreh the negligence of literary usage and form, in addition to a proliferation of colloquial terms, expressions and linguistic patterns, bear this out.[3] But this does not mean that it was not thought of as a literary entity, a small book, and as such it would have a definite composition. Such composition, together with the outward, physical features of the text and the stylistic devices used by the author, could supply us with an indication of the purpose of the text.

The manuscript of the MS Mudda consists of a text of twenty-six folios held together with string, creating a small book, consisting of fifty-two pages. The outer leaf (fol. 1ab, 26ab) is somewhat stiffer than the rest. The inner leaf (fol. 12ab, 13ab) is slightly smaller than the rest and has a double frame in red ink, but the text on these pages does not follow the frame. One of the folios (fol. 6ab, 19ab) has a more glazed surface and the area on which the text is written is discoloured, perhaps indicating that the paper of this leaf has been reused. These features corroborate Moreh's suggestion that we are dealing with a draft, written on cheap, second-hand paper.[4]

The text itself is written in a clear handwriting. The quality varies, but it does seem to have been written by the same hand. The writing is in black ink throughout, except at one point: the words 'tafsir ma auda'hu hadda' ('here is an explanation') on folio 3b are written in red ink. This feature signals the beginning of the author's explanation of the French proclamation and as such points to the importance of this part of the text. The fact that the writer has taken the time to change the colour of the ink at this point, and only at this point in the whole text, indicates that the following interpretation of the French proclamation is the main feature of this booklet, if not the whole point of writing it.[5]

Two other physical features of the text stand out. First, at certain points lines have been put on top of the words, between the lines of text. Moreh has reproduced the length of these lines in his printed version very accurately. The significance of these lines will be discussed further below, but at this point it should be noted that their thickness, colour and course indicate that they were made while the text was being written. Second, the word *shahr* ('month') is written with a certain dash, which makes it stand out in the text. The same goes for the word *fi-hi* ('on this [day]'), but only in certain parts of the text.[6]

Additions have been made to the text, either between the lines or in the margins. The additions and corrections point to the conclusion that the MS Mudda is not a 'rough' draft, but rather a second (or finished?) draft, which has gone through a revision by the author, in the process of which he has corrected his text and added further items of information.

A review of these corrections and additions shows that the vast majority intend to clarify the wording in the text already written. But quite a few add new items of information.[7] This shows that in the process of clarification and addition, the author decided to change the meaning of his first draft at certain points in the narrative.[8] This is corroborated by the fact that most of the additions in the margins end with a *sahha* ('correct'). One of the additions has been struck out again, obviously because the author realized that his correction was wrong. In two places the corrections take the form of striking out a couple of lines in the original text.[9]

Some of the additions in the margins have been written upside down or partly so (fols. 11b, 16a, 16b, 17a, 20b, 25b). On folio 17a this becomes even more complicated. One part of the addition has been written by turning the paper 90 degrees, the other part by turning it 180 degrees back. The first has been struck out with two lines, the second with one line. This would indicate that the addition should be treated as two additions, both struck out. It is interesting to note that the second of these two additions contains a *sahha*. This feature points to the conclusion that the additions were inserted in the course of at least two revisions.

These corrections and additions seem to provide us with evidence as to how the author worked: having established a draft he reviewed his material, clarifying the wording and adding and subtract-

Realist, activists and loyalists in Cairo 1798

ing new information and, in the process, correcting the information and the opinions it provided. It would seem reasonable, then, to suggest that the MS Mudda came about in the same manner, the author starting with an even rougher draft than the one we have, and after checking it out and adding new items, rewrote it into the MS we now know as the MS Mudda.

From this, two points may be deduced. First, if the author worked as suggested above, the original composition could be expected to be blurred by later additions.[10] Second, and even more importantly, what Moreh terms the MS Mudda should really be treated as at least two separate texts: the rough first draft (i.e. the MS without the corrections and additions) and a second (and perhaps a third) draft (i.e. the MS including the corrections and additions). This will be the basis of the following analysis of the MS Mudda. The possibility that the additions in the second draft represent two or more revisions will be discussed in this connection.

LINES IN THE TEXT AS AN INDICATION OF AN OVERALL COMPOSITION

As already mentioned, the text of the manuscript has been supplied with lines above certain words. The natural explanation would be that they mark out transitions in the text, indicating some sort of division between materials of different nature. This would mean that the items of information between the lines represent sections with some sort of common content. If this is so, the lines could be an important clue to how al-Jabartī arranged his material.

The lines divide the text into forty-five or forty-six sections.[11] Some of them are easy to understand, as they mark the beginning and/or end of documents,[12] and so represent an attempt at what could be termed layout. An investigation of the dates indicates that only sections headed by lines and a definite date should be taken as an indication of a transition from one part of the text to another and, as such, of an original composition. Short sections headed by firm dates may be attached to the section before or after, as the content may indicate. Lines over other types of dates should be disregarded if there is no other obvious reason for accepting them as genuine transitions intended by the author. In some cases the existence of a marginal note in combination with a line would strengthen the argument for accepting the line as a genuine transition.[13] This would leave us with fourteen sections/blocs of text.[14]

Four could be said to contain separate, distinctive stories, but at the same time these sections also contain separate smaller pieces of information at the beginning or the end.[15] The suggestion made above, that the present MS is the product of one or more rewritings where new items of information have entered the text from the margins, could be the explanation for the character of these transitions.[16] Three sections constitute cohesive narratives of decisive events (the French descent on Egypt; the battle of Imbaba and its repercussions; and the insurrection in October); one contains analysis and comment, one a short story with a moral, and one a string of French orders, actions and decisions. The last two constitute well-defined sections with material grouped by the month.[17]

This points to the conclusion that the author attempted some sort of formal composition, especially at the beginning. His basis seems to be a strictly annalistic narrative, but four sections clearly represent an attempt to supply some sort of background and interpretation for the reader to understand what is going on. But somewhere in the process of arranging and integrating the many individual entries of his material, he decided on the monthly grouping, as the easy (and traditional and accepted?) way out of his difficulties: 'and so this month passed with its major and minor events, which are impossible to record because of their great number' (p. 114)!

These signs of formal composition should not make us disregard the fact that the other sections, although consisting of many subsections and being difficult to define, do show some cohesion and that, judged by their content, they show a pattern, providing the reader with the necessary background to understand and evaluate the narrative in the section about the rebellion in October 1798. Perhaps this pattern is only what the course of events would dictate. But still, these intermediary sections, although they do not have the cohesion and well-defined character of the first three, do show some signs of having been worked on in order to establish some sort of unitary composition.

THE BEGINNING AND END OF THE TEXT

The beginning of the text, though not a proper introduction, still has all the signs of an opening paragraph, echoing the traditional opening of historical chronicles of the sultan–pasha variety. As such it should be considered an important part of the composition, signifying that the author intends to concentrate on the actions of political leaders.

The end of the text is more difficult. As noted by Moreh, it lacks a proper colophon to indicate that the author was of the opinion that the work had come to a definite conclusion. If this is so, the text just peters out, without leaving any indications as to its purpose, as a traditional conclusion would. On the other hand, it should be kept in mind that the fact that January 1799 was not the end of the French occupation does not exclude the possibility that to al-Jabarti this might be the right moment to stop. Meagre as they are, the final Qur'anic quotations could still signify a conclusion. If this is the case, they should be taken as a very important part of the composition, with important implications for the interpretation of the character and purpose of the MS Mudda, as they point back to al-Jabarti's evaluation of the battle of Imbaba.[18] The point of the quotations would be that perhaps ('the final judgement is with God') the 'fires of hell and disgrace', which the Egyptian army had brought upon itself by its poor performance, was reiterated later and came to encompass the whole Egyptian people, as the information supplied in this/these last section(s) (or paragraphs) demonstrates.

THE AUTHOR'S TEXTUAL DEVICES

The author uses a range of textual devices: the annalistic approach; the position of the narrator; the quotation of letters and documents; direct speech and dialogue. These devices will be analysed one by one below.

The annalistic approach

Al-Jabarti's care for dating his information by the year, month, date and day of the week is stressed right from the start with the opening paragraph stating the year, followed by the meticulous wording of the dating of the first entry. In this way, the text of the MS Mudda seems to conform to the pattern of the sultan–pasha chronicle.

As noted above, until page 56, i.e. until the end of battle of Imbaba, the text is a running narrative, punctuated by the French proclamation and the author's analysis of its contents, and showing clear signs of having been arranged in order to enable the reader to get a clear picture of what is going on. But even in this part of the text, dates have a prominent place in the narrative. From pages 56 to 68, from 74 to 92 and again from 106 to 123 dates are the most prominent structural and stylistic element of the text.

Every item of information is connected to a day. A new piece of information starts with a new date (or a note saying that it happened 'on that [same] day'), in strict numerical order. There are several references to events mentioned before, but only a single reference to events at a later date.[19]

The dates separate the material into individual items with different content.[20] The events on a random day may consist of up to eleven such individual items. There seems to be no pattern in the use of different sorts of dates and no relation between the different sorts of dating and the content, except that most of the firm dates introduce some sort of action by the French; but as most entries are concerned with the French, this is hardly significant.

With a few exceptions, which will be treated below, the material consists of what Hathaway termed political events (*akhbar/waqa' i*).[21]

Most items are introduced by the verb in the third-person plural in the perfect ('they did'); a few are in the third-person singular, but still in the perfect. In 77 out of the 141 individually dated items, the subject is the French (either mentioned on implied), in 13 it is the French indirectly, in 12 the subjects are one or more of the emirs and in 13 one or more of the shaykhs. The remaining 26 are shared by a motley group: news (*khabar*), the people, the rebels, a certain man, a gang and so on.

Each individual item starts out with a short statement on what happened, followed by one or more of the following parts:

• additional information enlarging the short statement;
• the author's comment, with or without arguments;
• a factual account of what followed.

An example, chosen at random, of such an item, containing all four parts, could be this one on page 60:

> On Tuesday they [the French] summoned the guilds of merchant-men in the bazaars and imposed upon them a large sum, which they were unable to pay claiming that this was to be a loan to be repaid after sixty days. So they [the guilds] raised a hue and cry and asked for help, going to the Mosque of al-Azhar and the shrine of al-Husayni where they called upon the Shaykhs who spoke with [the French] interceding on their behalf. As a result the loan was reduced to half and they also extended the payment.

There is no hard-and-fast pattern as to how many of these elements are used in the individual items. If they all occur, they usually follow one another in the sequence mentioned above.

However, there is a clear difference between the entries in which either the emirs, their people or the French take action and

Realist, activists and loyalists in Cairo 1798

the entries in which the shaykhs take the initiative. When the shaykhs act, we usually get a factual, often detailed, account of what followed, marked by direct speech or pieces of dialogue. This is the case in nearly all items where the shaykhs are involved. If the emirs or the French take action, and the shaykhs are involved, the proceedings are told in detail, often with the use of direct speech and dialogue, and the outcome stated. We only hear of what the emirs and the French said when the shaykhs are present. This important feature will be investigated further below.

The annalistic approach constitutes the fundamental narrative strategy of the MS Mudda: people act, things happen and the author's duty is to record these facts meticulously in the right order. He may enlarge upon certain more complicated initiatives; he may comment upon them, and usually does so in one way or another – especially when they happen to be concerned with money, taxes or trade. But the author does not want, or is not expected, to arrange his material in any order other than the one supplied by events themselves. The proceedings of the General Diwan,[22] just to mention one instance, are recorded day by day, punctuated by other items with nothing to connect them except the dates.

This represents a conscious choice on the part of the author. In a few instances al-Jabarti reveals that he is quite aware of the bigger issues and forces behind the events he records.[23] But it is significant that these instances are connected with circumstances outside Egypt, in Istanbul and Europe: the reader is not expected to be acquainted with these issues!

Al-Jabarti chose to present events in this annalistic, fragmented way. This was how the historian should present his material: a recording of events in strict chronological order. He may enlarge on the individual events, comment upon them, but he is not allowed to draw conclusions of a general nature and he is not allowed to use such general conclusions as a basis for his composition, at least not to such a degree that it would ruin the annalistic framework. The idea seems to be that such behaviour in a historical narrative would be trespassing on the domain of God: The historian may comment, but the real answers, those that may influence the actions and morals of men, belong to God, as al-Jabarti himself notes, when he is on the verge of doing just that![24] The historian should present his material faithfully in the right chronological order. The reader will have to make his own judgement and draw his own conclusion. The author may help him with additional information and comments, and by inserting lines in the text to signify transitions, but not more.

It is evident that if the author abstained from organizing his facts to sustain his opinions of how the past came about, it is going to be difficult to define these opinions with any degree of certainty! But, fortunately, we are not left without clues. As noted above, within the annalistic framework, the author may work on the presentation and wording of the individual entries. In doing so he is obviously able to tilt the focus not only of the individual entries, but also of whole sections. By selecting which entries should be expanded with additional information, selecting the nature of this additional information and by commenting on it, he determines the focus of the reader and creates the sort of narrative flow and progression that the annalistic framework defies.

In two cases the author seems to deviate from his rule of presenting events in chronological order. The first is the accumulation of undated events at the end of the months of Jumada al-Thani and Rajab at the end of the text and the second is the story of Muhammad Kurayyim.

At the end of the month of Jumada al-Thani (p. 114) the author notes that 'this month passed with its major and minor events which are impossible to record because of their great number'. He then goes on to describe a place of amusement, a *tivoli*, instituted by the French, but open to all – Europeans, Muslims, Copts, Greeks and Jews alike – and the many changes in the city and its environs brought about by the French military and civilian constructions. In this connection he takes the opportunity to describe in some detail the library, school and laboratory set up for the French scientists, noting that this is an eyewitness account, as he went there himself. His comments on these institutions are favourable, in spite of the fact that they reveal activities that would pose a challenge to any Muslim.

With the beginning of Rajab, the author reverts to his annalistic narrative until page 122, where he notes that 'this month ended with the general and particular events that occurred'. As an example he relates an instance of burglary and murder committed by a group of French soldiers, noting that the French authorities showed interest in investigating the incident. The final entry of the month (and the MS) is another example concerned with the aggressive behaviour of the guards, insisting that the lamps in the streets be lit.

As already indicated, this arrangement is a new compositional departure. In the preceding narrative there is only one such indication of the beginnings or ends of months having any influence on the flow of the narrative.[25] At the end of Jumada al-Thani and Rajab he seems to take the opportunity to gather information which would otherwise have called for a host of additional individual entries. It

Realist, activists and loyalists in Cairo 1798

seems as if the author at some point lost track of the changes and decided to pool them together in a final entry. This incidentally allows him to use the eyewitness account, a new and strikingly different feature in his text, introduced for the first time only a couple of pages earlier. The entries at the end of Rajab are slightly different. The first does not differ from the preceding except for the missing date, while the content of the very last entry is of the same sweeping, undatable character as those at the end of the preceding month.

The nature of this feature brings to mind another of Hathaway's observations on the sultan–pasha chronicle: that the end of the term of the pasha was marked by an enumeration of his 'feats', i.e. the monuments he left behind and, in some cases, his physical and moral characteristics. The author seems to have found this feature useful to sum up the devastation brought about by the French. This would indicate that he wrote the text covering these two last months consecutively and perhaps separately from the preceding material, in an attempt to wind up his narrative. This suggestion would make sense of the fact that the preceding text is taken up by the aftermath of the insurrection, while the first entry of the month of Jumada al-Thani is the text of a letter in French, 'written through the mouths of the sheikhs', connected with the insurrection, but mostly concerned with expressing the French desire to get things back to normal. This would also make sense of the missing line between these two last months and would correspond with the suggestion made above: that the MS Mudda, although lacking the conventional ending, was actually intended to end where it does.

The second departure from the annalistic framework, the story of Muhammad Kurayyim (pp. 68–72), is, strictly speaking, not a departure at all: the story starts with a firm date and is termed a story (*akhbar*). What makes this entry different from the rest is the detailed background, the fact that it is supplied right from the start and covers nearly two pages, and the sweeping conclusion of the author at the end.

If we compare this story with the entry on page 87 about al-Hajj Muhammad ibn Qimuh al-Maghribi, which is of much the same nature (and even refers to the story of Muhammad Kurayyim), it becomes apparent that what makes the story of Muhammad Kurayyim stand out is the fact that the information supplied includes a much more detailed background and also that this background precedes the account of what took place on the date of the entry. In the case of the story of Muhammad Kurayyim this has the effect of adding suspense, preparing the way for the conclusion and the moral it expounds, which has a much wider, and quite different, purport from what one would have expected, turning its focus away from the actions of the French and concentrating on the internal affairs of the Muslim community instead. This would indicate that the author worked on the composition of the entry about Muhammad Kurayyim and in this process transformed it into a virtual short story with a moral. In this way the story, although not a departure from the annalistic framework, has been turned into something different from the usual entries, indicating to the reader that this entry contains something important. And in fact the story of Muhammad Kurayyim constitutes a warning to all Muslims: not only to avoid the French but also to stay clear of the temptations of being raised to power and influence by any master at the cost of truth and the well-being of the people.

The content of this story brings another of Hathaway's categories to mind: the *tarajim* (obituaries, necrologies). The MS Mudda does not contain any other examples of this feature, which corroborates the suggestion that the story of Muhammad Kurayyim is used consciously by the author as a compositional measure to convey a message.

The position of the narrator

The narrator of the MS Mudda does not introduce himself in his text. He is implied or just mentioned, as in the eyewitness accounts. As the narrator and the author are the same person by definition in non-fiction such as history, the reader is left to infer his identity and position from the way the story is told. This, of course, does not necessarily have to be so. The identity and position of the narrator should be considered just one of many devices on the part of the author to get his message across. As we shall see below, there is ample reason to believe that the voice of the narrator of the MS Mudda does not necessarily reflect the opinions of al-Jabarti alone.

Another point to keep in mind would be that as the whole point of writing history is to add past to present experience, the narrator should stick to facts. The choice of the annalistic approach as the framework of the story suggests just that – it supplies reality with all its confusing details: 'and the month passed with its major and minor events, which are impossible to record because of their great number'.[26] But the narrator has to make sure that the reality he reports is believed to be true. This is done by occasionally noting how the information became public: 'it was said', 'news and letters arrived', 'it was announced', 'they set up notices', 'his group brought

Realist, activists and loyalists in Cairo 1798

news' and so on. The point of this feature seems to be that from these hints the reader will create for himself the intended mental picture of the narrator meticulously gathering information, and would be prepared to accept items of information without such reference as gathered in much the same way. By carefully noting how information on events outside Cairo was obtained ('news and letters arrived') the narrator corroborates this impression. But it is significant that the reader is never allowed to know exactly how he came into possession of this information, except in two instances of eyewitness accounts[27] at the end of the MS, in which miscellaneous information, which he has been unable to record in other ways, is summed up. This leaves the reader with the impression of a narrator who does not rely on his own eyes, except in cases of information of minor importance. By his use of the objective third-person opening of the entries and by casually alluding to the available channels of information al-Jabarti underlines his position as the observant narrator, meticulously recording facts.

This does not mean that the narrator wants to hide behind the facts. He has no intention of concealing himself. On the contrary, by his comments he is very much present in the narrative, supplying necessary background, pertinent arguments and his own opinion of the importance of events on the country and of the merits of the different actors. His voice comes through in a steady commentary, usually leaving the reader in no doubt of his judgements. But although the reader normally has no difficulty in identifying comments of the narrator, he is never presented as such. Only once[28] does he mention himself in the connection with such comments. This feature has the effect of connecting the comments to the meticulous recording of events in the mind of the reader, and in this way lending them the authority of the implied observant and conscientiously working narrator.

His comments overwhelmingly concern individual items of information. Only rarely does he venture to comment on the total impact of the French invasion, and then in short, heated bursts, obviously called forth by events themselves.[29] He provides a running, often heated, commentary on individual events and, as we have seen above, this can turn an entry into a virtual short story with a moral. The quiet summary and impartial analysis are not expected of the sort of narrator al-Jabarti wants to convey to the reader, at least not in the first instance: when they do occur, they have all the signs of being later additions from the margin,[30] implying that it was only after assembling the text and reading it through that comments of this nature suggested themselves to him.

Al-Jabarti seems to take it as a matter of course that the narrator may comment on events. But he is not allowed to mix narrative with comment, i.e. to let the wording of the narrative be influenced by his opinion. He is obviously taking great pains to keep the two apart, although he finds it extremely difficult at times, and does allow his comment to intrude on the narrative more often than strictly necessary.[31] This, however, accounts for the wording only. As noted above, he has the possibility of selecting additional information with which to tilt the entry in the direction he wants.

In the example quoted above, the French imposition is not commented upon directly. No adjectives are added. But by adding the information on how the French occupation was received, he makes sure that the reader is left in no doubt as to the implications of this measure and of the point of view and loyalties of the narrator.

This distinction between the wording and the selection of information may seem trivial, but from the point of view of the reader and his conscious or unconscious judgement of the credibility of the narrator, it is quite crucial. It is this distinction that accounts for the fact that, although the vast majority of entries are taken up by French actions, the point of view of the narrator remains non-French (or Egyptian). Al-Jabarti seems above all to be concerned with the repercussions of the French occupation on Muslim, Cairene society. The French present the challenge, and the MS Mudda tells the story of how this challenge was met. Al-Jabarti is only interested in the French actions and intentions in order to present the true nature of this challenge.[32]

The use of letters and documents

In chronicles of the sultan–pasha variety, reference to letters and documents is one of the main compositional features. This is also the case in the MS Mudda. They turn up in the text with a dating, usually a firm dating or in the course of proceedings already fixed to a firm dating. They are treated as events or part of events, indicated by al-Jabarti's careful notes on the dating, publication or reception of these documents. The word used is *mukatiba* (correspondence), but more precise terms are used when appropriate: *waraqa* (paper, notice), *firman* (decree), *'ardhal* (report, petition), *tumar* (roll). The word *khabar* (news) is occasionally used in connection with *mukatiba*.[33] Nearly all letters and documents quoted are French. Compared to these, the contents of letters from other, especially Egyptian, sources are treated in a summary fashion.

Realist, activists and loyalists in Cairo 1798

This feature seems to have the function of providing the author with an opportunity to present information that would otherwise be difficult to handle within the annalistic framework, and its demand on the author/narrator for making plausible the accessibility of his information. Letters and documents provide information on events in other places than Cairo, and provide the author with the possibility of presenting and commenting on the intentions of the French.

This is borne out by the fact that the text of these documents is treated in very different ways. As Hathaway noted, the treatment of the text of such letters constitutes one of the author's devices to colour his narrative.[34] One, the French proclamation, is quoted *in extenso*, and given a thorough commentary.[35] Others, such as the rolls read before the Grand Diwan, are related in condensed form with a commentary.[36] Some are cited in full, with only short introductory remarks.[37] Others are presented in condensed form with certain parts quoted in full, usually without comment, except for one or two introductory remarks.[38] Yet another group are just given in condensed form, without comment.[39]

Obviously, the author was of the opinion that the treatment of these documents was one of the stylistic devices at his disposal. In the context of his narrative some of these documents would be in need of more careful handling than others. The openly stated reason is that al-Jabarti is highly critical of the style in which the letters of the French are written, and insists on explaining and commenting upon them, to enable the reader to understand them properly. The Special Diwan, called the Court of Cases, was set up by 'a decree (*firman*) in which they included clauses in a style revolting to one's nature and disgusting to one's ear and among these stipulations which can only be understood after much pondering on the meaning of their expressions'.[40]

But the different treatment would also indicate a difference in importance to the author's argument of the information contained in them. The introduction of the roll, read out to the new Diwan, established after the insurrection in October, is quoted in full over most of a page, in order to enable the reader to see for himself 'the falsifications and weak-minded deceit and its audacious presumption in claiming Mahdihood and Prophethood and proving these claims by their antitheses'.[41] A letter from Ibrahim Bey to the shaykhs is quoted in three terse sentences in a summary fashion that, although it is not stated in so many words, implies a want of importance.[42]

The author is also influenced by the necessity of finding the proper balance: the two letters written by the French 'through the mouths of the shaykhs' are quoted in full. They are accompanied by the explanation that the last 'exceeds' the first, referring no doubt to the fact that the last contains a different and more specific explanation of the present situation in Egypt,[43] and indicating that as the first has been quoted in full, the second with its wider and much more detailed interpretation should be given the same treatment.

This would indicate that the author, when introducing these documents, is aware of the fact that, by their mere presence and by the treatment he affords them, they convey an impression of the importance or significance of the information. Long texts quoted in full attract the attention of the reader, and this tilts the balance of his narrative in favour of the information and of the opinions expressed in the text of the document. This is obviously the reason for quoting the first letter written 'through the mouths of the shaykhs'. Although it is not stated in so many words, the lack of comment on its style and content indicates that the author has nothing more to add and therefore, by implication, is in agreement with the message contained in the letter.[44] But when necessary, he tries to counterbalance this effect with his commentary. Al-Jabarti is obviously of the opinion that the decree on taxation that the French put before the General Diwan is very important, forming, as he sees it, the beginning of a series of events that eventually sparked off the insurrection in October 1798. Accordingly, he provides a long and detailed summary of the stipulations, but lest the reader be misled into believing that, in doing so, the author is in favour of such a policy, he provides the necessary antidote of caustic remarks and pertinent arguments.[45] The same effect is created by summarizing part of the text of the document in connection with the quoting in full of special passages, which then take on the character of a comment so obvious to the reader that the author need not be explicit.[46]

The French proclamation is given a special treatment, being quoted in full and meticulously commented upon. The word used is *tafsir*, which means explanation or commentary, especially of the Qur'an, and al-Jabarti's comments on this document seem to be just that: a careful, but by no means neutral, explanation of words and constructions that would trouble the Arabic-speaking reader. When necessary he adds extra information on the behaviour of the French, in order to sustain his main argument that the proclamation is a ruse, meant to deceive the Muslims of Egypt into submission.[47]

What is significant, though, is the fact that in the case of this document al-Jabarti chose to supply the reader with both the original text and a thorough commentary – although, judging from his handling of other documents, he had other ways of presenting the information contained in this document at his disposal. The fact that he chose to write the words introducing the commentary in red ink here, and only here, in the whole MS lends additional weight to this observation.

The treatment of this document is obviously done on purpose, and several explanations suggest themselves. The first, already hinted at above, would be compositional, as a way of introducing the future masters properly and thoroughly. The second might be to stress the importance of a proper understanding of the contents and purposes of the document. To al-Jabarti it had far-reaching, fateful consequences for the people of Egypt, and the fact that the beginning of the commentary is signalled by red ink indicates that the real problem was the correct understanding of the contents. Some people in Egypt, perhaps the prospective readers of the MS Mudda, obviously needed enlightenment on this point, and judging from his line of argument, their mistake consisted in not fully realizing two things: first, that the principles the French professed in the document were unacceptable to Muslims; and second, that the French could not be trusted to act in accordance with these principles anyway. The conclusion to be drawn from these observations seems to be that to al-Jabarti some people had placed too much trust in the French and that one of the purposes of the MS Mudda, if not *the* purpose, was to persuade them to realize this and change their ways. The treatment of this document indicates that the MS Mudda was written as a contribution to a debate, and, judging from the wording of the comments, quite a heated one, on how to meet the challenge presented by the French invasion.

In addition to this, the reason for the special treatment of this document might also be to introduce the reader to al-Jabarti's way of explaining and commenting on a text, and, by implication, his ability to do so. By doing this al-Jabarti would strengthen his trustworthiness in the eyes of the reader and thus enable him to treat later documents in a more summary fashion without losing credibility as a careful Muslim historian.[48]

This suggestion could be carried even further: the juxtaposition of text and commentary could be a way, on the part of the author, of showing the reader how to handle the individual items in his annalistic framework. By having both the text itself and the commentary, the reader would be able to see which items are commented upon and which are not. In his commentary al-Jabarti is almost exclusively concerned with the way the French present themselves and with refuting their claim to being virtually Muslims. This is condemned as lies and deceit. But he never squarely confronts and refutes the main argument of the French: that the emirs had harassed French merchants and ruined the country, and by doing so had brought the French invasion upon the country. Noting this, the careful reader would conclude that this claim on the part of the French was true – the more so as he has been prepared for it by al-Jabarti's comments on the past behaviour of the emirs[49] on the preceding pages. The reader would conclude that when digesting the individually dated items, the information they provide should be taken as true, if the commentary has not modified or refuted them. By providing the reader with both text and commentary here, at the start of his narrative, al-Jabarti arguably not only provides an introduction to the new masters and establishes his credibility as a Muslim historian, but also provides a key for the reader to assess properly the wealth of information in the subsequent narrative.

So the letters and documents are not only a convenient means to present intentions and opinions otherwise difficult to handle inside the framework of the annalistic approach. The author uses them consciously as a compositional and textual feature, which allows him to turn the narrative in the direction he wants, within the annalistic framework. As such they have the same function as his wording of the individual entries and his decision to pose as the careful, well-informed Muslim/Cairene narrator. They allow him to tilt the balance of the narrative, stressing the importance of some information and/or interpretation of events without seriously breaking the annalistic framework and in doing so to provide the narrative with an additional momentum, which would otherwise have been difficult to establish. In addition, they arguably allow him to furnish the reader with a clue to his interpretation of the confusing wealth of facts that follows: every item of information should be pondered and thought about, carefully noting what the author finds to be in need of additional comment and information and what he does not.[50]

Direct speech and dialogue

A prominent feature of the MS Mudda is the frequent use of direct speech and dialogue. These features constitute drama: showing things instead of telling. As such, they greatly enhance the narrative, providing it with the same feeling of being there as the letters and documents, but in a much more readable form. Like letters and documents direct speech and dialogue allow the reader access to the minds of the characters in the drama; however, they do not account for themselves, and as such they pose a problem for the credibility of the narrative.

Realist, activists and loyalists in Cairo 1798

The cases of direct speech in the MS Mudda are mostly mere illustrations of the behaviour of the people of Cairo. They are usually short and poignant, lending additional drama to the story and corroboration to the author's conclusions and comments. For natural reasons they are especially numerous in connection with the aftermath of the battle of Imbaba and the insurrection.[51]

What could be termed proper dialogue, i.e. two or more sentences indicating a conversation, nearly always involves the leading shaykhs, in one case with the emirs, but mostly with the French, and never alone among themselves.[52] In a few cases the French alone are quoted, but this happens mostly in situations where the presence of the shaykhs is implied.[53]

An example is provided by the incident in which Bonaparte tries to persuade the members of the Diwan to carry a shawl-like garment in the French colours:

> On that day the members of the Diwan went to the head of the Diwan and they were invited to go to the Sari 'Askar [i.e. the French commander-in-chief, Bonaparte]. Shaykh al-Sharqawi, al-Sawi, and those who were present went with him. After sitting for a while, the Sari 'Askar got up from his seat and brought a three-piece taylasan (a shawl-like garment) of red, white and blue and put it on Shaykh al-Sharqawi's shoulder. The latter removed it with his hand and put it on the floor, asking to be excused from wearing it. The interpreter said, 'O Shaykhs! You have become dear friends of the Sari 'Askar, and his intention is to glorify you and to honour you with his attire and token, because if you are thus marked, the soldiers and the people will extol you and you will fill a great place in their hearts.' They answered, 'But our esteem may fail in the eyes of our Muslim brothers.' The Sari 'Askar became angry with Shaykh al-Sharqawi and said, 'This man is unsuited for leadership,' and some other words in his own language which have the same meaning. The rest of the group treated them politely and asked to be excused from wearing this shawl. The interpreter said, 'If you don't do this, you must put the emblem on your breast.' They answered, 'Grant us time to think it over,' and they agreed on a respite of twelve days.

The problem, especially with the dialogue, is that it implies the presence of the author/narrator, in one way or another. But the author never mentions himself in connection with these conversations, a fact which the two eyewitness accounts tend to stress. So the reader is left with the impression that somehow the author/narrator had a sufficiently close connection with one of the main participants, (the leading shaykhs) to be able to record the conversation in detail and by keeping the dialogue to the barest minimum necessary to convey the points he wants to make, he is able to get away with this device, without seriously endangering his credibility.

The passages containing dialogue focus the attention of the reader on the importance of the leading shaykhs and their role as mediators, protecting high and low against the greed and injustice of the new masters. As such they tend to outweigh the strong presence of the French in the narrative, conveyed by the many items on their initiatives, including their letters and documents. It is significant that the dialogue both in items where the French have the initiative and those where the shaykhs have raised a matter stresses the mediating role of the shaykhs. The author rarely comments on the outcome of negotiations between the French and the shaykhs, and only does so to defend the latters' position.[54]

So the dialogue represents more than mere illustrations, conveying the points of the narrative in a lively and readily accessible form. It is a means by which the author makes the endeavours and attitudes of the leading shaykhs come to the fore of a narrative otherwise dominated by the many initiatives and documents of the French. As such it represents the conscious use of another textual device to make the annalistic framework of the narrative conform to the ideas of the author.[55]

DESCRIPTION

Al-Jabarti did not seem to favour what might be termed proper description. A non-fictional narrative, dedicated to the faithful rendering of a confusing reality in strict chronological order, does not lend itself to colourful descriptions of scenery or how people look. In the MS Mudda, people act! This does not exclude description, of course. When the action becomes so intense that the mere recording of these actions makes them flow together, vivid scenes are created, either of horror and distress – as in the case of the aftermath of the battle or during the insurrection – or of a certain splendour – as in the case of the festivities arranged by the French (the Breaking of the Dam, the Birthday of the Prophet, the celebration of the Inauguration of the Republic). In these situations al-Jabarti notes how things and people look. But it is symptomatic that these descriptions nearly always seem to serve a purpose, and/or an argument on the part of the author.[56] According to Moreh he even breaks into rhymed prose and metaphors,[57] although the metaphors do not sound as if they come from

Realist, activists and loyalists in Cairo 1798

a man much used to expressing himself in this way.[58] But apart from these situations, it is significant that what could be called proper descriptions, how people or things looked, although not uncommon, are short and do not show any signs of being more than what ran into the author's pen, unnoticed. They do not seem to constitute a consciously used device, but are features called forth by the author's ambition to record what went on as clearly as possible.

CONCLUSION

This investigation of the composition of the rough draft, i.e. the text of the MS Mudda without the corrections and additions, has shown that to the author the annalistic approach, based on individually dated items, was the basis on which the past could be conveyed most faithfully and conveniently to the reader. At some point he seems to have decided to superimpose a monthly ordering of his material on this framework, either in order to conform to tradition or as a convenient way to relate information otherwise hard to include in his narrative. It has been argued that the MS Mudda has a definite ending and as such constitutes a textual entity.

Within this framework of strictly chronologically ordered entries, al-Jabarti had a string of devices at his disposal: the change of the colour of the ink, the use of lines, the wording and composition of the individual items, the rendering of letters and documents, the use of direct speech and dialogue. The individual items show signs of having been worked upon in varying degrees and in such a way that they become elements in a consciously composed narrative, subordinated to the writer's general opinion of how events should be interpreted.

This composition seems to indicate that what made al-Jabarti start writing a history of the French occupation was his concern with the fate of Muslim society and its rulers under the impact of the challenge posed by the French invasion. Two lines of thought seem to have been in his mind: to describe and analyse the nature of this challenge to the Muslim community of Egypt; and to show how the group nearest to his heart, the leading shaykhs of Cairo, coped with it. The basic interpretation of events, on which he tried to arrange his material, may run like this:

Faced with the French invasion, the old masters, the Mamluk emirs, fail completely, while the masters in Istanbul are only heard of by way of letters – beautifully written and expressing the right attitude to the French, but not by way of any significant action. This leaves the field to the leading shaykhs of Cairo to mediate between the new masters and the people. However, they can only accomplish this task if they have the foresight, the patience and the courage to stay unattached to any master. This is no easy matter: the new masters are full of deceit and greed. Their actions are often incomprehensible, even to themselves. The non-Muslim groups – the Copts and, especially, the Syrian Christians – take every opportunity to change their traditional lot in relation to the Muslim majority. The people, if not properly led, tend to turn into a headless mob. Outside the city gates the beduin and the *fellahin* will respect no authority except the sword and a solid guard! But as long as the leading shaykhs are able to stick together, they will be able to secure the unity of Muslim society and make the masters powerless and the people safe. If not, it will be the ruin of everybody, even the French masters, as was shown by the insurrection in October. After that fatal slip, things will never be the same: the French are scared and ready for new ominous initiatives. The shaykhs stand discredited and defenceless, steeped in 'the fires of Hell and disgrace'!

[1] Moreh, 'Introduction', p. 18. In the following, page numbers refer to the translation and folio numbers to the Arabic text in al-Jabarti, *Ta'rikh muddat al-Faransis*, ed. and trans. S. Moreh. Moreh's statement that MS Mudda was written some time during 1798 is borne out by the dating on p. 42 ('they rebelled against their sultan six years ago'), which points to a date between 21 September 1798 and 21 January 1799. But the last entries are introduced with 'This month [of Rajab] ended' (p. 122) and later 'other events of the month' (p. 123), which seem to indicate that the end of the month (7 January 1799) has already passed. This would point to a finishing date of the rough draft somewhere in January 1799. The changes made in the last passages of the MS Mudda, when it was turned into a part of the MS Mazhar (Philipp's trans., p. 127) seem to corroborate this.

[2] Moreh, 'Introduction', p. 12.

[3] Ibid., p. 26.

[4] Moreh's suggestion (ibid., p. 12) that the collation of the MS Mudda indicates that al-Jabarti was not fully aware of the total length of his booklet when he began to write it does not seem logical: the arrangement of the text on the leaves shows that he had twenty-six folios at his disposal when he set out to write, and that this is what he needed. The fact that the text uses all but one of these shows that he had a fairly accurate idea of the length of his text. This again points to the idea suggested further on, that the MS Mudda Leiden had predecessors in the form of even rougher drafts than the one we have.

Realist, activists and loyalists in Cairo 1798

5 In this light, the words used to denote the character of the proclamation – '*al-maktub al-mankub*' – become important. Moreh translates them as 'this miserable letter', a translation which points to the many errors and bad language it contains. A more fitting translation would be 'this ill-fated letter', stressing its unhappy consequences. This point will be discussed further below.

6 Especially from fols. 12–13b.

7 The corrections and additions will be dealt with in more detail below.

8 Fols. 51, 66–7 (which changes the dating of the following item), 73(?), 77, 81.

9 P. 89 (fol. 17a). The author seems to realize that he is confusing the first with the second Diwan (see pp. 119–21). On p. 35 (fol. 1b) a couple of words have been struck out to accommodate an addition. On p. 118 (fol. 25b) a couple of lines have been struck out.

10 An indication that this is the case is seen in the sequence pp. 48–9 and 63–4. On p. 49 the item 'Moreover, in the same month (*wafihi aidan*)' clearly breaks the sequence of dates. On pp. 63–4, the items of information describe the cutting of the canal, rumours about the battle of Aboukir and explain the essential features in the war between England and France. This is followed by an item on troops being sent to Alexandria and then, rather abruptly, we revert to the cutting of the canal, this time stating that the dam at Azbakiyya was closed to prevent water from damaging the French camp there. Seen in this context the paragraph on Aboukir and the war looks like an addition in a pre-Mudda draft. This means that the closing of the canal to Azbakiyya is depicted in the present text as taking place later than it actually did.

11 The last is on p. 113, but it is obvious from the flow of the text that the beginning of the month of Rajab on p. 118 marks the beginning of a new section. In the original MS the beginning of the months are not marked systematically: the beginning of the month of Safar (fol. 5b) is mentioned and marked with a line. The beginning of Rabiʿ al-Awal (fol. 10a) is more formally introduced and the word *shahr* is written with a dash, but there is no line and there is no interruption in the text. The beginning of Rabiʿ al-Thani (fol. 13a) is formally mentioned, marked with a line and the word *shahr* written with dash, while the text shows a break. The month of Jumada al-Ula (fol. 17a) is formally introduced and marked with a line and the word *shahr* is written with a dash, but there is no break in the text. The month of Jumada al-Thani (fol. 22b) is both formally introduced, marked with a line and *shahr* written with a dash and a clear break in the text. The month of Rajab (fol. 25b) is formally introduced and the word *shahr* written with a dash, while the text shows a clear break, but it is not marked with a line. This could point to the conclusion that the monthly headings – the formal introduction of the month and the word *shahr* written with a

dash – should be considered as a mere formality, while the lines have been superimposed on the text and so represent a secondary feature. If this is the case, the missing line at the beginning of the month of Rajab has been forgotten.

[12] Pp. 40–7, 110–12.

[13] Pp. 56, 59. On p. 117 it might account for the missing space at the beginning of the month of Rajab.

[14] 1: pp. 33–39; 2: pp. 40–7; 3: pp. 47–56; 4: pp. 56–61; 5: pp. 61–5; 6: pp. 65–8; 7: pp. 68–74; 8: pp. 75–8; 9: pp. 78–84; 10: pp. 84–92; 11: pp. 92–106; 12: pp. 106–12; 13: pp. 112–18; 14: pp. 118–23.

[15] Pp. 48–51 (on the fighting at Imbaba), 51–6 (on what happened on the eastern bank and in Cairo), 68–73 (on Muhammad Kurayyim), 92–106 (on the insurrection in Cairo).

[16] If the firmly dated items represent the backbone of al-Jabarti's chronology and the older part of the material, which went into the creation of the present MS Mudda, it would be pertinent to ask where he got those items and their dates. Dates are difficult to remember, and to be as precise as al-Jabarti is able to be would seem impossible without notes made during the events of the French occupation. A diary of some sort would be absolutely necessary. Now, it is not impossible to suppose that al-Jabarti kept a diary, considering his background and interest in astronomy. Lacking firm evidence of such a diary, the only way to get an idea of the source of these firm dates would be to investigate their contents in order to get some clues. This would point to a source or sources intimately concerned with the precise dates of the various actions of the French. As it is hard to imagine what use it would be to any Muslim to keep track of the French actions, the obvious suggestion would be that this source is French! But as the dates are according to the Muslim calendar, this would require a translation of the dates (and the contents, of course). We should therefore look for evidence of such a translation. The Coptic date, mentioned in connection with the Nile (p. 63), is evidence that al-Jabarti had a calendar of some sort at his disposal, although this double dating was the normal usage in Egypt at this time in connection with matters important to agriculture (Cyril Glassé , *The Concise Encyclopedia of Islam*, San Francisco 1989, p. 83). A manuscript in Leiden, written by the same hand as the MS Mudda, on astronomy and calendars, points in the same direction (Moreh, 'Introduction', p. 8 n. 29). According to Cardin, al-Jabarti produced a volume on arithmetic and astronomy (Ayalon, 'al-Jabarti and his Background', p. 247 n. 1).

[17] In the MS Mazhar, the changes made in the text of the MS Mudda, corresponding to the beginning of section 2 (p. 31) and section 4 (p. 55), underline the suggestion that the author saw these places as the beginning of something new and consequently corroborate the interpretation made above. See below.

Realist, activists and loyalists in Cairo 1798

[18] Pp. 52 and 123. Moreh has a different wording, and reference, in the translation for the two quotations, but the wording in the Arabic text is exactly the same.

[19] The reference to Barthelemy, p. 47. On p. 80 the text seems to indicate that al-Jabarti has some experience in how these stipulations came to work. But the wording of the Arabic text is not quite clear.

[20] There seem to be some discrepancies, though: on p. 60 there are two entries with firm dates: on Tuesday and on the 20th of the same month. But Tuesday *was* the 20th! The same thing happens on pp. 83–4: two entries (Saturday the 18th and Saturday) with separate firm dates actually concern events that took place on the same day. The strict sequence of dates is broken on p. 61: after events on the 28th we have a dating: late Sunday night, which must be the 25th. This lack of system may be explained by the way the MS came about, i.e. by the insertion of new items of information.

[21] Incidentally, the word news (*khabar:* news, story) has, in the plural (*akhbar*), the technical meaning of annals!

[22] Pp. 85–92.

[23] Pp. 37, 64.

[24] P. 45 is a good example.

[25] P.74. But the fact that the entry is singled out by lines makes it reasonable to suggest that this is the result of a marginal note entering the text.

[26] P. 114.

[27] Pp. 112, 116.

[28] P. 54.

[29] Pp. 54, 63 (where he summarizes the impact of the French occupation, called forth by the hostility toward the French demand for people to enjoy the Breaking of the Dam), 69, 101.

[30] P. 64; see note 10 above. The marginal note on p. 104 is actually one of these.

[31] The sequences on pp. 79 and 105.

[32] But this distinction may also stem from a more practical cause. If the MS Mudda came about from adding new items and comments to a rougher draft, as suggested above, such a distinction would be the natural result.

[33] Pp. 35, 36.

[34] Hathaway, 'Sultans, Pashas, *Taqwims*, and Mühimmes', p. 75.

[35] Pp. 39–47.

[36] Pp. 75, 86.

[37] Pp. 109, 110.

[38] Pp. 55, 75, 83, 119.

[39] Pp. 35, 36, 76, 108.

[40] P. 79.

[41] P. 119.

[42] P. 75.

43 Pp. 109, 110.

44 This interpretation is corroborated by the changes made in the MS Mazhar: see below.

45 Pp. 79ff. It is ironic that the author's final judgement in this matter (p. 81) in the uncorrected version of the MS Mudda is in favour of these measures. The mistake was duly corrected!

46 P. 83, in the report from the shaykhs to the sultan and the sharif of Mecca.

47 In doing this he mentions the appointment of the artilleryman Barthelemy to the post of Katkhuda Mustahfizan (p. 47). Barthelemy's investiture is mentioned on pp. 57–8, where he is introduced as a man of low status, who makes himself ridiculous by his pride in his new situation. But the specification of the appointment is an addition from the margin. Just previously al-Jabarti notes that this post was given to Muhammad Agha al-Muslimani. Later, at the end of the insurrection (p. 102), Barthelemy is placed in charge of the patrols who seek out those held responsible, and acts in the same ostentatious and ridiculous manner. This is one of the extremely rare cases in which events are mentioned and used before they actually occur. This indicates that the comment on the proclamation (and by implication, one of the first drafts of the MS Mudda) was put together some time after the French had settled in Cairo or, more likely, after the insurrection. This would strengthen the case for the insurrection as the event that motivated al-Jabarti to write the MS Mudda.

48 These interpretations of the significance of the French proclamation and its commentary are corroborated by the changes made in the comment in the MS Mazhar, and the fact that the whole commentary is deleted in the MS Aja'ib: see below.

49 P. 37.

50 Hathaway, 'Sultans, Pashas, *Taqwims*, and Mühimmes', p. 76 notes that in the case of her eighteenth-century chronicles the quoting of letters and documents suggested 'the crystallization of one form of narrative history through the dialogue between central and provincial administrations', i.e. a dialogue between Istanbul and Cairo and the Turkish and Arab scholarly-bureaucratic elites in the Ottoman Empire. Following this train of thought the inclusion of French documents and letters in the MS Mudda would indicate the existence of a similar dialogue between the French and the scholarly-bureaucratic elite of Egypt to which al-Jabarti belonged, and the emergence of a common historical tradition, based on common sources. This was already hinted at above in connection with the discussion of the possible source of the many dated items concerned with French actions. That the dialogue worked both ways is indicated by the fact that a text by al-Khashshab on the history of Egypt was incorporated nearly verbatim in the *Description de l'Egypte*: see Gran, *Islamic Roots of Capitalism*, p. 226 n. 11, and below.

Realist, activists and loyalists in Cairo 1798

[51] Pp. 48, 51, 52, 53, 63, 66, 75, 94, 97, 98, 99.

[52] Pp. 37, 55, 57, 60, 63, 67, 71, 72, 73, 89, 92, 96, 103, 104, 107.

[53] Pp. 62, 65, 66, 72, 75, 106, 118.

[54] Pp. 37, 67. Curiously, the only other group that seems to get the same treatment is the wives of the emirs, Sitt Nafisa, the wife of Murad Bey, and the wife of Ridwan Kashif al-Sha'rawi. The mixture of gallantry and clever accommodation they put up in defence of the property of their husbands clearly conveys the impression to the reader that in al-Jabarti's opinion these women are worthy members of the Muslim community: pp. 66, 77–8. Actually, the case of Sitt Nafisa also involves the shaykhs.

[55] This use of the dialogue in medieval Muslim histories of the annalistic variety is noted by Rosenthal, *Muslim Historiography*, pp. 66ff.

[56] P. 76 is a good example.

[57] Morch, 'Introduction', p. 28.

[58] 'Like a swarm of locusts' is used both of the French army (p. 36) and of the women protecting the graves in Azbakiyya (p. 83). 'Abdallah is a 'human devil' (p. 88), the French are 'devils sent to this land of kings and sultans' (p. 45) and enter the city like 'the demons of the Devil's army' (p. 100), the 'host of Satan, allowed to move freely' (p. 101).

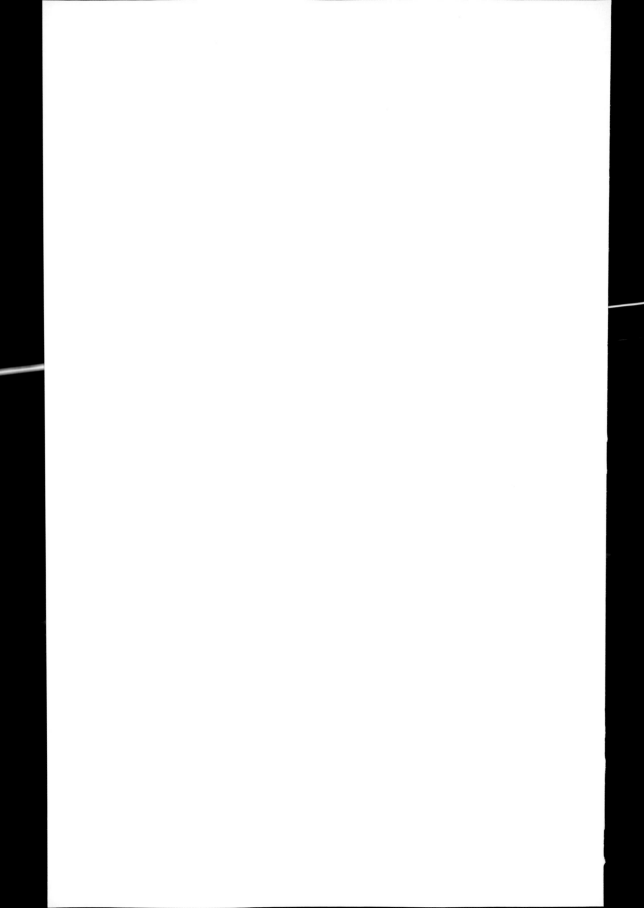

9 Al-Jabarti's interpretation of events in 1798–9

On the basis of the traces of composition, textual devices and the basic interpretation of events in the MS Mudda, al-Jabarti's interpretation of events in 1798–9 would run like this:

The old masters, listed in the opening paragraph, fail completely when faced with the French invasion. Murad Bey, Ibrahim Bey, the other emirs, their *mamluk*s and henchmen are presented as completely taken by surprise.[1] They have been too engrossed in the traditional local power game to act decisively in the new situation created by the French invasion of Egypt. Long-term mismanagement of military matters in order to appropriate funds to show off their power and wealth has left the country's defences in ruins. The passage relating the meeting of the emirs and shaykhs in Cairo in the opening pages of his narrative is marked by free dialogue and caustic comment. Al-Jabarti shows how the emirs, being quite aware of this situation, try to enrol the local Ottomans and the leading shaykhs in a common responsibility for the defence of Cairo, and that the shaykhs have the courage to resist and to safeguard their freedom of judgement. In the end they all agree to send an army against the French under the command of Murad Bey – a man of some repute among the people, but to al-Jabarti just another vain and ambitious *mamluk* trying to play the local sultan, handing out grand, but impossible, orders. Gloom settles over Cairo. The *agha* of the Mustahfizan and the *vali* have to order the shops to stay open and let the lights burn in the city.

Who is this new threat to Egypt? The French wanted to present themselves as friends of the Muslim community and its rightful leaders, the shaykhs and the sultan in Istanbul, simply professing an intention to eliminate the parasitic emirs, who had harassed the French merchants and laid Egypt waste in their irresponsible greed. It seems to be important to al-Jabarti to dismantle this attempt to delude the inhabitants of Egypt at the earliest possible moment in the narrative. This is done by reproducing the full text of the French proclamation and giving it the thorough treatment of a careful al-Azhar scholar, and by evoking his experience with the French during the following months of uneasy cohabitation. The message of his interpretation of the proclamation, the beginning of which is marked with red ink to stress its significance, is clear: these new people are no better – and perhaps even worse – than the emirs. They are not real Muslims; on the contrary, they are pure materialists. Their profession of veneration for the Muslim creed is a smokescreen. Their principles of liberty and equality are mere words, bent and broken whenever circumstances demand it. This is made clear by their disgustingly vulgar Arabic, the appointments they make and their general lack of tact and common decency. This analysis is framed by small notes on the advance of the enemy to suggest the coming catastrophe.

Having presented the two adversaries and introduced the third actor in the drama, the shaykhs, al-Jabarti proceeds to relate the decisive battle at Imbaba and the ensuing flight and panic. Without seriously altering the annalistic framework, but carefully selecting facts, description and direct speech, he conveys the story of the Egyptian defeat and its repercussions. The first skirmish with the French forces the Egyptians into action. A plan of defence is decided upon. Ibrahim Bey and the Pasha are to command the forces on the eastern bank of the Nile, while Murad Bey makes a show of preparing defences on the western bank of the river. But, as al-Jabarti notes in passing, both are quietly preparing for a hasty retreat to the south and east. The population of Cairo is easily fooled into an all-out mobilization. The description of the pitifully armed, naive and badly organised masses who throng on the eastern shore of the river is supplemented with the havoc this mobilization creates in the city itself.

On the banks of the Nile the two adversaries, the emirs and the French, confront each other. In the eyes of the author the difference between them is reduced to the painful fact that the French army possesses the cohesiveness and discipline of the Muslim army in the golden days of early Islam, while the Muslims do not. The outcome is a resounding defeat for the Muslims. Al-Jabarti carefully notes the reasons: the emirs' lack of imagination and their inadequate preparations. He also notes that the losses on the Egyptian side are conspicuously few: only one emir is killed and one drowns, trying to cross the river, while twenty *mamluk*s and common soldiers are killed in battle. Al-Jabarti's judgement on the outcome is low-key but final: 'So the Egyptian army altogether disappointed whatever hopes had been placed upon it and brought upon themselves the fires of hell and disgrace' (p. 52).

At the first signs of impending defeat, the two leading emirs, Murad and Ibrahim, make their expected retreat. Al-Jabarti carefully notes that by doing so, they are the direct cause of the ensuing general panic. In a series of vivid scenes, created by use of pertinent detail and direct speech, al-Jabarti makes it perfectly clear that in this crisis there are no heroes. The rich and powerful as well as the poor and simple people lose their heads and run, without a thought for their neighbours, squandering the wealth of Egypt in the process. Even the leading shaykhs (al-Jabarti makes a point of telling who) show that in

Realist, activists and loyalists in Cairo 1798

a crisis they are just as easily carried away by their fears and lack of courage as anybody else. The beduin and the *fellahin* show their true treacherous and greedy nature.

To al-Jabarti this is the real catastrophe: 'During that night, things happened the like of which had never occurred in Cairo, neither did we ever hear of anything, which resembled any of them in earlier histories' (p. 54). It is against the background of this devastating panic, which laid bare the fragility of the Muslim community in Cairo, that a handful of (unnamed) 'ulama of al-Azhar try to initiate a truce; but, perhaps significantly, it is only thanks to a Maghribi that the armistice is brought about. To al-Jabarti the shock of seeing the community falling apart overshadows the defeat: in a final scene he recounts the pitiful encounter between the victorious French commander and the frightened 'ulama, who have to admit that their leading shaykhs panicked and so have to ask the French to repeat their promise of safe-conduct. In addition they have to agree to join a consultative body, a diwan, for the new masters.

After this piece of close and integrated narrative al-Jabarti sets out to tell how the new French masters went about arranging the occupation of Cairo and its immediate surroundings. This part of the story does not lend itself to the same cohesive narrative, but al-Jabarti's wording of the entries makes the message come across to the reader clearly enough: The French attempt to prevent further plunder, through a diwan of shaykhs and the appointment of officials, is punctuated by a description of how the French take over the palaces of the emirs. The comment on page 58 – 'Their soldiers entered the city gradually, until the streets were full of them. They lived in the houses and the quarters stank of them, but they did not disturb anybody' – stresses the initial impression: the new masters are ill-mannered and ignorant, but essentially harmless.

This judgement is modified somewhat when the French proceed to raise money and conclude a settlement with the wives of the emirs. As al-Jabarti notes, this turns the function of the Diwan into something much more simple: to lend a veneer of legality and order to the French greed and plunder.

In the entries on the armistice and the Diwan, the leading shaykhs of Cairo hold centre stage. The proceedings of this, the first Diwan, introduce the reader to the second basic theme of the MS Mudda: the leading shaykhs of Cairo and their task of mediating between the masters and the people. Al-Jabarti clearly sees them as the cornerstone of the Muslim community. But only if they have the foresight, the patience and the courage to stay unattached to any master can they perform their duty. This is no easy task. These shaykhs are no

Plan of the city of Cairo, published in Description de l'Egypte (Etat Moderne, vol. I, pl. 26). In the eighteenth century the city had spread to the west, engulfing the old silted riverbeds of the Nile, some of which (the Azbakiyya (1) and Birkat al-Fil (2)) were still flooded during the yearly inundations. The impor-

tant mosques of al-Husainyya (3) and al-Azhar (4) are situated in the north-eastern corner. The Citadel (5), built at the beginning of the thirteenth century, was built on an outcrop of the Muqattam Hills to south east. Photo: The Royal Library, Copenhagen

heroes, as their behaviour during the aftermath of the battle showed, and as the following entries clearly demonstrate. The new masters are full of deceit and greed. The non-Muslim groups – the Copts and the Syrian Christians –try to take advantage of the situation to gain the upper hand over the Muslim majority. The common people are quickly scared, and easily become a rampaging mob. Outside the city gates the beduin and the *fellahin* are a law unto themselves.

The shaykhs have no power except the respect they command as authorities on what is right or wrong in the community. They cannot police the streets or protect the returning pilgrim caravan from the depredations of the beduin, except by pointing out to the rulers that they have a duty to look after these matters. But in the situation created by the French invasion, with the emirs and French competing for their favour and fighting each other, the beduin have an easy game and the caravan is more or less annihilated.

The real challenge for the shaykhs, however, is to stay unattached. By agreeing to sit on the Diwan they have undertaken to collaborate with the new rulers, but how far should they allow the new masters to use them to cover their plunder with the necessary legality? The French make serious attempts to win their favour by insisting on celebrating the customary festivities of the Breaking of the Dam (to mark the rise of the Nile) and the *mawlid al-nabi* (the festival of Muhammad's birthday) and investing the shaykh al-Bakri as *naqib al-ashraf*. But to al-Jabarti, the French are full of tricks: Instead of just accepting the shaykhs' demands for salaries (very modest, al-Jabarti notes!), the French try to buy them off with an offer of tax-farms, an offer which the shaykhs refuse – with good reason, seeing that the French were already trying to squeeze the holders of *iltizam*.

At this point the French execute Muhammad Kurayyim from Alexandria, the man they hold responsible for the harassment and extortion of the French merchants in the previous years. Al-Jabarti takes the opportunity to turn this event into a story with a clear warning: the rulers use men like Muhammad Kurayyim to break the unity of the Muslim community, the people and their trusted shaykhs, by raising them to public power and wealth in their service. This is exactly what the French attempt by making the shaykhs carry the sash and the cockade of the French Republic, and the shaykhs refuse. But this creates a serious crisis, which threatens the shaykhs' access to the French masters, so essential to their role as mediators. The crisis is solved by the good offices of the shaykh al-Sadat, because 'of [his] good nature'. Al-Jabarti carefully notes that al-Sadat (who is not a member of the Diwan) turns up at the meeting, summoned by the French. A precarious compromise is reached.

Realist, activists and loyalists in Cairo 1798

But the French rule generates disaffection and fear. The emirs try to kindle the fire of unrest, and the French do not improve matters by parading both their might and their intention to stay on as rulers of Egypt, putting up symbols of their state and issuing decrees, which seriously upset the everyday life of the people but which they are unable to follow themselves.

In this delicate situation the French dismiss the first diwan and the leading shaykhs as their principal advisers and set up a new diwan, the Court of Cases, consisting of six Muslim merchants and six Copts, and entrusting them with such sensitive issues as commercial and civil affairs, inheritances and lawsuits. Al-Jabarti does not conceal his rage: 'In the form of this Diwan the French established a basis for malice, a foundation for godlessness, a bulwark of injustice, and a source of all manner of evil innovations' (p. 79). In his long and heated summary of the French proposals (pp. 79–81) to this diwan, he demonstrates just how harsh they are.

The inability of the French to coordinate their punitive, administrative and sanitary measures and relate them to their publicly stated principles irritates al-Jabarti. Not because of their duplicity and deceit – he is well aware of that – but it offends his intelligence that only when the women of al-Azbakiyya fall on the Sar 'Askar like the French army did in Alexandria ('like a swarm of locust' (p. 83)) do the French see the stupidity of the situation. The point he really wants to make is that the French now tend to exclude the shaykhs from their confidence and reduce them to mere rubber stamps. The reports that the French have the shaykhs write to the sultan and the sharif of Mecca are summarized without comment, only fully quoting the last telling phrases: the statements of Mustafa Agha as the present *vali* (pasha) of Egypt and the promise to supply the Pilgrimage with provisions are obviously without foundation. In doing this the French are making the task of the shaykhs steadily more difficult. Even the venerable shaykh al-Sadat is about to get into trouble, and has to celebrate the birthday of Husayn to safeguard himself.

At this point the French decide to reinstate the shaykhs in their proper positions by a reorganization of the consultative diwan. A new General Diwan with members from both Cairo and the rest of Egypt is set up with the purpose of enabling it to handle the big and controversial issues: the procedures of courts; *shari'a* cases; title deeds to real estate and inheritances; and the taxes to be paid in connection with these matters. To al-Jabarti the fact that after some initial misunderstandings the French agree to allow the leading shaykhs to sit on this diwan and accept them in leading positions is a step in the right

VUE DE LA PLACE APPELLÉ

The Citadel of Cairo in 1798–1801 (Description de l'Egypte, Etat Moderne, vol. II, pl. 67). Cairo was constructed in the 1170s by the Ayyubid sultan Salah al-Din (1171–93), the famous Saladin to the Europeans. Since 1218 it has been the official residence of the rulers of Egypt. The massive towers of the Bab al-'Azab gate in the centre was the scene of the massacre instigated by Muhammad 'Ali 1811, which eliminated the last beys and their mamluks.

Pl.67

MEYLEH ET DE LA CITADELLE.

To the left is the mosque, madrasa and tomb of Sultan al-Hasan, built after 1356 by the Bahri Mamluk sultan al-Nasir al-Hasan (1347–51, 1354–61). After the introduction of guns in the late fourteenth century the solid walls and roof of the mosque made an ideal surface from which to bombard the Citadel, a fact that various Mamluk commanders and Bonaparte were quick to grasp!
Photo: The Royal Library, Copenhagen

direction. When the General Diwan convenes, al-Jabarti relates its meetings in a day-by-day account, stressing their quiet cooperation. They stick to their task, without taking notice of the real or imagined warnings created by Murad's victories in the south or the collapse of the gate in Azbakiyya, accepting the strange custom of the French of wasting precious paper voting on things already settled. They agree to cooperate and do have some influence on the outcome.

However, when the new measures are put into effect, a fatal split develops among the shaykhs, giving the disaffected persons among the common people the leadership they have lacked. This was what al-Jabarti warned against in the story of Muhammad Kurayyim, and alluded to in the story of the story of al-Hajj Muhammad ibn Qumuh al-Maghribi (p. 87). He makes this perfectly clear in his account of the insurrection in Cairo in the month of Jumada al-Ula/October 1798. When the French proceed to put the new tax on real estate into effect, it creates an uproar. Those 'lacking in foresight' decide that they have had enough, and unfortunately, they are backed by a group of 'ulama. To al-Jabarti, this activism is sheer folly: although the French had raised the rates which the shaykhs of the diwan had set, the shaykhs ought to have had the foresight to realize that these taxes were lighter than the former impositions and easier to bear considering the circumstances. Instead, they turn it into a case of paying poll tax to the unbelievers[2] and call for a holy war against the French, totally forgetting that they were 'prisoners in the hands of the French, who occupied the fortress and its walls, the high hills and the low, fortifying them all with forbidding instruments of war, such as cannons on carriages, rifles, carbines and bombs' (p. 93).

By backing 'those without foresight', these 'ulama lend support to what in al-Jabarti's eyes constitute the worst elements of the Muslim community: the rabble, the ruffians, the inhabitants of the al-Utuf and al-Husayniyya quarters, as well as the Maghribis of the al-Fahhamin quarter (who, as al-Jabarti carefully notes on p. 105, show their true nature by joining the French as mercenaries as a way of evading punishment) and the Kafr al-Zaghari and al-Tamma'in quarters of the city.

Al-Jabarti is unusually circumspect when alluding to these 'ulama: they are not named and it is not quite clear whether they are many or few, or just one. The only *'alim* mentioned by name among the rebels is Badr al-Maqdisi, but to al-Jabarti he is no real leader, just the necessary figurehead – and, incidentally, the only one who escapes execution. The murder of General Dupuy, which turns the protests into a rebellion, is brought about, not by an *'alim*, but by a perfumer, in the guise of a *faqih*! Clearly, al-Jabarti wants to make his point, but does not want to inform upon his fellow 'ulama.[3]

So the insurrection develops, the rebels believing that they have the backing of the Muslim community, but forgetting 'that the cause of all these misfortunes and calamities was but the lack of unity and the extreme disagreement and dispute among them' (p. 95). Stray French patrols are massacred and the crowd goes berserk, looting and raping, inciting each other into ever greater atrocities against friend and foe alike.

The leading shaykhs (their names are faithfully recorded!) try to intervene and mediate between the rebels and the French. Al-Jabarti devotes much space to their futile endeavours to contain or stop the bloodshed. But their influence is gone, broken by the split in their own ranks. There is a definite shade of reproach in al-Jabarti's story: if they had acted with more courage, they might have overcome the difficulties created by the split in their ranks, but it seems that to al-Jabarti the shaykhs do not have the necessary personal courage to handle this situation. There are differences, though: al-Sharqawi, the shaykh al-Azhar and chairman of the Diwan, seems to fail completely, while other leading shaykhs do make a serious effort, but succeed only in the easy cases, i.e. in the quarters close to the French garrison.

To al-Jabarti, the outcome is never in doubt. When the leading shaykhs' attempt at mediation peters out, the French open fire on the city and, with bombs exploding all around them, 'sense returns to the heads' of the people and a truce is arranged through the shaykhs. But as it turns out, this is not the end – not even the beginning of the end. 'After the first watch of the night the French entered the city like a torrent rushing through the alleys and streets without anything to stop them, like the demons of the devil's army' (p. 100). Retribution is in the air. The French masters shed the last pretences of restraint and veneration towards the Muslim community and act as the enemies of the Religion they truly are. The Syrian Christians and the Greeks (but not the Copts?) seize 'the opportunity to take revenge on the Muslims and reveal openly what was in their hearts' (p. 102). Barthelemy, the Greek Resident, who had entered the French service to offset his lack of personal accomplishments, and the *agha* of the Mustahfizan both excel in beatings and forced confessions.

The leading shaykhs now set to work, rehabilitating the Muslim community from its ruins. But they meet with little understanding. They persuade French to evacuate al-Azhar, but on the real issue of preventing the French from punishing the shaykhs, they fail. A group of shaykhs (their names are carefully listed) are rounded up, imprisoned and executed. Al-Jabarti makes a point of showing that the French are so thoroughly shaken that they dare not admit it in public. But it is significant that he does not squarely state the innocence of these shaykhs: obviously he was not quite sure at the time of writing. On the innocence of one of the other suspects, Ibrahim Efendi, secretary of the spice trade (*kaiib al-bahar*), who for some reason is near to his heart, al-Jabarti is quite emphatic, however, seeing his arrest as the result of the ubiquitous scheming of the Syrian Christians.

After this fatal incident, things will never be the same: the French are scared, and busy themselves with fortifying their positions and removing the remaining gates to the alleys in the quarters, the symbol of the privacy and security of the community. The tax on immovable property, the source of all these misfortunes, is now levied as originally planned and 'no one opposed this or uttered a single word', as al-Jabarti carefully notes (p. 108)!

The leading shaykhs stand discredited and defenceless, reduced to mere mouthpieces of the rulers. At this point al-Jabarti quotes, fully and without comment, two 'copies of advice from all the 'ulama of Islam in Cairo' written by the French 'through the mouths of the shaykhs' (p. 109), but nonetheless signed by them (the names are carefully noted) and in the case of the last one written by the secretary of the Diwan. In these letters the shaykhs are made to glorify Bonaparte's magnanimity and wisdom in sparing the city from the wrath of his soldiers, to vilify the emirs as the willing tools of the Muscovites and to exhort the inhabitants of Cairo and Egypt to 'busy yourselves with your own livelihoods, fulfil the obligations of your religion and pay the taxes imposed on you' (p. 109). These two letters represent the visible proof of the folly of collaborating. The shaykhs are no longer disinterested mediators, but mere mouthpieces of the rulers. In the context, the lack of comment on these two letters and al-Jabarti's careful recording of the shaykhs responsible for signing and writing the documents has the air of a conclusion.

This is stressed by the fact that at this point al-Jabarti introduces a new compositional feature, over and above the annalistic recording: ordering events by the month, pooling them under general headings, avoiding dates and adding eyewitness accounts on curiosities such as the amusement park, the balloon and the library, the school and laboratory of the French scientists.[4] As suggested above, this may signify the author's attempt to wind up his story, now that he has made his point. It is not very elegant and smooth, but in line with the annalistic approach and the opening paragraph.

In these concluding pages of his narrative, he concentrates on the mood of the new rulers, stressing 'the audacious presumption in claiming Mahdihood or Prophethood' (p. 119) of their leader (Bonaparte) and his ominous propensity for riding about alone in the desert while, back in Cairo, his subordinates turn sensible requirements such as keeping the lights burning in the streets into a burden and a source of extortion. The insurrection, brought about by the collaboration of the shaykhs on the General Diwan and their failure to stay together, has brought ruin to everybody, including the French. With the mediating shaykhs reduced to mere tools of the new masters, the French seem to lose their grip on reality and slip into new attempts at lies and deceit, bringing upon themselves and Egypt 'the fires of hell and disgrace'!

Seen in this perspective, it seems reasonable to suggest that what made al-Jabarti start writing the MS Mudda was the fatal split in his own group, the leading shaykhs of Cairo, in October 1798, when some of them forgot their basic obligation to stay aloof from politics and joined the insurrection against the new infidel masters. The purpose of the MS Mudda would be to show those 'without foresight' the folly of this course of action in order to prevent its repetition.

[1] The sultan and his vizier in Istanbul are mentioned in passing (p. 106) with reverence (they write beautiful letters!), while al-Jazzar is introduced in a short item, concerned with the abortive French attempt to enlist his support. The author sees them as part of the general political picture, but not as important actors in the narrative – at least not at this juncture.

[2] The *jizya* was the traditional head tax, paid as a tribute by free non-Muslims to the ruling Muslim community, and as such a symbol of Islam as the victorious faith.

[3] This suggests that this part of the MS Mudda was written after the insurrection, but before the general amnesty issued by the French, i.e. in November 1798.

[4] Considering the place and context of the description of the amusement park it is difficult not believe that al-Jabarti forgot to mention that this, too, is an eyewitness account!

10 Al-Jabarti and the 'ulama of Cairo

As we have seen in the preceding chapter, the author, when writing the MS Mudda, seemed to have the 'ulama, and especially their leading shaykhs, at the forefront of his mind: He carefully supplied the reader with the names of these shaykhs, listing the names of those who joined the emirs in exile and those who stayed on. He carefully concealed the names of those responsible for the split in their ranks in the events leading up to the insurrection in October 1798 in Cairo, obviously feeling some obligation to protect them. His careful description of their actions, and the fact that he avoided commenting on them, point to the conclusion that the actions and motives of this group were still open for debate and that the author was part of this debate. He had no intention of making a break with them. To the author of the MS Mudda they were still members of his group.

Seen in this way, the MS Mudda shows all the signs of being part of a debate, in which the author has strong views on what the right path should be, but still wants to uphold the unity among the shaykhs and the 'ulama as the only way of protecting the Muslim community of Egypt.

VOCABULARY USED TO DESIGNATE 'ULAMA

A survey of the words used in the Arabic text of the MS Mudda to denote shaykhs, 'ulama and leading shaykhs show that the word *mashyakha* is used throughout as the term signifying any native leader. However, the word is used alone when it signifies leaders among the 'ulama, the religious experts and scientists in the Muslim community. Shaykhs of other groups are always mentioned with a reference to the group they lead (a village, the merchants, the ruffians (pp. 60, 61, 91). The narrator clearly belongs to, or is writing for, the 'ulama group.

The 'ulama are always mentioned as a group. The singular noun used is the standard term *'alim,* but in situations when this group acts (trying to initiate a truce (p. 54), inciting the insurrection (p. 93), following al-Sharqawi in order to restore peace (p. 98), being rounded up and executed by the French (p. 103)) the word *muta'amimmin* is used. Moreh translates it with the standard term 'ulama, on the grounds that al-Jabarti changes the word in these contexts into *'alim/*'ulama when writing the MS Mazhar and MS Aja'ib.[1] But this change does not constitute a valid argument for believing that *muta'ammimin* is a synonym of *'alim* or *'ulama* in the MS Mudda. On the contrary, the fact that the author preferred this word in these situations in his story may indicate that he was actually trying to make a point.

Unfortunately the word does not figure directly in the standard dictionary. It seems to be perfect passive participle of *'amma* (v.), meaning 'those who have been allowed to wear the turban'. A study of the possible connotations of this word should be made, as it may contain a clue to al-Jabarti's opinion of these people; in the context of the MS Mudda *muta'ammimin* is obviously a derogatory term. They are not distinguished by their learnedness (*'alim*), but by the outer sign of their position, the turban. By using this term the author seems to suggest that they are too much concerned with influence and power. In addition to this he is obviously not impressed by their political performance. The word is used to describe the 'ulama of al-Azhar who tried to arrange a truce, but did not have the courage to face the French guns and carry it through. It is used to denote those 'without foresight', who made the insurrection possible and so brought about the calamities of this incident. It is used to describe the followers of al-Sharqawi in one of the abortive attempts to arrange a truce. And finally, it is used to describe those shaykhs who were executed by the French for complicity in the insurrection in October 1798.

The *muta'ammimin* appear as individuals in two instances, both connected with this insurrection: Badr al-Maqdisi, the figurehead of the rebels who got away; and the group of shaykhs who were executed by the French after the insurrection (Sulayman al-Jawsaqi, shaykh of the blind men's guild, Ahmad al-Sharqawi, 'Abd al-Wahab al-Shubrawi, Yusuf al-Musaylihi and Isma'il al-Barawi)[2]. Their necrologies appear in the MS Aja'ib. From these necrologies it appears that, with the exception of shaykh Sulayman (who, significantly, is singled out from the group as shaykh of the blind men's guild and who (perhaps even more significantly), was not, in al-Jabarti's opinion in the MS Aja'ib, innocent like the others!), they were teachers of the Shafi'ite rite at al-Azhar. In the addition in the margin of the manuscript of the MS Mudda, on p. 89, the term is directly connected to five names: al-Sharqawi, al-Bakri, al-Sawi, al-Fayyumi and al-Mahdi. Three of these appear as connected to the General Diwan as chairman, deputy chairman, inspectors and the secretary of the General Diwan, while al-Bakri was made *naqib al-ashraf* by the French. From their necrologies in the MS Aja'ib it appears that, except for al-Bakri, they were all connected to al-Azhar as teachers,[3] but only two of them (al-Sharqawi and al-Sawi) were of the Shafi'ite rite. The common factor seems to be that they were teachers at al-Azhar, of which al-Sharqawi was the head.

The necrologies in the MS Aja'ib should be used with care. They belong to a later stage in al-Jabarti's work and often express a completely different attitude to the persons involved. But a detail in the necrology of al-Sharqawi may contain a clue to the *muta'ammimin* of the MS Mudda. According to al-Jabarti one of the peculiar features of al-Sharqawi was his weakness for wearing big turbans ('as his situation improved he began to dress well and his turban grew bigger and his turban increased so in size and grandeur that it became proverbial'[4]). Seen against this background the word *muta'ammimin* may be a derogatory term for someone who presumes to wear the turban: the pompous turban-wearers of al-Azhar, or simply: al-Sharqawi's gang of self-important turban wearers!

Among the shaykhs of the 'ulama some have the position as leading shaykhs (*al-mashayikh al-kibar*, p. 55). The shaykhs, when meeting with Bonaparte, have to admit that their 'leading shaykhs [*al-mashayikh al kibar*: chiefs of the shaykhs] panicked' (p. 55). When Abu Qasim returns from Bonaparte he tells them to send 'a group of your notables' (p. 55)· The word used here is *wajih* (eminent person, leader). But these terms are just the common words for leaders, and so do not help us any further. It seems that in the MS Mudda it is taken for granted that the reader would know how exactly these leaders have been recognised as such, and whom they represent.

So, on the basis of the vocabulary of the MS Mudda, we do not get a more definite picture of the 'ulama and their leading shaykhs, except for the fact that the narrator takes it for granted that the reader is fully acquainted with the usages of this group and the indication that among the 'ulama there seems to be a faction known as the *muta'ammimin*, the turban wearers. This term probably denotes shaykhs of the schools and *riwaqs* of al-Azhar, perhaps even a group around the shaykh al-Azhar, al-Sharqawi. The narrator of the MS Mudda clearly uses this term in a derogatory sense.

THE IDEAL *'alim* AND THE LEADING SHAYKHS

The author of the MS Mudda presents the reader with a fairly clear picture of his opinion of how the ideal 'ulama and, by implication, their leading shaykhs, should be and act.

In his comments, especially in the story of Muhammad Kurayyim, the author expounds his views on the ideal *'alim*. The Alexandrian *faqih* Shaykh Muhammad al-Masiri (al-Maliki) is clearly presented as the ideal *'alim.* He gave the people of Alexandria lessons and explained *fiqh* to them according to the Imam Malik, 'showing no interest in what they owned, refraining from committing any act which would raise suspicion and avoiding what was forbidden' (p. 69). This attitude generated respect and unity in the Muslim community: 'their hearts united in love for him and they devoted themselves to obeying him in such a way that he became an authority for them in all matters'. The ideal *'alim* is apparently a man who is devoted to truth and lets this truth guide his actions. He acts with the knowledge that the truth of his teaching is measured on his ability to act in accordance with it. The right of the *'alim* to guide the Muslim community depends on his ability to create this unity of theory and practice in his own personal life. This constitutes the only source of his authority and influence.

This is no easy proposition. To the author, he has to be wise (*'aqil*: reasonable, understanding, intelligent, pp. 72, 43). He should be content to live in moderation (*qana'*: contentment, frugality, moderation), in order to avoid the temptations of the rulers. He has to be able to intercede and mediate (*shafa'a*: to mediate, pp.60, 63, 71), and in doing so he has to be kind (*fadl*: kindliness, superiority, refinement, culture, p. 47, *latafa*: to be kind and friendly, p. 105).

The author of the MS Mudda allows the reader to judge for himself whether the leading shaykhs conform to this ideal. When the victorious French summon the leading shaykhs of Cairo to the first Diwan, some decide to go into exile with the emirs. 'Umar Efendi Makram al-Asyuti, the *naqib al-ashraf*, Shaykh Salim al-Mas'ud, the chief of the Maghribi *riwaq* at al-Azhar, and Shaykh Muhammad al-Amir al-Maliki do not trust the French promises of safe-conduct. The author notes this without comment (except perhaps, noting that al-Mas'ud lost all the valuables his women had taken along, to the beduin!), and we do not hear anything of this group of shaykhs in the rest of the narrative. Apparently, by removing themselves from Cairo, they abrogate any responsibility, and so lose all interest in the eyes of the author.

Among those who stay behind, the author singles out those ten shaykhs who agreed to cooperate with the French on the first Diwan, and the shaykh al-Sadat. Most of them (and only they[5]) turn up in the following narrative mentioned by name in specific situations. If we try to summarize the author's presentation of how they handle these situations, the following picture emerges:

Shaykh 'Abdallah al-Sharqawi is obviously *primus inter pares*. When the General Diwan convenes he is elected chairman as a matter of course (p. 86). But the author bears him no love: he is depicted as panicking (p. 52), and makes 'the good-natured' al-Sadat panic too (p. 52) and has to call in friends to protect him (p. 56);

Realist, activists and loyalists in Cairo 1798

he causes a crisis by openly refusing to wear the sash (p. 73); he is slow in taking action (p. 88); avoids responsibility in vital situations (p. 94); and lets himself (and the *muta'ammimin*!) be scared away by the mob (p. 98).

Shaykh Khalil al-Bakri joins the general flight, but returns and joins the Diwan. He tries to evade the French overtures, but soon agrees both to arrange the celebration of the Prophet's Birthday and to take the post as *naqib al-ashraf* at the behest of the French (p. 65). He shows the same cordiality towards the poor and destitute (p. 91), succeeds in preventing the people in his quarter from joining the insurrection (p. 94) and makes two serious attempts to put an end to the insurrection (pp. 96, 98), but apparently does not have the courage to carry them to a successful end.

The shaykh al-Sadat[6] joins the flight, but only on the instigation of al-Sharqawi. 'Because of a slight indisposition resulting from this affair and related events' he is not present at the meeting of the first Diwan and apparently does not take part in this or any of the other Diwans.[7] But he is in communication with the new masters, and his 'good nature' enables him to prevent a couple of unnecessary clashes, which threaten the shaykhs' access to the ruler (pp. 73, 84). He is presented as the leader of the shaykhs' attempt to intercede with the French on behalf of not only the shaykhs held prisoners by the French after the insurrection in October, but also of Ibrahim Efendi and the rest of the prisoners from the Muslim community. The French temporize and al-Sadat is quoted as expressing his frustration (p. 104). He is not among the eleven shaykhs who sign the letters of advice from the 'ulama of Cairo (p. 110).[8]

Shaykh Mustafa al-Sawi does not panic. On the contrary, he is one of the shaykhs who is able to arrange the truce (p. 55), and intervenes successfully to avoid a crisis (p. 63). He is chosen as deputy chairman of the General Diwan.

Shaykh Sulayman al-Fayyumi also stays in the city and joins the group arranging the truce (p. 55). He is chosen as inspector of the General Diwan, and during the insurrection he prevents his quarter from joining the rebels. A *mamluk* of Husayn Bey seeks refuge in his house. Al-Fayyumi hands him over to the *agha* of Mustahfizan (chief of police) in order to get a safe-conduct for him. But the *agha* informs the French and the *mamluk* is shot (p. 118).

Shaykh Musa al-Sirsi also stays. He successfully intervenes to help Murad's wife, Sitt Nafisa, in a difficult situation (p. 77) and joins al-Bakri in the first abortive attempts to stop the insurrection (pp. 96, 98).

Shaykh Muhammad al-Mahdi also stays. Together with al-Sirsi he mediates between Sitt Nafisa and the French (p. 77), he intervenes actively on behalf of al-Haijj Muhammad ibn Qimuh (p. 88) and is made inspector and secretary to the General Diwan (pp. 89, 92). After the insurrection he intervenes successfully on behalf of Ibrahim Efendi, secretary of the spice trade (p. 105).

Shaykh Mustafa al-Damanhuri, Shaykh Ahmad al-'Arishi and Shaykh Yusuf al-Shubrakhiti are not mentioned except as members of the first Diwan and as signing the letters of advice from the 'ulama of Cairo. The same goes for Shaykh Muhammad al-Dawakhili, except that he joins al-Mahdi in a second (and successful?) attempt to save the life of al-Haijj Muhammad ibn Qimuh.

When we consider the way these eleven are presented in the pages of the MS Mudda, two seem to stand out: al-Sharqawi and al-Sadat, the former as the *primus inter pares* who obviously lacks the personal qualities to act as such, and the latter, who does not accept official posts on the Diwans, but nevertheless performs valuable service to the community by mediating between the French and the leading shaykhs. The other leading shaykhs singled out in the MS Mudda as actively collaborating with the French are either mentioned as having successfully intervened or are passed over in silence. Those who intervene successfully are those who, along with al-Sharqawi, accept leading posts (al-Bakri, al-Sawi, al-Fayyumi and al-Mahdi). Seen in this perspective the incident on pp. 72–3 concerning the shaykhs wearing the French cockade takes on an added importance. Al-Jabarti's comment on p. 73 'and thus was their situation' is ambiguous, but it certainly seems to have something to do with the fact that al-Sadat (because of his 'good nature' (*akhlaq husna*: excellence, superiority, moral perfection)) succeeded where al-Sharqawi failed, arranging a compromise with the French on the issue of the cockade. It is significant that in the incident with the Maghribi al-Hajj Muhammad ibn Qimuh (p. 87), a possible henchman of the emirs with connections to Muhammad Kurayyim, he singles out al-Sharqawi for special and not very flattering treatment.

If as suggested above the MS Mudda is part of a debate on the actions of the leading shaykhs in Cairo during the French occupation, this treatment of the individual leading shaykhs points to the actions of al-Bakri, al-Sawi, al-Fayyumi and al-Mahdi, but above all al-Sharqawi, the shaykh al-Azhar since 1793, and al-Sadat as the primary focus of this debate. Seen in this light, the MS Mudda takes on the aspect of an investigative report, supplying the detailed and critical account necessary, in the eyes of the author, to put this debate on a more solid foundation.

The field may be narrowed a bit further. In his necrology on al-Sadat in the MS Aja'ib[9] al-Jabarti supplies two interesting pieces of information: first, that al-Sadat is the anonymous shaykh who took the emirs to task for their neglect of the country's defences at the meeting before the French arrival in Cairo; and second, that the author visited the French in the company of al-Sadat 'to look at their handicrafts, paintings, drawings and other curiosities'.

These pieces of information are difficult to handle, appearing as they do in a later version of al-Jabarti's chronicles (al-Sadat died in 1813, so at least fifteen years separate the text of the MS Mudda from the necrology in volume IV of the MS Aja'ib). In this necrology the venerable al-Sadat of the MS Mudda is presented as a proud, vain and greedy person. On the other hand, these pieces of information do not fit into and are not used in the argument of the necrology. They have the air of revelation, the author at last revealing a few secrets from the past that have puzzled his audience.

If we accept them as true, they add an additional argument to the suggestion that the MS Mudda was written some time between October 1798 and the beginning of 1799 as a contribution to the heated debate going on in the Muslim community in Cairo. The focus on the activities of the leading shaykhs of Cairo suggests that the participants in this debate should be found among this group. The critical attitude of the MS Mudda towards the shaykh al-Azhar, al-Sharqawi, and the very favourable attitude towards the shaykh al-Sadat, suggests that the debate was raging between at least two groups among the leading shaykhs. One group seems to have had al-Sharqawi (and perhaps al-Mahdi) as the leading spirit and was advocating a close cooperation with the French. Another group was headed by al-Sadat and included al-Jabarti himself. To al-Sadat and al-Jabarti such close co-operation endangered the unity and influence of the leading shaykhs and the security and well-being of the Muslim community. For this reason they did not want to get their hands dirty by openly and officially collaborating with the French as members of the consultative bodies the French set up to handle their dealings with the population.

These pieces of information also put the eyewitness accounts in the MS Mudda of the author's visit to the French library, school and laboratory in a new light. The author's open-minded, not to say enthusiastic, description of these matters now turns out to be part of the 'pro-al-Sadat' tilt of the MS Mudda, rather than a measure of the author's ability to appreciate the importance of European science. As noted above, in the set-up of the narrative of the MS Mudda they appear as curiosities, mentioned at the end together with other minor matters. Now we may see them as curiosities, mentioned to please the hero of the story, al-Sadat.

If we accept the MS Mudda as representing a vindication of al-Sadat's attitude to the critical question of collaboration, some details in the narrative take on a new significance. First, as noted above, the author rarely comments directly on the actions of the shaykhs. The great exception to this rule is on page 37, where the author's comments follow the lead given by the anonymous shaykh at the meeting with the emirs. This comment now turns out to be a vindication of the opinion of al-Sadat.

Second, knowing that al-Sadat was shaykh of the al-Husayni shrine, we can see the significance of the difference between the fate of those who relied on the shaykhs of the Diwan and those who went elsewhere for help: on page 59 it is noted that the Diwan agrees to a loan from the coffee merchants, the Syrian Christians, the European merchants and the Coptic secretaries, and that these people are unable to effect a reduction. But when, on page 60, it comes to the guilds of merchants in the bazaars, they go (first?) to al-Azhar and (then?) to the al-Husayni shrine, where the shaykhs speak with the French and the loan is reduced to half while the time of payment is extended. In this context the author's comment on the Diwan ('as a result the function of the Diwan became simply the prevention of criminal acts' (p. 59)) becomes a denunciation directed specifically at the activity of the shaykhs on the Diwan. By allowing themselves to be the official mediators and counsellors of the French they have renounced their freedom of action, and by doing so they have lost their ability to help.

Even more interesting is the incident on page 70. Here al-Sadat turns up at the meeting between the French commander-in-chief and the shaykhs and saves the situation. Now it becomes significant that the author carefully notes that al-Sadat was summoned by the French – indicating that, unlike the others, he has been asked to be present. The intention of this detail is clearly to account for the question, obviously very much in need of clarification if one did not like al-Sadat, of how this person happened to turn up in the commander-in-chief's residence at this critical hour!

The incident on page 84, where al-Sadat hurriedly arranges a celebration for Husayn but shortens the number of days spent on the festivities, can be seen as a similar, carefully worded excuse for this action on the part of al-Sadat: 'a certain hypocrite' (al-Sharqawi?) had engaged in intrigue among the French to discredit al-Sadat. To save himself from being associated with the emirs, al-Sadat arranges the celebration, but only within the bare minimum of days.

'Abdallah al-Sharqawi (1738–1813), shaykh al-Azhar, painted by Michel Rigo (d. 1815), shortly after 1801 for Bonaparte for the billiard salon in Malmaison, probably on the basis of drawings made in Egypt between 1798 and 1801. Chateaux de Malmaison et Bois-Preau. Photo: Réunion des Musées Nationaux – Daniel Arnaudet

Shams al-Din Muhammad Abu 'l-Anwar (d. 1813), shaykh al-Sadat, painted by Michel Rigo (d. 1815) shortly after 1801 for Bonaparte for the billiard salon in Malmaison, probably on the basis of drawings made in Egypt between 1798 and 1801. Chateaux de Malmaison et Bois-Preau. Photo: Réunion des Musées Nationaux – Daniel Arnaudet

The comment on page 87 that the French persisted in their demand, 'behaving in a most unsuitable way', which at a first reading would imply the disgust of the author at the behaviour of the French towards al-Sharqawi, now becomes a comment, showing that the co-operation of this shaykh did not prevent the French from treating him with disrespect. The French respect only those who are able to retain their freedom.

The description of the French behaviour, and by implication the use of their documents, especially the presentation of the French proclamation, also takes on a new aspect. The careful, but heated comment on the contents becomes an argument: the shaykhs who joined the Diwan ought to have been aware of the true nature of the French. They ought to have understood, when they read it, and if not, they ought to have seen, when the French entered Cairo, that these people were enemies of Islam (or any religion) and as such could not be trusted to cooperate in the true interest of the Muslim community. And if, this argument goes on, they did not realize it in the beginning, they ought to have been able to see it when the French desecrated al-Azhar after the insurrection – or at least when the French reorganized the new Diwan and their commander-in-chief presented himself as a Mahdi, a new prophet.

The supposition that the MS Mudda was written in order to promote the views and opinions of the shaykh al-Sadat, in op-position to those of al-Sharqawi and other leading shaykhs on the French Diwan, should be seen against the background of the situ-ation among the 'ulama in Egypt in the late eighteenth century. It suggests the existence of factions and rivalries among the leading shaykhs of the 'ulama. However, it also suggests that these rivalries were concerned not only with power and influence, but with the political position of the 'ulama and their leading shaykhs in rela-tion to the rulers and its repercussions on their ability to protect and promote the Faith and the Muslim community in times of crisis. The MS Mudda seems to be a contribution to a debate in which al-Sadat, the leader of the Wafa'iyya order, is being promoted as the proponent of a stand which warns against cooperating too closely with the rulers, while al-Sharqawi, the shaykh al-Azhar, is presented as a leader who by his ready cooperation all but ruins the Muslim community. It is interesting to note that at this point he, and not the shaykh al-Bakri, is singled out as the target for the polemics in the MS Mudda. The shaykh al-Bakri is presented as a person of second-ary importance compared with al-Sharqawi. This would suggest that the issue was primarily ideological and religious in nature, and was fought out between a group centred around the shaykh al-Sadat, the

Wafa'iyya order and the Husayni shrine and mosque, on one hand, and the shaykh al-Sharqawi and the shaykhs of al-Azhar in alliance with the shaykh al-Bakri, on the other. Apparently the old alliance between the shaykh al-Sadat and the leading Qazdagli emirs Murad and Ibrahim Bey had ceased to exist.

What they do not explain, though, is the fact that in the MS Mudda we find al-Jabarti, an Azhari 'alim, promoting the cause and position of al-Sadat against al-Sharqawi. We know that his close friend, the 'alim and poet Isma'il al-Khashshab, belonged to al-Sadat's circle, probably because he was a sharaf himself.[10] Obviously, some sort of patronage seems to be at work here, but its exact nature eludes us. It is generally supposed that al-Jabarti, having inherited a sizeable fortune from his father, Hasan al-Jabarti (d. 1774), was able to spend his life as an independent rentier.[11] Apparently this did not exempt him from being part of the web of kinship and clientage ties in society. Actually, such ties may have been the necessary condition for staying in the same social position as his father.

In the following chapters we will explore these groups and the kinship and clientage ties they suggest through a couple of contemporary sources, both inside and outside the works of al-Jabarti.

1. Moreh, p. 54, n. 51.

2. The *Courier de l'Egypte*, no. 15 (20th Brumaire, vii) notes the execution of the shaykhs and provides a list of five names. The names are mentioned in a different order. This would indicate that the *Courier* was *not* one of al-Jabarti's sources. But in the same issue another item, quoting an *ordre du jour* of 14th Brumaire, mentions the letters from Ibrahim Bey and others: 'Tous ces firmans sont faux'. This seems to echo the words used in the MS Mudda: 'The *mamluks* are liars.' Perhaps these *ordres du jour* provided al-Jabarti with the information on the French?

3. Sharqawi: MS Aja'ib, IV, 160; al-Bakri: IV, 86; al-Sawi: III, 216; al-Fayyumi: IV, 105; al-Mahdi: IV, 233.

4, MS Aja'ib, IV, 160.

5. The letters of advice from the 'ulama of Cairo are signed by eleven shaykhs. The eleventh, Shaykh al-Amir, has been mentioned as one of the shaykhs who panicked (p. 52).

6. Actually his title is 'khalifa of the noble (sufi order of) Sadat'. His name is Shams al Din Muhammad Abu 'l-Anwar ibn al-Rahman (MS Aja'ib, IV, 258). For the sake of simplicity, the title used in the MS Mudda is also used here.

7. Shaw, *Between Old and New*, p. 260, states, on the basis of the secondary literature, that al-Sadat was a member of the Diwans. Andre Raymond, 'Egyp-

tiens et Français au Caire, 1798–1801', *Institut Francais d'Archeologie Orientale,* *Bibliothèque Général* 18 (1998), p. 99 has checked al-Jabarti and has to acknowledge that this was not the case. According to Henri Laurens, *L'Expédition* *française de l'Egypte. Bonaparte et l'Islam: le choc des cultures,* Paris 1989, pp. 91–2, al-Sadat's participation in the Diwan was stipulated in the French *ordre du jour* of 25 July 1798. This may explain the confusion on this point.

8. In the *Courier de l'Egypte,* no. 14 (10th Brumaire, vii) the first of these letters is quoted and the names of the eleven signing shaykhs are reproduced (in a different order). Al-Sadat is mentioned as the twelfth and last shaykh who signed! I have not been able to verify this (the original probably exists in the French archives at Vincennes). But even if it is true, it would only add to the weight of the point I am trying to make here: that al-Jabarti does not mention al-Sadat as having anything to do with the Diwan and its shaykhs.

9. MS Aja'ib, IV, 192.

10. MS Aja'ib, IV, 239.

11. Raymond, *Le Caire de Janissaries,* p. 63.

11 The second draft of the MS Mudda

The corrections and additions in the MS Mudda testify to the fact that the text investigated in the preceding pages was reviewed. As such they represent a second stage in the development of the text.[1] Corrections and additions, by their nature, imply that the original text was in need of clarification and specification or change of meaning. If we follow this line of thinking, they allow us to follow in detail the points the authors wanted to stress, when they set about revising the text. They allow us to see which part of the picture painted in the rough draft, i.e. which arguments the author – and the possible authority behind him – had at the front of their minds at this juncture, keeping in mind that we are dealing with a contribution to a debate, and that by the passage of time arguments in debates usually move on and change. The corrections and additions show us in which direction the frontiers in the debate among the leading Cairene 'ulama were moving. They may also supply us with additional evidence as to the nature of the authority behind the author and the verification of the additions in the margin (the *sahha* mentioned above).[2]

The additions and corrections seem to be concentrated on the emirs and the leading shaykhs. These people were apparently still the focus of the author of this second draft of the MS Mudda. The author now wanted to make it clear that the emirs were duly warned of the impending attack by the French. He also wanted to stress that because they relied on unimaginative people such as Muhammad Kurayyim, the emirs missed the opportunity to secure the necessary assistance from the English fleet when help from Istanbul would clearly not be feasible.[3]

The rough draft accused the emirs of having thoroughly mismanaged the country's defences by their greed and vanity. This was explicitly stated, at the meeting in Cairo. Now it seems as if the argument has moved on to pointing out that despite this, it might have been possible to avert the catastrophe if they and their henchmen had been alert and quick, by letting the English do the job.[4]

This indicates that the shaykhs of Cairo not only had an opinion on who had the responsibility for defending the Egyptian part of the Ottoman Empire, but that they were now taking it upon themselves to explain just how this defence might have been conducted. They point out that besides long-term preparation and assistance from Istanbul, the conflict between the European powers could have provided the necessary help if properly handled. It is difficult not to see these additions on the emirs' handling of defence as a continuation of the ideas put forward in another addition from an earlier stage of the text on page 64 ('the story of these English'). Obviously, the debate was developing along familiar lines: suddenly everybody knew what ought to have been done! But it is nevertheless important as an indication of future options in this respect.

Perhaps the addition on the behaviour of the Maghribi mercenaries belongs to this part of the debate.[5] The rough draft made much of the French ability to act with discipline and cohesion in battle. But the obvious conclusion – that Egyptians should start training along the same lines – is rejected in this addition as ridiculous. Military training is evidently seen as a curiosity like the balloon and the scientific experiments of the French institute. The author of the MS Mudda does not seem to favour military solutions.

The author's position on the past and future role of the emirs seems to have hardened in the second draft of the MS Mudda: They are now seen as a definite liability, a superfluous layer between the rightful ruler, the sultan in Istanbul, and the Muslim community in Egypt and its natural leaders, the 'ulama. The emirs are not fit to rule and will come to a bad end, as evidenced by the Mamluks now living on charity in al-Azhar.[6] By stressing this, the author has moved on to a more definite stand on this issue. The emirs are not fit to rule, and they should be eliminated as rulers. The author of the second draft seems to be moving down the road which several years later brought Muhammad 'Ali to power with the support of the 'ulama.

As for the leading shaykhs, the additions seem to attest to the author's need to make it clearer, by showing their respect and affection for the French commander-in-chief, that they collaborated consciously and personally with the French masters.[7] This seems to indicate that the argument put forward in the rough draft has met with some difficulties, necessitating the addition specifying that they openly followed the commander-in-chief and dined with him, despite having been openly tricked by the French over their salaries.

This would cover al-Sharqawi, too, but the author clearly feels a need to stress, once more, and quite unnecessarily, that he was in charge of the Diwan at the critical moment when the insurrection was getting under way, but that he was not of the right mould as a leader. He was being too slow, and had too little influence and respect among the people and too little hold on the shaykhs of his group.[8] Clearly, the arguments in the rough draft seemed insufficient to shake al-Sharqawi's position, and were in need of being more openly and directly stated.

The same goes for al-Sadat's position. By adding the jibe to the shaykhs who refused to wear the cockade and reminding them of al-Sadat's wise and successful mediation on this issue, the author clearly wants to clinch the argument. He wants to illustrate that al-Sadat showed the wisdom and foresight demanded of the shaykhs in the new situation created by the French invasion. An allusion to those too lazy to flee the city seems to indicate that al-Sadat's behaviour on this fateful night is felt to be in need of further amplification. Both additions indicate that the author and al-Sadat feel on the defensive.[9]

The additions on the French suggest a similar hardening of the author's attitude to the invaders. The French are not merely new rulers and enemies of the Religion, but simple criminals, ruffians, who hire other ruffians (Barthelemy and Maggalon) among the Greek and European residents to do their dirty work.[10] This would add one more argument against the leading shaykhs: they ought to have seen this, and held themselves aloof from collaborating with mere criminals.

The additions on the Copts reveal a similar interest in dispelling any doubts about the position of this section of the people of Cairo towards the French by eliminating events that could be used to counter such an argument.[11]

The group of five or six additions, which as noted above have been written upside down, do not show a pattern. If, as suggested, they represent a second round of the review, the mind of the author and the authority behind him still seem to have been moving along the same lines as in the first review, stressing a string of facts which should have made the shaykhs aware of the French duplicity.

The additions in this second draft of the MS Mudda are nearly all taken up with corroborating and enlarging the critical line taken in the rough draft of the MS Mudda towards the emirs, al-Sharqawi and the leading shaykhs, and its correlation, the vindication of the position of the shaykh al-Sadat, as sketched out above. The obvious implication of this conclusion is that in these additions we are presented with al-Sadat's comments on the rough draft and that the *sahha* at the end of the additions constitute his approval. The fact that the additions only seem to amplify attitudes already present in the rough draft corroborates the suggestion already hinted at above that the rough draft, too, came about in close collaboration with this shaykh.

This interpretation of the additions in the second draft, seeing the additions as answers to open or implied criticism of the picture painted in the rough draft, allows us to form an idea of the frontiers in the debate among the 'ulama and in what direction they were moving. They indicate that the position taken by al-Sadat – that the proper behaviour of the leading shaykhs would have been to stay clear of the French – is defensive. Consequently, the attitude towards the future of the old rulers, the emirs, and on the old rivals, the Copts, becomes more defined.

As the split in the ranks of the shaykhs between the group headed by al-Sharqawi and that of al-Sadat (and al-Jabarti, of course) seems to be getting wider and more obvious, it is interesting to note that the position represented by the rough draft of the MS Mudda, which propounds the necessity of the shaykhs reverting to the traditional role of staying unattached in any circumstance, is now supplemented by a new and more clear-cut position on the issue of the responsibility of the former rulers, the emirs. The second draft suggests that the shaykhs of the 'ulama headed by al-Sharqawi were on the verge of engaging themselves in a debate on how Egypt should be ruled and defended. It also suggests that al-Sadat and his possible supporters felt themselves to be on the defensive when trying to persuade them of the wisdom of keeping clear of formal ties with the French.

The additions furnish no clear indication of the dating of the second draft. But the fact that Bonaparte is not mentioned in connection with the story on the investigation of the robbery committed by French soldiers[12] suggests that it was made while he was still absent in Suez, i.e. before 7 January 1799.

---

[1] In the investigation of the corrections and additions in the MS Mudda the following procedure was followed: the corrections and additions were found and checked in the Arabic text and their position noted in the translation. The evaluation was then made on the basis of the context in the translation. For this reason references are to the translation, supplemented by references to the notes of Moreh in the Arabic text (in italics). The additions in the margin have been checked with the original MS in Leiden. References to the original text are given by the number of the relevant folio. I apologize for the inconvenience this is bound to create for the reader.

[2] Al-Jabarti in his necrology of al Murtada al-Zabidi relates such a procedure. He notes that 'this was the method of the traditionists in previous times as we have seen in ancient books' (MS Aja'ib, II, 200).

[3] On pp. 35–6 (p. 2) a short note on the arrival of the English fleet in Alexandria is turned into a dialogue pointing out that 1) the Egyptian emirs were duly warned ten days before the French arrived; and 2) they were offered help and assistance, which could have prevented the whole invasion if it had not been for the lack of imagination and flexibility of their local henchman, Muhammad Kurayyim.

Realist, activists and loyalists in Cairo 1798

[4] It is interesting to note that in his chronicle Nicolas Turc has Murad acusing the pasha and the central government in Istanbul of having made secret arrangements with the French. In 1798 there were apparently those who blamed the Ottomans, and not the emirs, for the difficult situation created by the French invasion. The chronicle of Nicolas Turc (*Chronique d'Egypte* 1798–1804, ed. and trans. Gaston Wiet, Cairo, 1950) has a close affinity to the texts of all three versions of the al-Jabarti's chronicle, and the most sensible conclusion would be that Nicolas Turc and al-Jabarti shared a common source. However, this is complicated by the fact that there is a direct connection between al-Jabarti and Nicolas Turc, when they discuss the responsibility of Muhammad 'Ali in the political manoeuvres in 1803–4 (p. 249, (*193*)) . At this point in the narrative of Nicolas Turc, al-Jabarti is one of his sources. The version which Nicolas Turc had at his disposal was the MS Aja'ib, and, because of the anti-Muhammad 'Ali character of the text he quotes, probably the revised, four-volume edition. This would fit with the note by Gardin quoted by Gaston Wiet in his introduction to his translation of Nicolas Turc, Chronique d'Egypte, p.vii, that the text of Nicolas Turc is a summary written at the end of his life, i.e. in the 1820s (p. vii). As a hypothesis for further studies into the connection between Nicolas Turc and al-Jabarti, I would suggest that up until the time when Nicolas Turc left Egypt, i.e. 1801 or 1802, his narrative shares a common source with al-Jabarti. The nature of this common source is difficult to ascertain, but taking Gardin's suggestion that Nicolas Turc's text is a summary of his correspondence with his master, the emir Beshir, it would be natural to start by assuming that al-Jabarti had access to this correspondence and used it, just as Nicolas Turc had access to the MS Aja'ib when he set about writing the last part of his chronicle from 1801 or 1802 to 1804. The string of episodes that opens the narrative of the French invasion in both Nicolas Turc and al-Jabarti has the character of just such a piece of reporting.

[5] P. 105 (*p. 79*).

[6] Pp. 37–8 (*p. 5*), 59 (*p. 31*).

[7] P. 77 (*p. 50*).

[8] Pp. 92 (*p. 66*), 104 (*p. 78*).

[9] Pp. 104 (*p. 78*), 53 (*pp. 24–5*).

[10] P. 57 (*p. 30*).

[11] P.76 (*p. 50*).

[12] P. 123. See below in connection with the analysis of the MS Mazhar.

12 An Ottoman *firman* of 1798

When news of the battle of Aboukir reached Istanbul on 14 August 1798 the Ottoman sultan, Selim III, was ready to declare war on France. But the faction in the Ottoman government favouring France was strong and well entrenched. Only after Russian pressure was war declared, on 2 September 1798. A manifest was distributed to the foreign powers represented in Istanbul, in which the Ottoman government explained its break with a traditional ally. At the same time, the government made sure that its point of view was made known to the subjects of the empire. In the middle of September 1798 a *firman* from the sultan appeared in the streets of Cairo. This text is of considerable interest as both its timing and content would suggest a connection to the debate to which the chronicle of al-Jabarti seems to belong. In the following chapter we shall try to see how and in which direction this connection can be substantiated.

After the conventional invocation, the text of the Ottoman *firman* went like this (in the French translation provided by Martin:[1])

Le peuple français (Dieu veuille détruire leur pays de fond de comble, et couvrir d'ignominie de leurs drapeaux) est une nation d'infidèles obstinés et de scélérats sans freins. Ils nient l'unité de l'Être Suprême, qui a créé le ciel et la terre; ils ne croient point à la mission du prophète, destiné à être l'intercesseur des fidèles au jugement dernier, ou, pour mieux dire, ils se moquent de toutes les religions; ils rejette la croyance d'une autre vie, de ses recompenses et de ses supplices, ils ne croient ni à la resurrection des corps ni au jugement dernier, et ils pensent qu'un aveugle hasard préside à leur vie et à leur mort; qu'ils doivent leur existence à la pure matière, et qu'après que la terre a reçu leurs corps, ils n'y a plus ni résurrection ni compte à rendre, ni demande ni réponse.

—

Les livres divins, inspirés aux prophètes, ne sont, à leur dire, que mensonge et imposture, et ils regardent le Koran, le Pentateuque et l'Évangile comme des fables. Les prophètes, tels que Moïse, Jésus et Mahomet, ne sont, selon eux, que des hommes comme les autres, qui n'ont jamais eu de mission, et qui n'ont pu en imposer qu'à des ignorans. Ils pensent que les hommes, étant nés égaux, doivent être également libres; que toute distinction entre eux est injuste, et que chacun doit être le maître de son opinion et de sa manière de vivre.

The *firman* goes on to describe the French policies of subversion and then clinches the argument by quoting a letter from the Directory to Bonaparte, which is said to have been picked up by one of the secret agents of the Ottoman government. The letter is commented upon in the following way:

> C'est ainsi que finit cette lettre infâme, et puisse le Dieu puissant que nous adorons tourner contre eux leurs diaboliques dessins. Nous vous avons fait une peinture fidèle des Français, de leurs ruses, de leurs fourberies, et des moyens qu'ils emploient pour vous perdre. Jugez donc maintenant si tout Musulman, si tout homme qui professe l'unité de Dieu, n'est pas tenu de prendre les armes contre ces insignes athées.

The rest of the *firman* calls on the believers to unite and be ready to fight the infidel. But the Muslims are warned to watch out carefully for French attempts to bribe or buy Muslims of a weak spirit. The enemy no doubt believes that he may entice the Muslims in the same way as he has done with the Christians. Therefore, the believers should be ready and on their guard. Orders have been issued to assemble troops from all over the empire.

If we turn to the comment of the author of the MS Mudda on the French proclamation, it is plain that he follows the general line of argument in the Ottoman *firman*, pointing out the lies and perverted habits of the French. But more than this, the very words of the *firman* come through at the end of his comment.[2]

This strongly suggests that the Ottoman *firman* of September 1798 was known to the author of the MS Mudda – and more than that, it seems to have provided him with his main line of argument: The leading shaykhs had let themselves be lured away by the French, or, as it is more than hinted at in the *firman*, bought by the enemy with honours and influence. This was exactly the danger against which the *firman* warned. The disdain shown in the MS Mudda towards the participants in the insurrection in October 1798 suggests that the author did not find the situation ready for open rebellion either. The *firman*, too, suggested caution: the believers should be on their guard to avoid French attempts to lure them into cooperation while an army and a fleet was being prepared to crush the enemy. The author of the MS Mudda more than suggests that the insurrection was premature. The rebels should have waited until the Ottoman army was ready to move.[3]

It is probably stretching the point too far to say that the *firman* sparked off the debate and set al-Jabarti on the road as a historian.

The sad outcome of the insurrection in October still seems to be the natural point of departure for those whose hands were still clean. What went wrong? Who was to blame for this disaster? But the *firman* surely provided a useful platform for al-Jabarti and his patron, al-Sadat, from which to point out the failures of both the leading shaykhs co-operating with the French and the participants in the insurrection in October 1798.

The Ottoman *firman* of September 1798 suggests that the Ottomans were very much part of the debates and discussions that took place in Cairo among the 'ulama in the autumn and winter 1798 and in late 1801. The *firman* seems to have been known to the authors of the MS Mudda and to have provided them with their main line of argument against the position of the leading shaykhs around al-Sharqawi. The position taken by al-Sadat and al-Jabarti (staying clear of both the active collaboration of this group and those advocating open fight) should be seen not only as an attempt to formulate an alternative to the position of al-Sharqawi, but as a stand which followed the lead taken by the central Ottoman government. The cautious line suggested by the *firman* itself and the dangerous situation in Cairo in the autumn of 1798 can explain the fact that the Ottoman government does not figure prominently in the MS Mudda. Ottoman clients in Cairo had to watch their step!

1 Martin, *Histoire Scientifique de l'Expedition Francaise en Egypte*, Paris 1815, vol. IV 142-53; Shaw, *Between Old and New*, p. 263; J. Kabrda, *Quelques firman concernant les relations franco-turques lors de l'expedition de Bonaparte en Egypte*, Paris 1947; Laurens, *L'Expedition française de l'Egypte*, p. 136.

2 MS Mudda, p. 42.

3 This was what happened in April 1799. Unfortunately the French were too quick to lift the siege of Acre and to return to Egypt in time to defeat it.

13 A text by al-Sharqawi

Apart from the MS Mudda, another – very much shorter – Muslim narrative of the French occupation exists. Shaykh 'Abdallah al-Sharqawi composed a sort of catalogue of the kings and governors of Egypt, at the end of which he added two pages on the French invasion. This text was dedicated to the Ottoman grand vizier Yusuf Pasha. In the introduction al-Sharqawi relates that in Ramadan 1214 (27 January to 25 February 1800) after the first peace agreement with the French had been concluded (i.e. the convention of El Arish), he and some other 'ulama went to meet the Ottoman vizier Yusuf Pasha in the city of Bilbays. He was here advised by one of the companions of the vizier to write the history of the French occupation and present it as a gift.[1]

I have had access to the text in an extract translated and published by Delanou, which covers the last two pages on the French occupation.[2] However, considering the importance of al-Sharqawi in the chronicles of al-Jabarti and the fact that a later version of al-Jabarti's chronicle, the MS Mazhar, too, is dedicated to Yusuf Pasha, this text from the hand of al-Sharqawi is of considerable interest. How did the shaykh al-Azhar himself present the situation in Egypt under the French occupation?

Actually, in this work al-Sharqawi does not try to tell the story of the French occupation. His short text is a closely reasoned argument in which he seems to concentrate on making three points. First, the participation of the shaykhs in the French diwans was a blessing for the Muslim community. As his starting point he takes the French attitude to the Muslim and Christian creeds. To al-Sharqawi the French are a sect of philosophers who reject belief in the Divine Law, the prophets and God's messengers Muhammad, Jesus and Moses, and the resurrection. They have reached their belief in one God on the basis of reason. To the French, laws are simply practical rules set up to serve the needs of men in different historical periods. This rationalism, he goes on, is the explanation for the French decision to set up diwans in Cairo and the principal cities to regulate the affairs of the Egyptian population. Their decision to include several shaykhs on the Diwan of Cairo is seen as a favour from God to the people of Cairo, as it allowed the French to consult them on questions that did not affect the *shar'ia*.

Having stated his position on the intentions of the French, al-Sharqawi goes on to explain why the people of Cairo and the principal cities had to show some restraint and submission towards the

Jabarti did not remember the actual contents of these last two pages, which, as we have seen, do not have anything to say on the departure of the French and the coming of the Ottomans, but cover only the first period of the French occupation, until the aftermath of the insurrection in October 1798, i.e. they only cover a little less than the MS Mudda. Al-Jabarti's dating of al-Sharqawi's text is equally ambiguous: does he refer to the situation in the beginning of 1800, when Yusuf Pasha arrived, but the French did not depart; or does he have in mind the situation in late 1801, when the French had finally departed and left the field to Yusuf Pasha, the returning emirs and the British? Further studies, especially into the full version of al-Sharqawi's text, are needed to clear up these problems.[4] For the time being, we shall have to leave open both possible datings.

From the summary of al-Sharqawi's text made above, it becomes clear that, as suggested by Gran, al-Sharqawi not only echoes the Ottoman *firman* of October 1798, but actually quotes its initial statements on the religious beliefs of the French! However, as we have seen, al-Sharqawi uses these statements as an argument in favour of the collaboration of the shaykhs. In this way, his document becomes an open refutation of the position proposed by the Ottoman government towards the French. Al-Sharqawi evidently did not agree that the rationalism of the French precluded any collaboration.

Al-Jabarti's analysis and comment in the MS Mudda on the French proclamation were meant not only as an introduction to the French, but also as an argument in a debate on the possibility of cooperating with them. It seems to have been important to al-Jabarti to dismantle the French attempt to delude the inhabitants of Egypt into believing their profession of veneration and respect for the Muslim faith and community. The shaykhs who joined the Diwan should have understood this when they read it.

Seen in this light, al-Sharqawi's text indicates another position: To him the basic rationalism of the French was not in question. On the contrary, it permitted the French to engage the shaykhs in the ordering of affairs of the country and allowed the shaykhs to accept this. The proclamation actually worked, at least to such a degree that the shaykhs agreed to cooperate with the new masters on the basis of its promises. Unfortunately the French did not keep their promises, with the result that the country, its people and the venerated mosque of al-Azhar were plundered and nearly destroyed. The argument of al-Jabarti that the French started to break their promises right from the start is ignored. By separating his interpretation of the French beliefs from the words of the proclamation, al-Sharqawi implies that the promises contained in them, and the subsequent

Realist, activists and loyalists in Cairo 1798

breaking of those promises, had nothing to do with the shaykhs and the diwans. It seems obvious that he wants to convey the impression that to him and the other leading shaykhs on the diwans there were good and reasonable arguments for agreeing to co-operate, as long as the French stuck to their side of the bargain, even considering the religious aspects. Al-Sharqawi makes a point of stating that coopera- tion on the Diwan did not affect the *shar'ia*.

The suggestion made above, that al-Sharqawi's document be- longs to the debate of the autumn and winter of 1798 among the shaykhs of Cairo, takes on added probability if we take a closer look at his description of the French desecration of the al-Azhar mosque. This part of the text shows such affinity to the texts of the MS Mudda and the MS Mazhar (but not the MS Aja'ib, which lacks the fact that people found in the *riwaqs* of the mosque were killed) that they must be related, either directly[5] or indirectly, i.e. through a common source. Unfortunately this does not allow us to date the texts more precisely. But the fact that they are related makes the way they treat the desecration of al-Azhar significant: al-Sharqawi stops here with- out commenting on it, letting the details speak for themselves. In the MS Mudda the French behaviour in al-Azhar is presented as the final proof that they are enemies of Islam and, as such, another argument for the shaykhs not to collaborate with the French.

So, if al-Sharqawi's two pages on the French occupation were written as early as November 1798, it may be seen as the target of, if not the reason for, the arguments in the MS Mudda against the posi- tion of the leading shaykhs who were cooperating with the French. The MS Mudda will stand out as al-Jabarti and al-Sadat's (and behind them, the Ottoman government's) violent attack on the simple-mind- edness of al-Sharqawi and his gang of self-important turban wearers in collaborating with the French! Such ferocious attacks would call for an answer. Al-Sharqawi's text looks like such an answer.

---

[1] Moreh, 'al-Jabarti's Method', p. 353.

[2] 'Abd'Abdallah al-Sharqawi, *Tuhfat al-nazirin fi man wali Misr fi wilayat al- Salatin*, Cairo 189, published in Gilbert Delanou, *Moralistes et politiques mu- sulmans dans l'Egypte du XIXe siècle (1798–1882)*, Lille 1980, pp. 94ff.

[3] MS Aja'ib, IV, 163.

[4] The part of al-Sharqawi's text which al-Jabarti terms a catalogue of the kings of Egypt has until now been passed over as being without interest. But, as we have seen in the case of the MS Mazhar (and below in the MS Aja'ib), such summaries of the history of Egypt may be able to throw some light on the attitudes of the author.

5 In his necrology on al-Sharqawi, MS Aja'ib IV, 160, al-Jabarti adds the detail that al-Sharqawi simply copied his (i.e. al-Jabarti's) biographies of the modern Shafi'i jurists word for word in his works. This may also explain the relationship between the MS Mudda and al-Sharqawi's text on the French desecration of al-Azhar. See also Moreh, 'al-Jabarti's Method', p. 362. But considering al-Jabarti's general dislike for al-Sharqawi, it should be kept in mind that it might also be the other way around!

14 Hasan al-'Attar

Hasan al-'Attar, who became shaykh al-Azhar under Muhammad 'Ali, was a young man in 1798. A document he wrote, the *Maqamat al-'Attar*, clearly relating to the issues raised by the French occupation, has survived, but unfortunately it is undated, and is at present available only in an incomplete English translation, published by Peter Gran. But as the contents of the text seem to be of considerable interest in connection with the questions discussed in this study, it should be included here, if only on a preliminary basis.[1]

The title, *Maqamat al-'Attar*, means the 'recitations of al-'Attar' (*maqam* being a literary term which simply means 'rhymed prose'). The text is concerned with al-'Attar's decision on how his relations with the French orientalists should be handled, and how that decision was reached. It tells the story of how one day al-'Attar approached the house of the French scientists in their lodgings beside the residence of the French commander-in-chief. Rumours of the behaviour of the French made him hesitate, fearing the kind of reception they would give him. But the sight of these young and handsome men, and their open, friendly and eager manner soon put him at ease. He was invited to visit the house, and found himself engrossed in interesting discussions on literature and questions of the Arabic language and grammar. Their breadth of knowledge and devotion to these matters impressed him. One of them attracted him in particular by his faultless Arabic and good looks. The meeting affected al-'Attar strongly, and a passion for literature, 'which had once grown stronger, then weaker, was now revived'. Al-'Attar started composing poetry again, to the joy and astonishment of his new-found friends. They urged him to come and stay with them. But al-'Attar hesitated. He kept the offer 'a secret for lack of authorisation, knowing that if I had gone ahead with this matter, rebukes and hostility would have awaited me as well as the scorn of society. Thus I returned to my senses and made my decision. May God forgive me for what I have done.'

The point of this *maqamat* thus seems to be that there was a limit to how far Egyptians like al-'Attar might associate with the French without authorization. He might visit them, he might talk and discuss with them, but only on an informal, provisional basis. To do more would require him to seek out his superiors and get their permission. If he went ahead without doing so, he would be subjected to rebuke and hostility, as well as the scorn of society in general. He had been sorely tempted to cross the invisible line between interest and curiosity and formal collaboration, but checked himself just in time. The decision he made is not specified, but from the context it seems plain that it involved a break with the French. He decided to stay clear of them in the future, and deeply regretted that he had let himself be carried away. The proper attitude to the French, the one expected by his superiors and society, was not one of open friendship and cooperation, but apparently the opposite.

The *Maqamat al-'Attar*, taken as it stands, undated and incomplete, allows us to make some interesting observations. In the first place, it attests to the fact that the classic dilemma of collaboration existed and was fully understood in Egypt under the French occupation. Second, it illustrates the psychological mechanism discussed above, which sees the way of presenting the French as a function of the author's relations, not to the occupying power, but to his fellow countrymen. Al-'Attar's attitude to the French is circumscribed by his relationship to his superiors and his wish to avoid the scorn of society. We are reminded of the position of al-Jabarti in relation to the shaykh al-Sadat, suggested in the analysis of the MS Mudda.

Third, the work suggests the social circumstances of a men such as al-'Attar and al-Jabarti. The document does not mention who the 'superiors' are, and gives us no indications as to their identity. But al-'Attar clearly sees himself as being under the authority of more powerful people than himself, i.e. what has been termed a 'patron'. This is apparently how things worked: people, and especially up-and-coming people such as a young poet and grammarian of modest origins like al-'Attar,[2] were expected to seek out the necessary permission before taking important steps in the social sphere. Al-'Attar and the author of the MS Mudda had to respect the bonds of patronage.

In the next version of his chronicles, the MS Mazhar, al-Jabarti employed poems composed by al-'Attar. As he was still under the patronage of al-Sadat at this stage, there seems to be good reason to believe that the superiors alluded to by al-'Attar may have been the same, i.e. al-Sadat.

The *Maqamat* has the character of a piece of autobiography. Al-'Attar looks back from the point of focus, i.e. the point when he returned to his senses and made his decision to stay away from the French. However, it is important to note that he still remembers his fascination for the French as something positive. He has not felt the need to let his regrets and bad conscience turn the French into the tempting devils of the Ottoman *firman*, who deploy clever ruses to weaken and annihilate the Muslim community. His situation at the time of writing the *Maqamat* does not demand a denial of former attitudes.

This raises the tricky question of when this text was written. Gran finds that it must have been written in 1801[3] on his return from his long exile in Asyut in Upper Egypt, in a situation in which the normal sanctions of social behaviour were relaxed. But this rests on the supposition that al-'Attar returned to Cairo before the French left for good, which is contrary to the information supplied by al-Jabarti. According to al-Jabarti, al-'Attar left Cairo after the second uprising in Cairo in May 1800 and stayed away for eighteen months until no French were left in Egypt, i.e. late 1801.[4] As al-'Attar apparently left Egypt early in 1802 for Turkey and Syria, only to return in 1815,[5] it would be reasonable to place the situation referred to in the *Maqamat* in the early part of the French occupation, i.e. 1798 or 1799. This would fit in with the fact that the content of al-'Attar's poems in the MS Mazhar, especially in the preface, follows the same anti-French line taken by the al-Jabarti in this chronicle. We know that al-Sadat and al-Jabarti visited the French Institute and that this was still considered a proper thing to do, while the MS Mudda was being written. From the way this visit is treated in the MS Mazhar, it must be concluded that this was not the case in December 1801, perhaps even as early as January 1800, at the time of the convention of El Arish, five months before al-'Attar left for Upper Egypt. The way the French commander-in-chief is mentioned suggests that Bonaparte was still in Cairo. So the most appropriate date for the decision taken by al-'Attar seems to be some time between January and August 1799.

But it is one thing to make a decision to stay away from the French, and quite another to feel a need to communicate it in writing. Why and when did al-'Attar compose this memoir? Why did he feel the need to communicate his regrets and ask for forgiveness? Several situations suggest themselves, the most obvious being during the siege of Cairo, after the battle of Heliopolis, when retribution was in the air. After this siege al-Sadat fell out with the French in earnest. This would explain why al-'Attar left Cairo: with al-Sadat out of favour with the French, there would be good reason for his retainer to disappear in order to avoid unpleasant repercussions.

Unfortunately it is not possible to date the text of the *Maqamat al-'Attar* more accurately, except for the fact that it clearly belongs to the period of the French occupation. But even then it still constitutes an important source of information for our understanding of the psychological situation of intellectuals on the fringe of upper-class Cairo at this time. Al-'Attar's connection with al-Jabarti suggests that the ideas and arguments propounded in the chronicles of the latter were produced under the same conditions of patronage, and possibly the same patron, al-Sadat.

¹ Gran, *Islamic Roots of Capitalism*, pp. 189–91. According to Gran, the text was published together with another *Maqamat* composed by 'Abd al-Rahman al-Suyuti in a manuscript, preserved in the Dar al-Kutub (7574 Adab), and translated by Oscar Rescher, in *Orientalische Mizellen*, Constantinople 1925, pp. 229–334. It is not clear whether Gran translated it from the original or from Oscar Rescher. The text is incomplete (dashes in some passages indicates this), but it is not clear what these passages contained and why they were deleted.

² Gran, *Islamic Roots of Capitalism*, p. 78.

³ Gran is not clear on this point: on p. 89 he states that the *Maqamat* was written in 1798 or 1799, but on p. 90 that he wrote down in his autobiographical fragment an explanation of his motivations in the same free spirited fashion that reigned in Egypt at his return from Upper Egypt, i.e. late 1801.

⁴ MS Mazhar, Philipp's translation, p. 279

⁵ Gran, *Islamic Roots of Capitalism*, p. 78.

15   Conclusions

The investigation of the composition of the MS Mudda indicates that in spite of the fact that most of the entries in al-Jabarti's annalistic chronicle are taken up with the actions of the French, the MS Mudda seems to have been written with the clear purpose of supplying the necessary pertinent facts to vindicate the stand taken by the shaykh of the Wafa'iyya sufi order and the al-Husayni shrine, the shaykh al-Sadat, in the situation created by the French occupation. Unlike the shaykh al-Azhar, al-Sharqawi, and his followers, al-Sadat stayed free of the official French diwans on the ground that such a commitment to and cooperation with the enemies of Islam would seriously imperil the power of the shaykhs to intervene with the new rulers to alleviate the plight of the people. The MS Mudda propounds the view that, as the only source of power of the 'alim stems from his personal conduct and his ability to live and act by his own advice, it is important that he remains unattached to any ruler.

The group of shaykhs who agreed to collaborate with the French, and especially their leader, al-Sharqawi, are presented as people who panic and, in consequence, find themselves to be mere tools in the hands of the French, providing justification for their plunder, brutality and extortion. By their actions they allow the French a free hand to try to change the system of taxation, and at the critical point they do not even have the necessary cohesion as a group, nor the personal courage and initiative, to prevent the people of Cairo from committing the folly of an insurrection against the French. They are seen as responsible for the loss of life and property that this rebellion brought about for the people of Cairo. But in spite of this, they carry on and let themselves take part in a new reorganised diwan, and in doing so allow the French to assume positions that can only be the cause of new calamities in the future.

The author of the rough draft of the MS Mudda argues that the Muslim community of Cairo (and Egypt) is fragile and confronted with many dangers: the traditional ones from the Copts, Jews and Syrian Christians; and the new one, the French. The emirs have lost their ability to defend the country, squandering its riches in their petty power games, and the rightful master, the sultan, is too far away. In this situation the leading shaykhs are the only ones left to defend the Muslim community. However, the MS Mudda presents the case that an important section of the leading shaykhs, the group around al-Sharqawi and al-Azhar, have taken the wrong path. They did not re- alize that the French were enemies of Islam, and committed a grave mistake in seeing them as friends, who honestly wanted to respect the community.

The rough draft of the MS Mudda should be seen as part of a debate among the 'ulama of Cairo. The dating of the manuscript is difficult, especially as the text shows signs of having been preceded by other drafts. But considering the content, it seems most likely that this debate was sparked off by the insurrection in October 1798. The first drafts were probably written some time in October–November 1798, with the present rough draft, i.e. the MS Mudda without the additions and corrections, probably coming about no later than late December 1798.

This debate, judged by the wording and comments of the rough draft of the MS Mudda, is heated and incriminating. But it is important to note that it is still carried on within the 'ulama. The author's attempt to avoid informing on the shaykhs who lost their patience and joined the insurrection testifies to his willingness to cover for these people, even though their 'lack of foresight' has placed them in opposition to his hero, the shaykh al-Sadat. To the author it is still a matter of some importance to preserve the unity of the 'ulama and its leading shaykhs.

It follows from this that the MS Mudda should be used with great care, both as a source for Muslim opinions of the French and the emirs and for minor matters, as the treatment of these aspects in the narrative seems to be subordinated to the author's wish to present his arguments properly. The main interest of the MS Mudda as a source for the history of Egypt around 1800 is the fact that it supplies us with an idea of how the leading shaykhs in Cairo handled the issues created by the French invasion.

The additions in the MS Mudda illustrate how the debate moved on. In these additions we are presented with al-Sadat's comments on the rough draft. They indicate that the position taken by al-Sadat – that the proper behaviour of the leading shaykhs would be to stay clear of the French – is a defensive one. Consequently, the attitude towards the future of the old rulers, the emirs, and the old rivals, the Copts, becomes more defined.

As the split in the ranks of the shaykhs between the group headed by al-Sharqawi and that of al-Sadat (and al-Jabarti, of course) seems to be widening, it is interesting to note that the position represented by the rough draft of the MS Mudda, which propounds the necessity of the shaykhs reverting to the traditional role of staying unattached in any circumstance, is now supplemented by a new and more clear-cut position on the issue of the responsibility of the former rulers, the emirs. The second draft suggests that the group of shaykhs headed by al-Sharqawi were on the verge of engaging themselves in a debate on how Egypt should be ruled and defended. It also suggests that al-Sadat and his possible supporters felt themselves to be on the defensive when trying to persuade them of the wisdom of keeping clear of formal ties with the French.

The additions furnish no clear indication of when the revision of the second draft took place,[1] but a date before 7 January 1799 seems to be the most likely.

This picture of the situation among the 'ulama in Cairo is corroborated by external evidence. The corroboration is supplied by three texts, which have survived outside al-Jabarti's chronicles. The wording of an Ottoman *firman*, which appeared in the streets of Cairo in September 1798, strongly suggests that the stand propounded in the MS Mudda echoes the Ottoman government's position, which advised staying free of the offers of cooperation made by the French. This implies that al-Jabarti and his patron, the shaykh al-Sadat had decided, in the precarious situation created in Egypt by the French invasion, to stay loyal to the Ottoman government. Al-Sharqawi's short statement at the end of his history of Egypt presents the arguments of the group of leading shaykhs willing to cooperate with the French in order to protect Muslim society. The content of this text strongly suggests that it actually came into existence as part of the debate among the 'ulama in Cairo in the winter of 1798–9. The same does not seem to be the case with the last text, the *Maqamat* of al-'Attar, which was probably put into writing at a somewhat later date, but clearly relates to early days of the French occupation and attests to the fact that the classic dilemma of collaboration was very real to educated people. The text highlights implications of the ties created by patronage for the freedom of persons such as al-'Attar and al-Jabarti, and in this way helps to explain the fact that in the MS Mudda we find al-Jabarti acting as the mouthpiece of the shaykh al-Sadat.

So, the picture that emerges from the pages of the MS Mudda seems to be a familiar one. On one hand, we have the 'realists' (al-Sharqawi), who agree to cooperate, probably with varying degrees of enthusiasm (al-Mahdi, al-Bakri). On the other, we see the 'activists', who reject any cooperation with the invaders, divided into a group of *exilès* ('Umar Makram) and what could conveniently be termed the 'home front' (Badr al-Maqdisi). In this scheme of things the shaykh al-Sadat (and al-Jabarti) would represent a stand somewhere between the 'realists' of the main body of leading shaykhs and the 'home-front' activists!

What made al-Sadat choose this position is not explained. At the crucial moment, when the French formed the first Diwan of

III

IN SUPPORT OF
THE OTTOMANS:
THE MS MAZHAR AL-TAQDIS

16 Composition of the MS Mazhar

Al-Jabarti finished a new version of his chronicle, the MS Mazhar al-Taqdis ('A clear view of the sanctifying will of God in the departure of French rule') at the end of the month of Shaban 1216/December 1801 and dedicated it to the commander–in– chief of the Ottoman army in Egypt at this time, the grand vizier Yusuf Pasha.[1] The text is divided into a preface, an introduction, and an account of events in Egypt from 10 Muharram 1213 (24 June 1798) to the end of Shaban 1216 (December 1801). The part from 1798 to January 1799 is based on the MS Mudda. To this he added a short epilogue.[2]

The MS Mazhar is a voluminous work,[3] and a detailed investigation of the entire text lies outside the scope of this study. The analysis will be confined to a survey of the composition of the new chronicle, an examination of the content of the preface, introduction and epilogue (i.e. the beginning and the end) and finally a more detailed analysis of the changes made in the part based on the MS Mudda.[4] This should provide sufficient evidence to draw conclusions about the perspectives and purpose of this new version.[5]

Al-Jabarti did not change the basic composition of his chronicle when he set about revising the MS Mudda in order to include it in his new version. Naturally, the fact that an independent entity (or the draft for one) was being turned into a part of a larger work required some compositional changes: the opening paragraph and the final Qur'anic quotations had to be deleted, as they were superseded by the preface/introduction and the epilogue. However, minor but telling differences do occur in the part covered by the MS Mudda. In the continuation, i.e. the part of the MS Mazhar that covers the period from January 1799 to December 1801, the author did not have a pre-existing text to encumber him. He used this freedom to develop new ways of presenting his material.

THE ANNALISTIC FRAMEWORK

The annalistic framework with dated entries in chronological order is still the compositional backbone of his chronicle. The changes in this respect merely consist of deletions and additions of entries or parts of them, without touching the basic composition found in the MS Mudda. However, the sheer size of the text presented him with new opportunities.

The division by month, which he developed in the later part of the MS Mudda, now covers the whole text. The flow of dated entries is systematically punctuated at the end of every month with the summaries of undated events and general conditions. There are some exceptions,[6] but the author seems to favour this feature, whenever circumstances allow him to use it. Only when the narrative becomes too eventful is the division into months reduced to a mere formality.

In a few cases the month is introduced with a short summary of the events to be described,[7] indicating that at the time of writing the author had an idea of the following events, perhaps even a plan for his work. The latter is indicated when the reader is promised a final (and better!) poem in praise of the vizier further on, in its proper place.[8]

The nature of the material in the concluding summaries is much the same as in the MS Mudda, i.e. general conditions and undated stories which tend to stress the oppressive nature of the French occupation. However, new material is brought in, obviously to highlight the social and moral disruption of Muslim society. The end of Shaban 1213 is used as a summing up of the heresy of the people.[9] This topic was introduced previously in conformity with the usual annalistic pattern, with a dated entry followed by background information and a comment on its significance. What sets it apart from the other entries is the length of the entry. The first instance relates the story of how the festival of the birthday of Husayn came to be celebrated again under the French.[10] The second concerns the celebration of the birthday of Sayyid 'Ali al-Bakri, buried in the al-Sharaybi mosque in Azbakiyya.[11] To the author, these festivals are pure heresy, providing the Cairene people with an opportunity to display their natural superstition and its organizers with a handsome income.[12] The author is quite obviously of the opinion that the French support of the festivals is a ruse to lure away the people from their spiritual leaders, the shaykhs: 'The French permitted this to the people since they saw in it transgression of Islamic law, pursuit of carnal desires, public gathering of women, diversion and the committing of sins!'[13] These items seem to have the nature of what Hathaway terms *aja'ib*, curious incidents, taken from local lore and used to furnish the narrative with colour and perspective,[14] in this case the subversion of the morals of the people by the French.[15]

The general use of divisions by the month has not interfered with the tentative division of the text into 'chapters' (i.e. sections/subsections) in the part of the text covered by the MS Mudda. One of the changes is clearly intended to strengthen this feature.[16]

Because of the length of the period covered in the MS Mazhar, the author comes up against a new chronological feature, the start of a new year. The year 1213 is closed with a short summary of events: As the most important, the author points to the disruption of the Pilgrimage from Egypt. Neither the *kiswa* (the ceremonial cloth with which the Ka'ba is covered) nor the money for Mecca was sent. The author notes that nothing comparable had happened under the rule of the Ottomans.[17]

At the close of the year 1214, the author starts with a short summary of the most important events, similar to that of the previous year: the blockade of the ports, the suspension of all travel on land or sea and the disruption of the Pilgrimage. However, he then proceeds to describe at some length the tribulations caused by the behaviour of the beduin highwaymen and the French in the villages. This is followed by a string of undated entries: a short note on the low rise of the Nile and a story of the clash between the French and the citizens of Minufiya, Tanta and Mahalla al-Kubra, the French seizure of Ottoman ships in Alexandria, the French looting of Suez, Murad's support for the French and the exactions of the Coptic tax-collectors in the provinces.[18]

When the year 1215 is closed, the author does not note whether the events of the year are important or not, but simply sets out to describe, first and at some length, the continued destruction of landmarks in the city caused by the French activity and the fighting, then the licentiousness of the women, the activity of Yacub the Copt, the cutting down of trees and smashing of boats by the French, the extreme inundation of the Nile and the disruption of traffic, which caused high prices. Finally he describes the plague which broke out in Egypt and Syria by quoting a letter from his friend al-'Attar in Asyut.[19]

Judging from this sequence, the author originally set out to sum up the most important events of the year in a short conclusion. At the end of 1214 he finds it necessary to add a list of some of the major disasters and problems caused by events, and in 1215 he simply forgets the summary. As for the content of these conclusions, he is purely concerned with events that changed conditions in Egypt for the worse. There seems to be a sort of progression in these conclusions, not only in the length of the text, but also in the content: a steady broadening of the disasters and calamities caused by the French occupation, starting with the disruption of the Pilgrimage and ending with the plague. The lively letters of al-'Attar, quoted at the end of 1214[20] and at the very end of 1215, are obviously used to make the reader visualize the disasters. It is difficult not to see these features as a means to create a fittingly dramatic background of mounting disasters for the return of the Ottomans and the second, final recapture of Egypt. Things are going from bad to worse!

NECROLOGIES

At this crucial point, at the end of the year 1215,[21] the author introduces an entirely new compositional feature: necrologies. Until this point people who have died are mentioned and commented upon at the appropriate dated entry.[22] There is no elaborate introduction. Following al-'Attar's letter describing the plague in Asyut, the text just says 'And then for those who died in this year among the notables'. In the following entries the reader is presented with the life and personal characteristics of the deceased and the author's opinion of their personalities. Seventeen emirs or retainers of emirs, headed by Murad Bey, are mentioned. The length of the individual necrologies vary from several pages (on Murad Bey) to the mere mentioning of a name. The common feature seems to be the fact that they are *mamluk*s and, with a few exceptions, died of the plague in this year. The author apparently sees them as a group: Ayyub Bey al-Kabir is mentioned as 'one of the better among them', [23] and as this remark indicates, the author does not think highly of them. In fact, except for Ayyub Bey, Yahya Kashif and a few others, who are only mentioned by name, they are all denounced for their personal deficiencies and deplorable actions. Only Salim Kashif was 'courageous, forceful, resolute and reckless' and 'generous and hospitable'. He was also, however, 'tyrannical, an oppressor and ready to spill blood'.[24] The more discriminating judgement on this emir seems to spring from the fact that one of his freed men, Ahmad Kashif Sha'rawi, was a friend of the author! The author ends the list by noting that 'others too, died whose names I do not recollect'.[25]

The most straightforward explanation for the introduction of this feature seems to be that at the end of the year 1215 the plague did away with Murad Bey and other emirs. This provided the author with an opportunity to comment on these people. In the case of Murad Bey it further afforded him an opportunity to retain some of the material that had been deleted from the MS Mudda (e.g. his connection with Muhammad Kurayyim). As part of the end-of-year summary, this feature seems perfectly natural.

But the fact that the author limits himself to emirs and makes a point of showing that, with a few exceptions, they were men of bad character indicates that this feature is also used compositionally to stress the author's argument. In the general scheme of the MS Maz-har, this point, the end of the year 1215, just before the final victory of the Ottomans and the following showdown between the vizier and the Egyptian emirs,[26] seems to be a fitting place to stress that the Egyptian emirs, and especially Murad Bey, the main culprits in the story on the Muslim side, were unfit to rule and incapable of the nec-essary leadership! It seems as if these necrologies in the MS Mazhar developed by chance, but that once they were in place, the author re-alized their potential as a compositional device to stress an important theme in his account.

The introduction of this feature is of considerable importance for our understanding of the development of al-Jabarti's work. As we shall see, it inspired the author to further innovations in the MS Aja'ib, where it seems to have provided him with an opportunity to use the material he had written on famous 'ulama for his friends al-Zabidi and al-Muradi,[27] as well as the chance to demonstrate, by way of the necrologies of the shaykhs (in the MS Aja'ib significantly placed before those of the emirs), that there were people more wor-thy of the rulers' trust than the emirs. Hathaway's observation that al-Jabarti's contribution to the development of necrologies as a feature of the chronicles seems to be 'one of separation and elaboration, rather than one of synthesis'[28] is borne out by this. This contribu-tion apparently came about in connection with al-Jabarti's attempt to transform the MS Mudda into the MS Mazhar (and, as we shall see, the MS Mazhar into the MS Aja'ib).

TEXTUAL DEVICES

In the process of adapting the MS Mudda to the MS Mazhar, the position of the narrator has not changed. Apart from the change in the line of argument (or, as we shall see below, because of it!), his comments have become more restrained, subdued and factual in content.[29] Entries containing unconfirmed or speculative mate-rial,[30] as well as much of the heated polemic, have disappeared,[31] even against the French.[32] In the case of the French, the polemic has been replaced by short epithets such as 'infidel' or 'accursed' joined to the name, a feature which, consequently, takes on the air of a token, conventional condemnation.[33] Many details on the more disgusting – or downright obscene – habits of the French have been moved and/or deleted.[34] The author seems to have found these de-tails too vulgar and inappropriate, even in a description of the infidel French! In the continuation the implied author relates events in the third person (singular or plural). Openly stated comments on events are restricted to one or two short remarks, correcting unfavourable – but obviously unavoidable – phrases about the Ottomans in the documents quoted. Instead, perhaps as a more fitting substitute, his friend al-'Attar is quoted, either directly[35] or indirectly, through his poetry and letters.

Some of the changes in the MS Mudda are best explained as an attempt to bring some order and method into parts of the narrative. Changes of this nature are not confined to the analysis or the summaries of documents, which, as we have seen, clearly needed to be straightened out.[36] They can be found throughout the narrative, where passages containing many details have been superseded by comprehensive remarks stating the point the author wanted to make.[37] He apparently had no intention of altering the basic compositional character of his narrative, only to straighten out the more turbulent or inappropriate passages. His endeavours in this respect suggest a different readership with a more considerate and refined taste.

The use of French documents is retained, but with a tendency to quote them in full. In the part of the text covered by the MS Mudda, there is virtually no change in the way the author renders these documents. In the two cases where he does change the text, the reason can found in the content.[38] It is the same with the speech read out to soldiers at the celebration of the inauguration of the French Republic.[39] As this is not a document, the author may have felt free to delete it altogether. But in the continuation, comments and analysis on the documents become rare.[40] The documents are mainly left to speak for themselves, and as such they tend to stress the deceitful intentions of the French.

However, two new kinds of letters turn up: the letters from al-'Attar in exile in Upper Egypt; and, most appropriately in the light of the dedication of the MS Mazhar, a decree from the sultan, issued by the vizier Yusuf Zia Pasha himself, providing the beduin of Buhayra with the right to settle in the province. This letter is reproduced *in extenso* at the very end.[41]

The use of direct speech is obviously more restricted. In the coverage of the doings of the people of Cairo many of the lively details, using direct speech, have disappeared.[42] Although this cannot be attributed solely to the author's attempt to suppress this feature, in many cases it does seem to be the major reason. However, direct speech used to visualize the thoughts and temper of the common people appears during the author's description of the siege of Cairo in 1800 after the failure of the Convention of El Arish, obviously to

In support of the Ottomans: The MS Mazhar al-Tagdis

corroborate the courage and zeal of the Muslims. So the author still seems to cherish the use of direct speech as a stylistic device.

In the part of the MS Mazhar covered by the Mudda, much of the dialogue has disappeared. However, as we shall see shortly, it is evident that the reason is to be found in the author's intention to change some of the arguments and points contained in the dialogue, not the feature itself. Wherever the dialogue conforms to the new line of argument in the MS Mazhar, it has not been touched.[43] In the continuation, the use of dialogue is kept on the same restricted level, but only until Menou sets up a new Diwan.[44] From this point onwards, the deliberations and discussions of this Diwan are covered in much detail, quoting not only the French commander and his commissioner's letters and speeches, but also the point of view of the shaykhs. This dialogue is presented according to the pattern established in the MS Mudda. The names and point of view of individual members are usually not supplied; the shaykhs are presented as a group. But the picture presented of the French is significantly different from the preceding account. The strong anti-French vocabulary disappears and the new governor, Menou, and his commissioners are shown as sincerely listening to the advice of the shaykhs. A letter from Menou is quotedin full,[45] but without comment. According to this,

> the best order for organising this world entirely is the one that pays heed and follows completely the order emanating from the wisdom of God Most High. You [i.e. the shaykhs of the Diwan] know that the land and regions considered successful, happy and prosperous are so only because its inhabitants are rightly guided by the principles of the *shar'ia* and laws which emanate from men of astuteness and understanding and are prepared for the path of justice and equity.[46]

From the MS Aja'ib, (but not from the MS Mazhar), we know that al-Jabarti himself was a member of this Diwan. The author's direct access to the deliberations of the Diwan may explain the richer detail. However, the fact that the author points out that this Diwan consisted only of Muslim shaykhs and devoted much attention to securing a Muslim perspective in the ordering of affairs, and his subsequent lack of anti-French invective, suggest that he had a more definite purpose. From the use made of such comments and dialogue in the MS Mudda, we know that the author favoured this feature, i.e. open, detailed but uncommented-on dialogue, when he wanted to convey important arguments in his narrative to the reader. It seems reasonable therefore to suggest that this deviation from the established pattern of the MS Mazhar represents an important component of the message the author wanted to convey to the reader. By providing a detailed description of the deliberations of this Diwan, the author is able to show that the French, under Menou, seem to have come around to the right understanding of the duties of the ruler: to uphold the *shar'ia* and to consult those who know what this entails, the shaykhs, and that this way of handling things is to the benefit of all, the rulers and the Muslim community. As we shall see, this fits the thoughts expressed by al-Jabarti in the preface and introduction.

POETRY

The author decided to include poetry by his friend Hasan al-'Attar, 'so that he may be well remembered with us'. This is done right from the start of the preface,[47] where he quotes a poem by al-'Attar on the French occupation. Al-'Attar turns up again further on with a poem on the beauties of Azbakiyya [48] and on Abu'l-Qasim, shaykh of the Maghribi *riwaq* at al-Azhar,[49] and in praise of the vizier, on the occasion of his parade through the city.[50]

But al-'Attar is not the only poet quoted. Al-Jabarti quotes Sayyid 'Ali al-Sairafi al-Rashidi, a resident of Acre, for a poem praising al-Jazzar for his defence of the city against the French.[51] In a somewhat cursory fashion he quotes another friend, Shaykh 'Ali al-Sharanfishi, distinguished as a literary expert, for an ode to the *kapudan* Husayn Pasha.[52] This ode was offered to the pasha at the latter's visit to the Husayni shrine, for which the shaykh was richly rewarded! Al-Andalusi is also quoted, on the beauties of Birk al-Fil.[53]

Obviously, the author feels that poetry is necessary in a work like this and, as he is no poet himself, he has to rely on his friend al-'Attar and other (great or small) luminaries to supply the necessary material. However, the author's use of al-'Attar goes further. Al-'Attar is not only able to supply him with poetry of the necessary quality, but also with some qualified criticism of other poets![54] Al-Jabarti has clearly made an effort to summon all possible forces to make his narrative and its arguments conform to the refined taste of the prospective readers from Istanbul.

The similarity between the general line of argument of the MS Mazhar and al-'Attar's poems poses some interesting questions. From the content of al-'Attar's poems, especially in the preface, it appears that he takes the same line of argument as the author. Did the author inspire al-'Attar or is it the other way around? From the comments supplied in the text,[55] it seems most likely that this famous poet not only supplied al-Jabarti with his poems, but also shared – or perhaps even inspired – the author's interpretation of history generally, and the events in Egypt under the French occupation in particular, or, in other words, that al-'Attar acquired the status of the author's spiritual mentor!

---

[1] Moreh, 'Introduction', pp. 17–18, 21.

[2] The MS Mazhar al-Taqdis seems to have come about in much the same manner as the MS Mudda. According to Moreh the author's autograph (MS Maz.Cam), contains many passages from the margins of the MS Mudda

[3] Apparently, some further notes were added to the autograph of the MS Mazhar before it was rewritten into the finished version of the MS Mazhar (represented by MSS. Maz. Bay., Ram., BM.)

[4] The printed edition of the MS Mazhar was based on these MSS

[5] Moreh, Introduction, pp. 8, 17-18

[6] Moreh, 'Introduction', pp. 8, 12. The MS Mudda consists of 26 folios with an irregular number of lines, between 22 and 32, per page, while the autograph of the MS Mazhar, the MS Maz.Cam, contains 128 folios with 25 lines per page.

[7] The changes from the MS Mudda to this part of MS Mazhar have been identified on the basis of the translations and verified in the Arabic text of the MS Mudda and its footnotes and the printed Arabic edition of the MS Mazhar. Unfortunately there seem to be minor discrepancies between Moreh's footnotes and the translation, probably indicating further changes between the MSS at the disposal of Moreh and the printed version. For these reasons the following will have the character of a preliminary investigation, to be further verified and corroborated. References to MS Mazhar will for the present be to the printed edition (in italics) and the translation by Thomas Philipp. The term MS Mudda in the following signifies the second draft of the Mudda, i.e. the text with additions and corrections.

[8] The investigation is made on the basis of the following texts: Moreh's edition of MS Mudda and its footnotes, the printed edition of the MS Mazhar, and a translation by Prof. Thomas Philipp, covering the period until the end of the year 1214/may 1800, which is based on the printed edition of the MS Mazhar from 1969. For practical reasons I have used Philipp's English translation of the MS Mazhar to the end of the year 1214. For the rest I have used the Arabic edition in the following way: the Arabic edition was checked against the English translation of the MS Aja'ib version and the differences noted and/or translated. This provided me both with a complete translation of the MS Mazhar, necessary for this survey, and with a fairly accurate idea of the changes made in the MS Mazhar when it was transformed into the MS Aja'ib, necessary for the analysis of the MS

Aja'ib. For this reason references are to the Arabic text of the MS Mazhar (in italics) and Philipp's translation until the end of 1214, and after that to the printed version of MS Mazhar, in italics, and to the English translation of the MS Aja'ib (and, incidentally, to the printed text of this version in Arabic, as the English translation very conveniently has stuck to this pagination).

9 Muharram, Safar, Rabi' al-Awwal Rajab, Shaban, Shawwal 1214, Rajab, Ramadan, Shawwal, Dhu al-Qa'da 1215, Muharram, Safar, Rabi I, Rabi II, Jumada II, Rajab, Shaban 1216.

10 *113*, p. 142; *185*, p. 221; *259*, III, 139;*278*, III, 146.

11 *103*, p. 190

12 *111*, p. 139.

13 *103*, p. 128.

14 *183*, p. 220.

15 *111*, p. 139.

16 *184*, p. 221.

17 Hathaway, 'Sultans, Pashas, *Taqwims*, and Muhımmes' p. 64.

18 In the MS Mazhar the development of the celebration of the birthday of Husayn into a major public event is attributed to the overseer of the *waqf* of the mosque of Husayn, Sayyid Badawi al-Qabani, in the most unflattering way. This story is repeated nearly verbatim in the MS Aja'ib (III, 40ff.). In the necrology of al-Sadat (IV, 189ff.), the author has done a u-turn: Now Sayyid Badawi is portrayed as the innocent victim of the ambitious intrigues of al-Sadat and the responsibility for the deplorable development of the festival of Husayn is placed on him. This is a good example of the strong anti-al-Sadat tilt of the necrology of al-Sadat, which will be discussed below.

19 45, p. 55. Unfortunately, it is not possible to ascertain from the available texts whether this feature is used in the continuation, but a look at the MS Maz.Cam would clear this up.

20 *146*, p. 182.

21 *241*, p. 283.

22 *304*, III, 159.

23 The letter is placed just before the conclusion of the year (*237*, p. 279) in order to illustrate the plight of the refugees from Cairo.

1 *314*, III, 167–76.

25 Some examples: *113*, p. 142: Shaykh ad-Damanhuri; *255*, III, 136: *Mustafa Pasha*; *277*, III, 151: *Muhammad, agha of the Mustahfizan*; *293*, III, 154: *Shaykh Muhammad ibn al-Jawhari*; *296*, III, 156: *Murad Bey*.

26 *320*, III, 172.

27 *330*, III, 176.

28 *331*, III, 176.

In support of the Ottomans: The MS Mazhar al-Tagdis

[29] Only alluded to in the MS Mazhar, 372, III, 202.

[30] Philipp, in al-Jabarti, *History of Egypt*, vol III: *A Guide*, p. 2.

[31] Hathaway, Sultans, pashas, Taqwims, p. 64

[32] 27, p. 29 is a good example.

[33] *74, 86*, pp. 91, 106.

[34] 26, p. 30 and *84*, p. 104 are worthy examples.

[35] *69*, p. 84.

[36] *72, 85*, pp. 88, 105 may serve as examples.

[37] *34*, p. 37/40, *69*, p. 85.

[38] *153, 164*, pp. 189, 202.

[39] *35*, p. 37, *95*, p. 118.

[40] *80*, p. 98 may serve as an example.

[41] In the letters from the shaykhs to the people of Cairo and Egypt, 89,.92, p. 110, 114.

[42] *63*, p. 77.

[43] The comment of al-'Attar provides one of the few examples (164, p. 202).

[44] *376*, III, 204–6.

[45] *26, 43, 79*, pp. 29, 50, 98 are good examples.

[46] *46*, p. 55 may serve as an example of this point.

[47] *260*, III, 137.

[48] *268*, III, 142.

[49] *271*, III, 143.

[50] *13*, p. 12.

[51] *210*, p. 256.

[52] *302*, III, 158

[53] *361*, III, 190.

[54] *139*, p. 185.

[55] *358*, III, 188.

[56] *307*, III, 161.

[57] *153*, p. 190.

[58] *164*, p. 201: 'Our already mentioned friend said [in a comment on a letter from Bonaparte to the 'ulama] that the statement of the cursed "inform the people of Egypt that the Ottoman rule over Egypt has ceased" shows the ambitions of the soul travelling in the realms of hope, clinging to the tails of desire, which hit the neck of men without ever reaching; the abandonment of the soul of the wicked on the pastures of sin and error; the distortion of the mind from the right path, ineffectuate with the opposition of darkened imagination and corrupted fantasy.'

17 The preface, introduction and epilogue

In his preface to the MS Mazhar, al-Jabarti sets out to explain to the reader what finally made him 'gather these notes and put them into proper order'. As the title: 'A clear view of the sanctifying will of God in the Departure of French Rule' (Philipp's translation) indicates, he has seen the hand of God in these events. An interpretation of his line of argument would run like this:

In the old days, Egypt was able to defend its borders – even against the Mongols, who until then had brought down every dynasty they had faced. Like the Mongols, every enemy who tried to lay his hands on the riches of Egypt had been destroyed. The Ottoman government had relied on the local Egyptian rulers to defend the country. But these rulers forgot their responsibilities and allowed the infidel French to occupy the country. The French spread through the country like poison, wiping out its beauties and loosening the foundations of her venerable kingdom.

In this situation Egypt, like Andalusia in former days, seemed about to be lost to Islam. However, the Ottoman sultan stepped in and dispatched his troops under the leadership of the grand vizier Yusuf Zia Pasha. The author sees this as another sign: whenever Egypt is in danger, it is saved by someone by the name of Yusuf: Yusuf the Righteous (i.e. Josef, the son of Jacob), who erected dikes and provided a livelihood for the people during the seven years of drought; Salah al-Din Yusuf, who saved Egypt from the Fatimids and their heresy; Yusuf Pasha, the vizier of the late sultan Selim (I) the Great; and now the vizier Yusuf Zia Pasha, who has put an end to the rule of the infidels and re-established the government of the best men. The author sees his arrival as the fulfilment of God's word: 'Surely the earth is God's and he bequeaths it to whom he will among his servants. "The issue ultimate is to be godfearing" (Koran VII: 125) and for Egypt this "issue ultimate" was the arrival of the vizier and his army.'

To the author, the aim of history is to inform the intelligent reader of events, so that future generations may understand their pattern and remember the lessons to be learnt from it. Basically, history is deterministic: God's will is behind everything. Historical events have followed one upon the other ever since God created the world, in a pattern arranged by God:

They occur in accordance with the Divine Self-Revelation and manifestation of his names and attributes. They become differentiated and fall within the realm of Creation in accord with the properties, which God consigned to the heavenly influences in their conjunction with each other and in accord with the hidden harmony between the latter and events on earth. And this comes about in accord with the course of Divine Custom, whose occasions and causes may be inferred from these circumstances and aspects. (P. 1)

But to be able to see this pattern is no easy matter. Only 'certain pure human souls and spirits, free from bodily attachment and egoistical passions' are able to do that, either by inspiration or by the acquisition of knowledge from the study of astrology. This apparently explains the title: the author intends to provide the story of events in such a way that these people will be able to get a clear view of what has happened in the past, and learn the lessons indicated in past events.

The author obviously feels that he has seen such a pattern. When he sets about writing the preface of the MS Mazhar, the French occupation has actually come to an end. Ottoman rule has been restored! Islam reigns supreme again! The outcome has changed his perspective on the intervening period. While the occupation was still in force, it seemed likely that Egypt would forever be cut off from the world of Islam under the rule of the French, like Andalusia under the Spanish Catholics. And as we have seen in the analysis of the MS Mudda, under those circumstances the perspective, at least among the shaykhs, was how to accommodate the new rulers and find the right balance between independence and collaboration. Central to this perspective was the role of the shaykhs and how they were to use their power to bestow legitimacy on the rulers. This does not imply that the return of the Ottomans has restored the author's faith. In the MS Mudda, too, he saw events as the will of God. But not knowing how they would end, he could not see them as a punishment, a sign of God's wrath to be endured by his community until God's will had been fulfilled. The arrival of the Ottomans has created a new perspective, and this implies a new future. History contains a lesson for the future regulation of affairs.

The opening paragraph in the MS Mudda contains a list of the people in power in Istanbul, in Syria and in Egypt. Common to all these was the fact that they seemed to have no impact on the fate of Egypt. In the MS Mudda the author saw things as a manifestation of a new reality in which the only people of authority left in the country, the leading shaykhs of the 'ulama, groped for a new definition of their position in the power vacuum.

In the MS Mazhar this paragraph has been replaced by a preface (and an introduction) of considerable length. The author has turned historian because events have made him see the past in a different light. But as a contemporary historian he is also fully aware of the fact that the new perspectives imply a new future: the 'reestablishment of the government of the best men'. The implications of this are hinted at in the characterisation of Yusuf Zia Pasha, the grand vizier, and his lieutenants: They, and especially the vizier, are 'a company of men devoting their lives to strengthening and supporting the faith – they were unrelenting in applying and enforcing the shar'ia, and to rescue it, they took the lives of those who opposed it' (p. 8). The author sees the arrival of the Ottomans in Egypt as a chance to restore the *shar' ia* to its proper place as the foundation of society.

This, of course, entails the cooperation of the shaykhs of the 'ulama. The new preface suggests a new political programme: the shaykhs, and not the emirs, should be the new local guardians and administrators of Ottoman power in Egypt. The emirs have proved unworthy of this trust: 'they erected palaces. Instead of manly heroes, they went in for ladies of the boudoir, instead of valiant knights, beautiful boys. In their pride and vanity they competed in the arena of wine-drinking and in the racetrack of licentiousness and pleasure' (p. 3). Seen in this light, the MS Mazhar, like the MS Mudda, seems to be written with a purpose, and the preface suggests that the purpose of the MS Mazhar had to do with impressing on the new Ottoman rulers how well the group of leading shaykhs would fit the role as the local guardians of Ottoman power in Egypt.

As Moreh pointed out, the praise lavished on the grand vizier Yusuf and the fact that the story is taken right up to the month of Shaban/December 1801, i.e. after the re-establishment of Ottoman rule in Egypt, point to the end of the year 1801 as the time when the author set about to 'assemble his notes' and turn them into the MS Mazhar. But it should be kept in mind that over a year before, in the beginning of 1800, the convention of El Arish created a situation very similar to that of 1801. After El Arish the Ottoman forces proceeded to enter Cairo. The grand vizier moved his camp to Bilbays, where he received a deputation from the leading shaykhs of Cairo. If the MS Mazhar was written in order to influence the new Ottoman ruler, this would have been the right moment to present it. When investigating the MS Mazhar further, the possibility of an earlier version, an intermediary version so to speak, from the beginning of 1800 should be kept in mind.

At the end of the preface, the author states that he has included material composed by his friend al-'Attar. The first example has

However, to what al-Jabarti would have termed 'the informed and intelligent reader', this view of history would imply that the ruler listens to and lets himself be guided by people who are acquainted with the *shar'ia*, i.e. the 'ulama and their leading shaykhs, who are the people trained in this field. As the author presents the task of the ruler, he will not be able to perform his duty without the advice and recommendations of this group. So, by defining the task of the ruler as the upholding of the *shar'ia*, the author implies that the ruler is obliged to support and protect this group of experts, without whom he would fall an easy prey to the two enemies of every ruling dynasty: heresy and decay.

In the preface the author praised the vizier Yusuf Pasha for establishing a government of wise men in Egypt. In the introduction he presents the ruling Ottoman dynasty as the only one to have avoided the pitfalls of power. This implies a close cooperation with, and support and protection of, the 'ulama class that is not stated in so many words. But to the author and his readers, this implication is unavoidable, and presents the criterion by which any ruler should be judged. The implications of the preface and introduction for the purpose of the MS Mazhar would be clear to any 'informed and intelligent' reader: The following narrative is intended to show that the 'ulama and its leading shaykhs are worthy of this task. As we have seen in the end-of-year summaries and the necrologies, the MS Mazhar is an account of the disasters brought about by the French occupation. But the use of dialogue in the Diwan of Menou also showed how the 'ulama and the leading shaykhs worked, unselfishly and incessantly, to prevent and contain the worst calamities of this disaster, and as such it implies that under the strong Ottoman rule of Egypt, the 'ulama and their leading shaykhs will be admirably suited to fill this role.

The preface and introduction contain no doubts as to the ability of the Ottomans. The author's assertion that the Ottomans, unlike the preceding dynasties, have avoided decay is only possible to uphold because he leaves out the history of the Ottoman sultans from the reign of Süleyman the Great.[3] And as we shall see in the part of the MS Mazhar covered by the MS Mudda, the author goes to great lengths to avoid any implication of lack of faith in the Ottomans' ability to perform their task in Egypt. He is clearly prepared to select his facts to make them fit his purpose, i.e. to make the returning Ottoman rulers look favourably at the leading shaykhs of the 'ulama as their future advisers and administrators in Egypt.

The epilogue starts on p. 380, but already from the solemn parade of the vizier through the city on 5 Rabi' I 1216 (15 July 1801),[4] the narrative takes on the appearance of a conclusion, in which the author makes a point of showing how all the usual Muslim/Egyptian celebrations (the birthday of the Prophet, the Breaking of the Dam, the procession of the *kiswa*) are carried out in proper fashion by the Ottoman authorities, and how these people work hard to restore order and justice.

As promised, the author provides, in a suitable place, a poem of praise by al-'Attar for the vizier, i.e. in connection with the vizier's parade through the streets of Cairo. In this connection he summarises his hopes for the future: 'Praise and gratitude to God for this favour. We hope that in his bounty He will restore hearts gone astray and will move those in power toward charity and the requisite justice, inspire them to follow the right and straight road, and guide them in the straight path.'[5]

Seen in the overall context of the MS Mazhar this appears to be an important comment, not only suggesting the mood of the author when concluding writing of the MS Mazhar, but also pointing to the purpose of this version. The author's attention in these concluding passages is directed towards the future, towards those whose allegiance to the cause of the Muslims has been in doubt ('hearts gone astray'). He is concerned that the future actions of the new Ottoman masters ('those in power') follow 'the right and straight road of charity and requisite justice', i.e. the *shar'ia*, as mentioned in the preface and introduction. It is significant that these thoughts are expressed as hopes, and not convictions. The author is by no means certain that the new masters will fulfil his expectations. The past actions of the Ottomans (as presented in the introduction) and the first weeks of their rule in Egypt have been promising, but whether they will be able to stick to the 'straight path' is still an open question. They will need inspiration and guidance in this task.

The subsequent incident involving Yusuf Efendi, who arrives with a *firman* from Istanbul appointing him *naqib al-ashraf*, may be seen in this context: The point of the story seems to be that the leaders of the empire, the new masters, are fully capable of following 'the straight path' of justice. They just have to be guided to the truth.[6]

The account of the MS Mazhar is terminated with the month of Shaban 1216/December 1801 (380). To the author, this is a fitting time to conclude his narrative. Its conclusion will add to the blessings of the coming month of Ramadan, and he takes the opportunity to express his hope that the benefits for Egypt brought about by the arrival of the vizier will last and be reinforced, just as the faith of the believers is reinforced by the fast of the month of Ramadan. Just as the faithful celebrate the fulfilment of their expectations at the end of the month of Ramadan, on the Night of Power/Laylat al-Qadr, so the author hopes that the expectations aroused by the arrival of the vizier will be met. In alternating prose and poetry (by al-'Attar) he expresses his hopes that the vizier will stay and be able to continue his efforts to reform and unite the Muslims. The author intends to present him with his work, i.e. the MS Mazhar, in the hope that the vizier will look upon it with approval. If this happens, the book and the lessons which can be learned from it will become widely known, to the benefit of Egypt.

The point of this epilogue seems to be the wish of the author to see the vizier carry on the task of re-establishing the prosperity and security of the Muslim community of Egypt. All the hopes and expectations invested by the believers in the celebration of the month of Ramadan are transferred to the vizier.

As such the epilogue seems to corroborate the interpretation of the purpose of the MS Mazhar that has emerged in this preliminary survey of the MS Mazhar as a whole: this version is a plea in support of the re-establishment of a Muslim government based on the principles and laws of the *shar'ia*, made to the vizier as the deputy of the rightful ruler, the Ottoman sultan and his dynasty, as part of the guidance and inspiration he will need in order to follow 'the straight path' of the *shar'ia*.

---

[1] *237*, p. 280

[2] Moreh ('al-Jabarti's Method', p. 353) is aware of this possibility.

[3] It is significant that when trying to find a parallel to the situation of Egypt, he alludes to Andalusia, which was lost to Islam before the Ottomans reached the pinnacle of their power, and not the losses in the Balkans in the seventeenth century.

[4] *360*, III, 189.

[5] *364*, III, 190.

[6] *374*, III, 203.

18   The MS Mudda and the MS Mazhar

In this chapter we will compare the part of the MS Mazhar covered by the text of the MS Mudda to the MS Mudda. For the sake of convenience we will stick to the sections used in the MS Mudda.

In the MS Mazhar the opening section (section 1, 24-7, pp. 27-31) has retained its compositional function of introducing the principal participants on the Egyptian side, but the presentation has been radically altered. The emirs loom larger in the picture but the narrative has lost some of its animosity. They are still unprepared and still misjudge the French strategy, but the fiery attack on their negligence and vanity has disappeared. The shaykhs still take part in the meeting in Cairo, but they do not utter a word, and the author's comment is much more rational and subdued. Significantly, the British offer of assistance has almost disappeared, while the fact that Egypt belongs to the sultan is stressed, perhaps implying that any help will come from him. The people still play a part, but their anxiety and doubts have been suppressed. The changes suggest the new line of argument: the French invasion is an attack on the Muslim community of Egypt, the sultan's loyal subjects. The military are unprepared, but everybody acts as best he can in the circumstances. Everyone misjudges the French strategy. However, God had already determined this ('that God might determine a matter that was done', 24, p. 28

In the MS Mudda, section 2 contained the French proclamation and the author's comment. In the MS Mazhar (27-35, pp. 31-41), it has been the subject of extensive changes. The section has been turned into a much more cohesive analysis which concentrates on showing that although they pretend to be Muslims, the French are mere materialists and rationalists, without any basic principles at all. While clearly feeling the need to put more order and method into this section, the author seems to have stuck to his original opinion of the French: a people without principles or respect for common decency. By deleting the background information on the French, the author now presents an uncompromisingly anti-French attitude. The fine words of the proclamation are just one of their many ruses to delude the Muslim people: 'all his talk is incorrect and its author be cursed' (35, p. 41)

In the MS Mazhar the character of section 3 (35-45, pp. 41-55) as a separate piece has been stressed. The author has been at pains to highlight the general unity and willingness to fight among the Muslims. He has retained the failure of the emirs to shoulder their responsibilities as military leaders. Nevertheless, the defeat is presented as partly due to bad luck on the part of the Muslims. The praise of the French military ability has disappeared, and Bonaparte seems to be a man with little respect for the leading shaykhs. Any allusion to the conduct of specific shaykhs during the flight from the city is deleted. Their responsibility for the terms of the truce is reduced. In the process, the character of the text as a separate section has been strengthened. But it has obviously lost some of its descriptiveness and has become more restrained in its comments.

In the following sections the changes are few but not insignificant. In section 6 (55-6, pp. 67-9), for example, the entry on the shaykhs and their salaries has been totally deleted. The author of the MS Mazhar wishes to present the story as a confrontation between two groups – the French and the Muslims – and to delete or reduce all evidence to the contrary. In this scheme of things, the shaykhs' demand for salaries obviously implies a far too close cooperation with the new rulers, and has been deleted.

Given this background, it would come as no surprise that section 7 (56-61, pp. 70-4), which in the MS Mudda was used to tell the story of the death of Muhammad Kurayyim, has been thoroughly revised in the MS Mazhar. The story of Muhammad Kurayyim has been reduced to half its original size, making him a victim of the lust for revenge of the French, while Maggalon, 'the greatest criminal of them all' in the MS Mudda, is now 'the accursed'. In line with this, Muhammad Kurayyim is now presented as a respected and well-liked member of the community. All indications to the contrary have disappeared, and anything which might be construed as a resemblance between the conduct of the emirs and that of the French has been deleted. As a consequence, the elaborate moral has disappeared. In the following description of the encounter between Bonaparte and the shaykhs on the question of wearing the sash and the cockade, all names have been deleted. The shaykhs' dislike for these signs of collaboration and submission has been retained, but the note on the people's eagerness in this respect has been changed into the complete opposite: now most of the people are described as abstaining from wearing it. Even more significantly, the incident explaining how 'the good nature' of al-Sadat brought about a compromise has disappeared. The main theme of the MS Mudda was how the leading shaykhs should cooperate with the rulers, whether emirs or French, in order to protect the Muslim community. The line taken in the MS Mazhar is to highlight the greed, oppression and duplicity of the French. Where possible the collaborating shaykhs have been reduced to an anonymous group, trying to alleviate the plight of the Muslims.

In support of the Ottomans: The MS Mazhar al-Tagdis

The most significant change in section 8 (*61-5*, pp. 74-9) is the assertion that Bonaparte came to al-Sadat's house, not just to visit a friend, but with the purpose of investigating the rumour of another letter from Ibrahim Bey to the shaykhs. This turns al-Sadat into just another, not very cooperative, shaykh: the shaykhs, and especially al-Sadat, collaborated with the French only out of necessity.

In section 10 (*70-8*, pp. 87-95) the changes seem to follow the now familiar pattern: the names of the shaykhs have been deleted or, if mentioning them is unavoidable, as in the case of al-Sadat and al-Sharqawi, the description of their actions has been shortened or significantly changed in order to present their cooperation with the French as a case of limited collaboration, forced upon them under the circumstances.

The important section 11 (*78-85*, pp. 96-106), containing the story of the insurrection in October 1798, has seen extensive changes. Some of these can be seen as attempts at shortening and clarifying a long and detailed narrative. Many lively details have disappeared, especially on the behaviour of the rebels. This has made the narrative more factual and dry. But the extensive – and mostly unfavourable – description of the leading shaykhs' activities during the insurrection has been cut down to a minimum. The author does not conceal or condone the fact that the shaykhs supplied the rebels with moral support, but because he focuses on the single known shaykh and deletes his comments on the lack of unity, this fact loses the importance it had in the MS Mudda. By deleting all reference to the intervention of al-Sharqawi and the leading shaykhs, except at the end, and by deleting the addition on the cockade, he divests this section of most of its polemical nature. In the process the insurrection has become proof of the true nature of the French as enemies of the Faith. The mob is still a mob, and its behaviour deplorable. But the picture painted in the MS Mudda of the French, as people who only reluctantly resort to bombs and cannons to secure their power, has disappeared. In the MS Mazhar they stand out as the brutal oppressors of the Muslim community.

There are only small changes in section 12 (*85-92*, pp. 106-14). Some of these changes, the deletion of the signatures of the shaykhs in particular, fit the already established pattern. Others present new departures. Up to now, the author has not ventured to make significant changes in the text of the documents, quoted in full. The reason for doing this here could be that he considered it unwise to remind the readers of the existence of a pro-French party in Istanbul and equally unwise to talk about the Ottoman's new allies, the Russians, in derogatory terms! The reason for the inclusion of the new entry on Caffarelli is equally dubious. The death of this colourful French officer at Acre in the spring 1799 is commented upon by the author further on in his account of the campaign in Syria. A reason may also be found in the fact that a shaykh was martyred while destroying the French instruments, as we shall see below.

Section 13 (92-6, pp. 114-19) has been the subject of many changes. Again, while some of these changes are clearly intended to put some order into a not very coherent narrative, the majority conform to an already established pattern. The author is at pains to clean his narrative of details that could put him in a dubious light (the amusement park), or associate him with people with an unhealthy interest in the materialism of French scientists (the French Institute). The destruction of the instruments in Caffarelli's house and the death of a shaykh in this connection in the preceding section could be seen as such, i.e. as additional corroboration of the narrator's dislike of these matters. The addition on Hasan Kashif is curiously out of line with the general trend of the MS Mazhar, and feels more like the old animosity towards the emirs in the MS Mudda.

The final section, 14 (96-102, pp. 119-27), has seen a few changes. Significantly, the change in the Qur'anic quotation fits the new scheme in the MS Mazhar. As the same quotation at the end of the description of the battle of Imbaba has disappeared, and a new part taking the narrative to its happy end in 1801 has been added, the quotations do not serve their old purpose and have been changed accordingly. Incidentally, the change corroborates the suggestion made above that this feature constituted a conclusion in the MS Mudda.

From these examples of the changes made in different sections of the MS Mudda to make it fit the new version of the chronicle, it is clear that it contains little new material. Most of the changes consist of deletions. But both the deletions and the additions show a clear pattern, in which the main actors in the drama have changed their roles.

The most conspicuous element is the author's attempt to change and/or reduce the role played by the leading shaykhs. They are no longer quoted as attacking the emirs' negligence.[1] On the contrary, they now assemble in al-Azhar to promote the common cause with prayers and recitations.[2] The part played by the leading shaykhs in the negotiations for a truce has been reduced to receiving the dictates of the victorious French.[3] They still figure by name as members of the first Diwan, but their refusal to take part in restoring law and order has been retained,[4] as has the intervention of the shaykhs on behalf of members of the Muslim community, often specified by name.[5] The author does not try to conceal their part in the celebrations of religious festivals and appointments to important positions;[6] but wherever possible he has cut out such items[7] and deleted any allusion to a more intimate collaboration between the leading shaykhs and the French.[8] Bonaparte and his staff no longer visit their houses and dine with them,[9] or if they do, the entry has been elaborated with new information stressing the point that the shaykhs only collaborated under pressure.[10] They do not ask the French for their salaries.[11] They no longer sign letters.[12] But the fact that they had a hand in the new taxes has been retained.[13] The part played by the 'ulama in the instigation of the rebellion has been concentrated on one man, al-Maqdisi.[14] The many abortive attempts on the part of the shaykhs to intercede in the insurrection have disappeared,[15] as has their attempt to reach a compromise with the French on the imprisoned shaykhs.[16]

Not surprisingly, in the process of changing and reducing the role of the leading shaykhs, the arguments against the way they collaborated with the French, so important to the author of the MS Mudda and his mentor, al-Sadat, have virtually disappeared. Al-Sharqawi and al-Sadat still figure by name in the narrative, but reading the MS Mazhar, no one would guess that its predecessor insisted on proving that under the leadership of shaykh al-Sharqawi, the leading shaykhs jeopardised the Muslim community by accepting the formal constitutional framework set up by the French. They would not guess that the preceding version tried to vindicate the more detached position of al-Sadat in this matter. The story of Muhammad Kurayyim has been deleted from among the passages presenting the fundamental ideas of this position,[17] and the point that the compromise on the wearing of the cockade was reached through the good offices of al-Sadat has been deleted.[18] Most significantly, the addition in the second draft of the MS Mudda exposing the hypocrisy of the people in wearing the cokarde and vindicating al-Sadat's wise counsel on this point has been entirely removed.[19] Even now, when the question is not how to collaborate with the French, but proving that the shaykhs only did so hesitatingly and under strong pressure, the author seems to be at pains to vindicate al-Sadat. He makes quite sure that Bonaparte's visit to his house is properly understood and interpreted by the reader by adding new information.[20] His part in celebrating the birthday of Husayn has been purged of all incriminating evidence in this respect,[21] and his celebration of the birthday of Sayyida Zainab has been deleted.[22] It should be noted that the author makes sure that al-Sharqawi is similarly protected.[23]

In line with these changes the author of the MS Mazhar has changed his attitude towards the conduct of the emirs. They are still held responsible for the lack of defensive preparations[24] and they are still accused of failing to grasp the nature of their shortcomings in the face of the French[25] and of accepting defeat too easily.[26] The vicious personal attack on the conduct of Murad and Ibrahim has, however, been deleted.[27] They are shown as preventing the rich and important people from fleeing the city and the people from killing the Christians and Jews.[28] Murad is no longer the direct cause of the panic.[29] Later on, in the incident with the Pilgrimage caravan, Ibrahim's ability in fighting the French cavalry is stressed.[30] Murad's successful attack on the French in the south has been retained and somewhat elaborated,[31] and the author does not refer to '*mamluks*', but simply to 'Muslims'.[32]

The openly expressed disappointment with the Egyptian army has been deleted,[33] and the description of its encounters with the French army has been augmented with much detail, stressing the martial qualities of the rank and file.[34] Instead of bad planning and confusion the author now stresses the unity and general willingness among high and low to cooperate in order to defend the country and the Muslim community,[35] and the defeat is now described as partly caused by the strong westerly wind.[36] The dead emirs are mentioned, but the author no longer makes a point of showing how few the casualties were on the Egyptian side.[37] In a piece of new information the author praises a group of Albanian soldiers, who fought and died on the battlefield.[38] Albanians were prominent in the army that finally forced the French out of Egypt in 1801, but how this group happened to be in Rosetta in 1798 is not explained.

'This is the Sultan's land. Neither the French nor anyone else has access to it.' This proud statement by Muhammad Kurayyim to the English in Alexandria seems to be the key to the new line of argument developed by al-Jabarti in the MS Mazhar.[39] Faced with the French invasion, the Muslim community of Egypt, of which Muhammad Kurayyim himself is now shown as a worthy and respected member, and its religious leaders unite and prepare to do their duty as the loyal subjects of the sovereign. The local military leaders fail to perform their duties, but the rank and file, aided by the few, valiant Albanians from the sultan's army, put up a fight worthy of respect and praise. Actually, the defeat is brought about mainly by bad luck, disguised as the strong westerly wind![40] Possibilities of help from the British and the background on the war in Europe have disappeared from the narrative,[41] implying that the Muslim world is able to take care of itself. It does not need allies to repel the attacks of the infidel French! The allusion to the fact that the sultan had been intimately allied to the French for many years and that the new situation had necessitated a change of government in Istanbul is deleted,[42] as are the derogatory remarks about the sultan's new allies, the Russians![43]

In line with this perspective, the ignominious part played by the religious minorities – the Copts, the Syrian Christians, the Greeks and the local Europeans – has not been changed. They are still presented as exploiting the situation[44] and as taking part in the celebration of the Inundation of the Nile[45] and the celebration of the French Republic, although the description of their provocative dress has been reduced.[46] The behaviour of Yacub the Copt and the Coptic moneylender is still vilified.[47] They figure as the willing tools of the French, and as such they too become 'cursed'.[48]

To the author of the MS Mudda the common people of Cairo were an aimless crowd that needed constant and firm leadership. If this was lacking, they turned into a mob, committing atrocities far worse than the French. In the MS Mazhar this is only slightly changed. When the French advance towards Cairo, the people are provided with the leadership of the shaykhs and behave as valiant defenders of the faith; but later, when no proper leadership is available, they revert to their true ways.

The attitude of the author to the beduin and *fellahin* seems to be unchanged. They are still unreliable, dangerous people, outside civilization. Their behaviour during the chaos after Imbaba and towards the returning pilgrims remains deplorable.[49]

Changes affecting information or comment on the French are small but frequent, the most extensive and prominent being those connected with the French proclamation. The author has retained the character of this section as an initial presentation of the nature of French invaders. The proclamation itself, however, is now dismissed as a ruse to deceive the Egyptians into submission.[50] To corroborate this, the author adds a piece of new information on their use of spies.[51] This theme is repeated further on in the narrative.[52] In the MS Mudda the author seemed to make a sincere effort to get down to the truth behind the bewildering statements in this document. In the MS Mazhar he has no need for such things. The background information on the French, their government, history and political ideas has been deleted. Instead he concentrates on proving that their profession of respect and veneration for Islam is simply a cover, a ruse. To prove his point he adds a new piece of information, a short didactic story, illustrating their lack of sensitivity in these matters.[53] He now concludes that they are not interested in any religion. Each of them follows a religion which he contrives by the improvement of his mind.[54] They are materialist and rationalist, but to the author this only means that they will act without principles, according to their whims.[55]

Part of the argument in the MS Mudda had to do with the proper understanding of the nature of the French attitude. The author clearly wanted to show the grave dangers inherent in formal collaboration with people like the French. They simply could not be trusted not to interfere with the Muslim community. The leading shaykhs ought to have realized this and held aloof from the diwans. In the new line of argument in the MS Mazhar this is no longer an issue. The leading shaykhs are forced to cooperate, but drag their feet as much as possible. Apparently there is no room in a confrontation between the Muslim community and the infidel invaders for discussions on which form of collaboration would be most beneficial to the position of the shaykhs and the Muslim community. As a consequence, there is no need to point out that more or less from the start, the French behaved as enemies of the religion.[56] They are simply 'accursed' and 'infidels',[57] even Caffarelli, who clearly impressed the author with his technical knowledge, energy and ability to command the affection of his subordinates.[58] Comment on the reasons for their military success is now irrelevant and, as such, deleted,[59] while their number is greatly augmented.[60] In this scheme of things it seems only natural that Bonaparte should be presented as a man who does not even pretend to respect the shaykhs.[61] The celebration of the French Republic is still explained by referring to the execution of their sultan, but the creation of a republic is now openly condemned as 'the heresy, which they initiated and with which they deviated from the proper way and other nations'.[62]

The author consciously widens the gap between the two camps: the speech to the soldiers on this occasion, faithfully rendered in the MS Mudda on the basis of the interpreter's words, has disappeared in the MS Mazhar, on the grounds that nobody was able to understand it![63] Documents are no longer sent to the notables[64] or posted in the streets.[65] The procedures of the General Diwan have been shortened.[66] The author still deplores the insurrection. But by leaving out General Dupuy's intention to make amends,[67] the massacres of groups of French soldiers,[68] the failure of the shaykhs to face the mob and the story of the people in the Utuf quarter bringing up guns,[69] he presents the French as a great deal more brutal and uncompromising in suppressing this revolt. In this context it comes as no surprise that the author has deleted a large part of his favourable description of the French Institute.[70]

In the MS Mudda the author openly expressed his animosity towards and disgust with certain aspects of the French behaviour, but the relationship between the Muslim community of Egypt and the invading French was not made clear. Both sides were presented as

In support of the Ottomans: The MS Mazhar al-Tagdis

people prepared to compromise and cooperate in order to find some common ground. Attitudes were apparently supposed to change, and actually did so. As we have seen, the very existence of the MS Mudda was a part of this ongoing debate on the Muslim side.

In the MS Mazhar this debate has clearly come to an end. The French invasion is now seen as an open violation of the sovereign rights of the sultan and the Muslim community, a brutal invasion by deceitful infidels. The Muslim community faces the challenge in unity and faith. The negligence of the local military commanders and sheer bad luck turn the invasion into an occupation. The MS Mazhar is the story of how the Muslim community handled this situation. Left without leaders, the people committed the folly of insurrection, but to the author, the important point now seems to be that the Muslim community never succumbed to the temptations of actively collaborating with the infidels, even on an informal basis, except under strong pressure.

In the preface to the MS Mazhar, the author summarized his work in transforming the MS Mudda by noting[71] that he 'had set down on paper in a somewhat disorganised and random way notes on events since the beginning of the French occupation of Egypt until the arrival of our master the Vizier. I frequently thought about gathering together these notes and putting them into proper order, although I am hardly up to such a task, so that it would be a history informing the intelligent reader about "astonishing reports and marvellous memorials", and a reminder to all generations after.'

In the light of the relations between the MS Mudda and the MS Mazhar, this would seem an understatement: some of these notes had already been gathered together into the text of the MS Mudda, i.e. into a proper order, but one quite different from that used in the MS Mazhar. Transforming the MS Mudda into the MS Mazhar not only entailed the addition of an introduction and additional material taking events right up to the departure of the French in 1801, but a thorough revision of the text of the MS Mudda, in order to make it fit the author's new perspectives.[72]

In the changes made in the MS Mudda to turn it into a part of the MS Mazhar we are able to follow the transition to the new perspective quite closely. The French invasion is now seen as posing a challenge to the sultan's dominion in Egypt. Faced with this challenge the Muslim community unite to face the enemy, but unfortunately the military leaders, the emirs, are not properly prepared and Egypt falls into the hands of the infidels. Under the French occupation, the shaykhs, as the only leaders left, cooperate with the new masters, but only when strictly necessary to protect the people and the Muslim community. The insurrection is a tragic, deplorable event, initiated by people who did not fully realize the weakness of their position.

To the author, the occupation seems to constitute a contest between the Muslims and the infidels. The French intend to lure the Egyptian people away from the Muslim faith by their ruses in order to weaken the Muslim community in general and the power of its rightful ruler, the sultan.

This is not far from the position propounded in the MS Mudda on behalf of the shaykh al-Sadat in the debate among the leading shaykhs of the 'ulama on how to react to the new challenge. In this debate the author and his patron tried to convince its readers that the French were basically hostile to the Muslim community. For this reason, the leaders of this community made a mistake when they entered into formal cooperation with the French. They ought to have stayed aloof from the new rulers, merely keeping the lines of communication open in order to be able to perform their basic duty of interceding and mediating to alleviate the stresses and dislocation caused by the presence of the new masters in order to preserve the faith and its community. The main difference between the position of the author and al-Sadat in the MS Mudda and the new perspective represented by the composition and style of the new chronicle and the changes made in the MS Mudda in order to fit it into the MS Mazhar seems to be that the loyalist stand of al-Jabarti and his patron is now openly stated. Egypt was part of the general Muslim community and the Ottoman Empire – a powerful empire, protected by God and the sultan.

Seen from this new perspective, the behaviour of the shaykhs as presented in the MS Mudda – especially those under the leadership of al-Sharqawi, but also the more informal collaboration of al-Sadat and the very existence of the MS Mudda itself for that matter – would signify a conspicuous lack of faith in the empire and its ability to preserve Egypt as part of the Muslim lands. This behaviour might even be construed as an attempt on the part of some of the shaykhs to fill the power gap left by the emirs. These aspects of the MS Mudda therefore had to be thoroughly deleted – both the formal, realistic stand of al-Sharqawi and the shaykhs on the French diwans and the more informal and, as it proved, loyalist stand of al-Sadat, as well as any allusion to the fact that the shaykhs did not entirely agree on the nature of the French intentions. If these elements could not be entirely deleted, it was stressed that the shaykhs were forced into this. They had had no choice but to cooperate. The text of the MS Mazhar obviously tries to make it very clear that in doing so they acted strictly as religious leaders of the Muslim community, in order to protect the *shar'ia*. The author has obviously found it necessary to dispel any doubt as to the intentions of the shaykhs in this respect and to stress the fact that the shaykhs act as a united and a cohesive group. Any allusion to the heated debate among the shaykhs in 1798–9 is carefully avoided. The position propounded in the MS Mazhar seems to be that the shaykhs may disagree among themselves, but never to such a degree that they appear divided in the eyes of the ruler. In the MS Mazhar, dedicated to the Ottoman vizier, the author and his patron select their facts accordingly. It is interesting to note that both the emirs and the people seem to have benefited from this attempt to present the shaykhs as a united group. The emirs were the targets of the author's vicious attacks in the MS Mudda. They are still the main culprits, but the attacks on their behaviour in this part of the MS Mazhar seem more subdued. It seems that, being Muslims (and the traditional local rulers) who carry on the fight against the infidels, they are viewed with more respect. Even the people of Cairo are presented as capable of behaving as faithful Muslims in certain circumstances.

As for the way the French are presented, few changes were needed. Having deleted any allusion to the fact that the shaykhs did not entirely agree on the nature of the French challenge, the only task left was to make this perfectly clear by restructuring the analysis of the proclamation, adding small epithets to the names of the French leaders and their local accomplices and deleting any hint of interest in the military and scientific innovations of the infidels. As we noted, the second draft of the MS Mudda already seemed to have made a stand in the question of military reform by ridiculing the training of the Maghribi soldiers in the service of the French. Now this position could be made perfectly clear by deleting the favourable comment on the French military organization. For the same reason the description of the French Institute could be shortened to a mere note on its existence.

[1] 26, p. 30.
[2] 36, p. 42.
[3] 45, p. 54.
[4] 46, p. 55.
[5] 54, 58, pp. 65, 71.
[6] 55, 75, pp. 66, 92.
[7] 78, 86, pp. 95, 106.
[8] 55, 60, 62, 71, 74, 75, 96, pp. 66, 72, 75, 87, 91, 92, 119.
[9] 55, 96, pp. 66, 119.
[10] 63, p. 76.

This, surely, is different from trying to 'relieve his own conscience'. By presenting the facts in the way he does in the MS Mazhar, the author argues that the cooperation of the shaykhs was the outcome not of a conscious political choice of individual shaykhs, but French pressure, and he protects the group of leading shaykhs as a whole. Later, under Menou, when the French grew more amenable and understanding, the shaykhs succeeded in monopolizing the role of financial advisers to the rulers with respect to the Muslims, and turned their position into something which, under the circumstances, could be seen as an advantage for the Muslim community.

Shaykh Ibrahim, the former owner of the MS Maz.Cam, has been identified as the European J.L. Burckhardt, who cannot be expected to have been able to appreciate the circumstances of the 'ulama of Ottoman Egypt in 1801. Furthermore, he wrote his comment fifteen years after the events, at a time when other things had superseded the issues of the French occupation. To him (or his sources) the French were now remembered mainly for their scientific endeavours and the danger of retribution, not for the challenge and possibilities they presented to the leading shaykhs of Egypt. For these reasons his statement on the purpose of the MS Mazhar cannot be regarded as a reliable source.[5]

Rather, the MS Mazhar should be seen as part of the complicated political situation in Egypt in the autumn of 1801. The French had capitulated in Cairo in July, and the last French forces had left Egypt at the end of August. The Ottoman vizier and his army had been masters in Cairo for several months when the MS Mazhar was finished in December 1801 and presumably handed over to the vizier. Actually, in the autumn of 1801 the Ottoman vizier found himself in a difficult position. He and his government were firmly resolved to use the French withdrawal to eliminate the power of the emirs and re-establish the power of the central government in Egypt. However, the British who commanded the only effective army in Egypt did not trust the Ottoman government to defend Egypt effectively against a future French attempt at conquest, and for this reason supported a return of the emirs. In October the vizier and his deputy mounted a concerted campaign in Cairo and Alexandria to round up and imprison the emirs. They were prevented from carrying this action to its logical conclusion by the vehement protests of the British commander-in-chief, General Hutchinson. The general insisted that the emirs be set at liberty, and the Ottomans had to comply. In November 1801 the position of the Ottoman vizier was seriously weakened.[6] At this point al-Jabarti finished his chronicle with its lavish praise of the Ottomans and the vizier, as the legitimate rulers of Egypt and promoting the shaykhs of the 'ulama as the loyal supporters of the Ottoman government. Against this background the MS Mazhar takes on the aspect of a conscious decision on the part of al-Jabarti and his patron al-Sadat openly to confirm their loyalist leanings, not from a position of weakness, but from one of strength.

However, the unity among the 'ulama suggested by the MS Mazhar did not reflect reality. The split in their ranks still existed. When the vizier arrived on the outskirts of Cairo in July the French allowed the shaykhs to visit him and pay him their respects. But they did not go together. The shaykhs were delayed by the last meeting in the Diwan. When they finally arrived in the Ottoman camp they found that al-Sadat had got there before them! Later, in connection with the showdown between the vizier and the emirs, the vizier had the shaykhs meet in the house of al-Sadat to compose a letter admonishing the emirs to remember their promises. Apparently the vizier was making use of al-Sadat as his major supporter among the shaykhs. The pledge made in the MS Mazhar seems to have been honoured.[7]

But, as we have seen, al-Sharqawi, too, had composed a text dedicated to the Ottoman grand vizier Yusuf Pasha, a sort of catalogue of the kings and governors of Egypt, at the end of which he added two pages on the French invasion. In the introduction al-Sharqawi relates that in Ramadan 1214/27 January to 25 February 1800, after the first peace agreement with the French (i.e. the convention of El Arish), he and some other 'ulama went to meet the Ottoman vizier Yusuf Pasha in the city of Bilbays. He was here advised by one of the companions of the vizier to write a history of the French occupation and present it as a gift.[8] But the truce following the convention of El Arish broke down, and al-Sharqawi had to wait more than a year before a similar situation occurred, in June 1801, to present his gift to the vizier Yusuf Pasha. In this way his text becomes a parallel to the MS Mazhar.[9]

Both groups of leading 'ulama in Cairo wanted to present their case to the Ottomans. It should be noted, however, that al-Sharqawi's text only supports the suggestion that the split in the ranks of the 'ulama between the group of al-Sharqawi and al-Sadat still seemed to exist in 1800, at the time of the convention of El Arish. The fact that a finely decorated copy of the MS Mazhar is found in the sultan's library in Istanbul, while al–Sharqawi's account is found in the Bibliothèque Nationale implies that it was never handed over to the vizier, a suggestion which seems to be corroborated by the unfinished character of al-Sharqawi's text. This fact would suggest that the split had been resolved in the difficult period from January 1800 to June 1801. The appointment of al-Jabarti, a client of al-Sadat, to the Diwan of Menou in late 1800 would point in this direction. All the same, the unity among the 'ulama professed in the MS Mazhar did not prevent al-Sadat from going to meet the vizier separately and in this way position himself as the uncontested leader of the Egyptian 'ulama.

1 As already noted, the fact that al-'Attar is said to have left Cairo at the end of 1214, only to return eighteen months later, when the Ottomans had returned, i.e. in May 1801, and that the circumstances after the convention of El Arish in January 1800 presented a situation more or less identical with that in 1216 (although only for a time), suggests that the MS Mazhar should be investigated further in order to see whether there is any indication of part of the MS being written in connection with this earlier date. On *188*, p. 225 al-Jabarti quotes the agreement of El Arish in full, followed by a description of how the representatives of the Ottomans arrive in Cairo. On *200*, p. 239 the visit of the 'ulama and other Cairene dignitaries in the camp of the vizier is recorded. They are well received and return to Cairo with robes of honour. Somewhere around this point a first version of the MS Mazhar would have come to an end, at the latest. The following text starts with an incident with a firm date and then jumps to a new incident with a very loose date (in the middle of the month), followed by two items with firm dates, the latter relating the beginning of the battle of Heliopolis and the end of the truce. The item with the loose date is a not-very-precise summary of the news of the English refusal to accept the terms of the convention of El Arish. These passages show a resemblance to the composition (or lack of composition) which marked the point where the continuation in the MS Mazhar takes over from the revised MS Mudda (*103*, p. 128). However, without firmer evidence, perhaps from the autograph, MS Maz. Cam, this point will remain an open question. See also Moreh, 'al-Jabarti's Method', p. 353.
2 Moreh, 'Introduction', p. 8.
3 Ibid.
4 Ibid., p. 18.
5 Gran, *Islamic Roots of Capitalism*, p. 80, sees the MS Mazhar as a result of al-Jabarti's good connections in Istanbul: 'Yusuf Agha (presumably Yusuf Zia Pasha, the grand vizier) turned to him to write a history of the recent troubled times. Al-Jabarti wrote the book which Yusuf Agha requested and included in it material by al-'Attar perhaps as a way of rehabilitating a friend.' In support of this interpretation Gran refers to the note in the preface on al-'Attar, and to the very end of the epilogue (*382*). Phillip, 'The French and the French Revolution in the Works of al-Jabarti', in Crecelius (ed.), *Eighteenth-century Egypt*, p. 132, supports the suggestion that the MS Mazhar is a political report 'requested by the (Ottoman) government'. Although

In support of the Ottomans: The MS Mazhar al-Tagdis

the texts of the preface, introduction and epilogue are very flowery and difficult to handle, I have not found any evidence that could substantiate this interpretation.

6 Sorby, 'The Struggle', pp. 174ff.

7 MS Aja'ib, III, 202, 203.

8 Moreh, 'al-Jabarti's Method', p. 353.

9 As the example of the MSS Mudda and Mazhar shows, it is perfectly possible that the two pages were written in the autumn of 1798 and reused in 1801. In that case, al-Sharqawi, like al-Jabarti, added a dedication and an introduction.

21 Conclusion

Compositionally, the author of the MS Mazhar sticks to the general pattern developed in the MS Mudda. But at certain points he deviates from this pattern in significant ways and, in the process, develops new features. The end of the year is used as a summary of events, the ever-widening calamities providing a fittingly dramatic impression of the mounting disasters created by the French occupation, culminating in the plague in 1215. The deaths of Murad Bey and other emirs in this connection afford the author the opportunity to state his opinion on these former rulers of Egypt. With a few exceptions the emirs, especially Murad Bey, lacked the personal qualities needed to rule. This critique is accomplished by summarizing the actions and personal characteristics of the emirs in the necrologies, incidentally including some of the material deleted from the MS Mudda and in this way reasserting the author's profound dislike of these people in the MS Mudda. It is suggested that the opportunity afforded by the death of many emirs in the plague in 1215 gave the author the idea of using this feature, with which he was well acquainted through his work on the lives of famous 'ulama for al-Zabidi.

The use of direct speech and dialogue is more restricted, except when it comes to the deliberations of the last diwan established by Menou. It is possible to account for the rich detail in this connection by the fact that al-Jabarti himself was a member of this diwan. But the evidence afforded by the use of dialogue in the MS Mudda suggests something more – a political, ideological message on the part of the author: at long last the French rulers had come to understand that the proper way to rule a Muslim country like Egypt would be to establish a diwan consisting entirely of shaykhs and to follow the advice presented by this group.

The preface, the introduction, the concluding parts of the text and the epilogue provide a key to the understanding of these features. In the preface the author praised the vizier Yusuf Pasha for establishing a government of the best men in Egypt. In the introduction he presented the ruling Ottoman dynasty as the only one to have avoided the pitfalls of power.

The MS Mudda was used as a basis for the new version. Its transformation into a part of the MS Mazhar entailed a thorough revision of the text in order to make it fit the author's new interpretation of events and the perspectives they present for the future.

The French invasion is now seen as a challenge to the sultan's dominion in Egypt. Faced with this challenge the Muslim community unites to face the enemy, but unfortunately the military leaders, the emirs, are not properly prepared and Egypt falls into the hands of the infidels. Under the French occupation, the shaykhs, as the only leaders left, are forced by the terms of the armistice to cooperate with the new masters. But they are shown to do so only when it is strictly necessary to protect the people and the Muslim community. The insurrection is presented as a tragic, deplorable event, initiated by people who did not fully realize the weakness of their position.

The MS Mazhar is an account of the disasters brought about by the French occupation, which the author presents as a contest between the Muslims and the infidels. It tells the story of how the infidels tried to part Egypt and its Muslim community from its rightful ruler and the *shari'a* by all sorts of ruses, deceptions and coercions. The text is intended to show that the 'ulama and their leading shaykhs are the worthy advisers of any Muslim ruler who wants to make the *shari'a* the foundation of his rule, and how they worked, unselfishly, incessantly and united, to prevent and contain the worst calamities until at last the French, under General Menou, realized the truth of this message. Seen in this way, the MS Mazhar contains a political programme for the future of Egypt, consisting of strong Ottoman rule, guided by the 'ulama and its leading shaykhs.

So, faced with the task of presenting events in Egypt during the French occupation to the returning Ottoman masters, the author decided to suppress or diminish not only the fact that leading shaykhs took an active part in the French administration, but also the disagreement between them on this matter. This wish to stress the importance of the unity of the Muslim community was one of the main arguments of the MS Mudda. In the MS Mazhar the author has decided to present events as if this unity were a matter of course, right from the start.

As for the way the French were presented, few changes were needed to fit this new perspective. Since al-Jabarti had deleted any allusion to the fact that the shaykhs did not entirely agree on the nature of the French challenge, the only task left was to make this perfectly clear by restructuring the analysis of the proclamation, adding small epithets to the names of the French leaders and their local accomplices and deleting any hint of interest in the military and scientific innovations of the infidels.

The emirs were subjected to vicious attacks in the MS Mudda. In the MS Mazhar they are still the main culprits, but the criticism of their behaviour seems more subdued. It seems that being Muslims who carry on the fight against the infidels, they are viewed with more consideration.

The author's assertion in the preface and introduction that only the Ottoman dynasty has avoided decay is only feasible because he leaves out the history of the Ottoman sultans from the reign of Süleyman the Great.[1] And as we have seen in the part of the MS Mazhar covered by the MS Mudda, he goes to great lengths to avoid any implication of lack of faith in the Ottomans' ability to perform their task in Egypt. Derogatory remarks in letters and speeches by the French are either deleted or corrected by additional comments. The author is clearly prepared to select his facts, or at least rearrange them, to make them fit his purpose of getting his message on behalf of the shaykhs of the 'ulama across to the Ottoman rulers.

The author's attention in the concluding passages and the epilogue is directed towards the future, towards the actions of the new Ottoman masters in the hope that they will follow 'the right and straight road of charity and requisite justice', i.e. the *shari'a*, as mentioned in the preface and introduction. It is significant that these thoughts are expressed as hopes, and not convictions. The author is by no means certain that the new masters will fulfil his expectations. The past actions of the Ottomans (as presented in the introduction) and the first weeks of their rule in Egypt have been promising, but whether they will be able to stick to the 'straight path' is still an open question. They will need inspiration and guidance in this task.

In the MS Mudda the general purpose of the text was developed in close cooperation with the venerable shaykh al-Sadat. The purpose of the MS Mazhar is different, but the shaykh al-Sadat still stands out as a prominent figure in the story and is presented as a person who conforms to the new perspectives: a staunchly pro-Ottoman shaykh, severely victimized for his convictions. But the position of spiritual mentor to the author seems to have been shared with his friend, the poet and linguist al-'Attar, whose poems and comments, propounding a strongly anti-French and pro-Ottoman stand, have been afforded a prominent place in the narrative. Whether this signifies a loosening of the ties between the author and al-Sadat, or just comes from the fact that the author is writing for a different and more discriminating readership, cannot be determined. As already indicated in connection with the MS Mudda, the necrology of al-Sadat in volume IV of the MS Aja'ib shows a different, and rather unfavourable, opinion of the shaykh al-Sadat. Some time between January 1799 and 1813 a breach between this shaykh and the author seems to have taken place. But in December 1801 al-Sadat is still seen as one of the eminent leaders of the Muslim community of Egypt, although he no longer seems to be the only person influencing his work on the chronicle.

Conclusion

The purpose of the MS Mazhar appears to be a plea for the reestablishment of a Muslim government, based on the principles and laws of the *shari'a* and performed by the representative of the Ottoman dynasty in close cooperation with the shaykhs of the 'ulama. The text of the MS Mazhar should be seen as part of the guidance and inspiration the Ottomans are going to need from this group, if they are to follow the 'straight road' of the *shari'a*. The MS Mazhar becomes a memorandum to the Ottomans, strongly supporting their wish to establish direct rule in Egypt. But it is important to note that in the situation in December 1801 this pledge of support was made from a position of strength on the part of the shaykhs. The vizier acknowledged it and used the good offices of the loyalist al-Sadat to promote his policies of curbing the power of the emirs in the autumn of 1801.

It seems clear, however, that the unity among the 'ulama presented in the MS Mazhar could not have been deeply rooted. The way al-Sharqawi is presented in the MS Mazhar shows that the author and his patron still have serious doubts about al-Sharqawi's ideas of the true political position of the 'ulama. However, events seem to have narrowed the gab between the two groups. Al-Sharqawi has had to acknowledge that cooperation with the French is at best a dangerous game, while al-Sadat has had to admit that his loyalist stand has made him an enemy of the French and threatens to deprive him of any influence on the future of the Muslim community of Egypt. The fact that they both decide to cooperate with the French under General Menou, al-Sharqawi directly as a member of the Diwan, al-Sadat through the membership of his client al-Jabarti, suggests that some sort of compromise has been reached. Still, when they go to pay their respects to the Ottoman vizier after the French capitulation in Cairo in June 1801, they do so separately! The fact that only the MS Mazhar is found in Istanbul, while the text composed by al-Sharqawi ended up in Paris points to al-Sadat, as befitted a staunchly pro-Ottoman shaykh, as the leader of the Egyptian 'ulama in 1801.

1 Al-Jabarti has shown that he is well aware of the idea of decline. The fact that he leaves out the history of the Ottomans after the reign of Süleyman the Great is best explained by such tactfulness.

IV

IN SUPPORT OF
MUHAMMAD 'ALI, 1805

22 Composition of the MS Aja'ib

Al-Jabarti's third version of his work, *Aja'ib al-athar fi tarajim wa'l-akh-bar*, is even more voluminous than the MS Mazhar. The printed version, the so-called Bulaq edition, contains four volumes. The most recent translation, edited by Thomas Philipp and Moshe Perlman, runs into 2,164 closely printed pages.[1] The author's autograph, MS Aj.Cam, consists of three volumes: the first, 295 folios; the second, 179; and the third, 300. Each page contains 27 lines. The manuscript contains numerous passages in the margins. These additions are in the same hand as the text and seem to have been introduced during a general revision of the text.[2]

From the last entries in the third volume of the printed version, it appears that this volume was finished some time in the year 1221/1806 and that a fourth volume would follow.[3] However, a marginal note in the MS Aj.Cam informs us that the MS was already in the possession of another person in 1806–7.[4] This would indicate that the general revision of the autograph took place some time around 1806, probably in connection with the release of the 1805 edition, which is represented by the three-volume editions.[5]

The MS Aj.Cam , that is his personal autograph , contains the first three volumes only. Moreh states that the other copies of MS Aja'ib included in his investigation contain the first three volumes.[6] On the other hand, he notes that the printed Bulaq edition of the MS Aja'ib, which covers all four volumes, is based on a revised version of the MS Aj.Cam 'with a few passages added'.[7] This would indicate that the fourth volume was added to the 1805 edition with only a few changes in the first three volumes. The last passages in the fourth volume cover the end of the year 1236/1821. A note in the Bulaq edition states that al-Jabarti did not write any more.[8] This information would indicate that al-Jabarti released the third version of his work in a three-volume edition, covering the time up to the year 1220/1805–6. After this he went on writing a fourth volume, and in the process added a few passages to the first three volumes already released in 1805–6, but had to stop in 1821, leaving it unfinished.[9] However, Moreh notes that many passages in the Bulaq edition are missing in the MSS Aj.Cam, BN, BM.[10] In addition, he has been unable to identify the MS on which the Bulaq edition was based. This would indicate a rather large revision of the first three volumes in connection with the writing of the fourth.[11] If this is how the printed Bulaq edition of the MS Aja'ib came into existence, the four-volume version of the MS Aja'ib, i.e. the Bulaq edition (and its father, and a very favourable comment on the last governor Mustafa Pasha's term of office (1754–8), 16 necrologies follow, shaykhs first, emirs and others – the sultan Mahmud I among them – second. A second group of 16 necrologies of 'notables other than Husayn Bey' is added. Many long poems are included. The necrologies in part III amount to 60 out of 63 printed pages!

Part IV covers the period from 1171 to 1181 (1757–68), and is mainly concerned with the rise of 'Ali Bey al-Kabir and ends with the prediction of his victory in 1768 over opposing forces. Where possible, the entries are dated. At the end necrologies of 37 shaykhs, emirs and other notables follow. The longest is devoted to Shaykh Salim al-Hifnawi, imam of the Khalwati order, to which the author belongs. Necrologies take up four-fifths of the text.

Part V takes the story year by year from 1182/1768–9 to 1189/1775–6. Each year is followed by a group of necrologies, shaykhs first, emirs and others second. Seven-eighths of the text are taken up by 80 necrologies (96 out of 112 pages), among them the author's father and the emirs 'Ali Bey al-Kabir and Muhammad al-Dhahab. The part (and the volume) ends with the death and necrology of Muhammad Abu al-Dhahab (I, 417–18). Al-Jabarti has a high opinion of this emir, apparently because he treated the 'ulama according to his precept ('given to good deeds, he loved the 'ulama and was by nature inclined to them – the best of the emirs of Egypt I know').

Taken together the 358 necrologies of volume I amount to three-fourths of the text (313 out of 420 pages).

After a short introduction, similar to the one in volume I (a list of people in power but here mentioned from the sultan down, noting that the retainers of Muhammad Abu al-Dhahab, especially Ibrahim and Murad Bey, wielded absolute power), volume II takes the account from 1190/1776 to 1212/1798. The material is arranged year by year, with a short text, usually only a couple of pages, followed by necrologies, until 1200/1786. In this and the following three years the text swells, and in 1201–3 the account is divided by month. This is caused by the arrival of the Ottoman grand admiral Hasan Pasha and his attempt to enforce Ottoman rule in Egypt in 1786–9. To all intents and purposes the author's account of events in volume II stops with the year 1209/1794–5, as the last three years contain only necrologies of various 'ulama. This implies that the volume ends with an agreement between the 'tyrannical and unjust' emirs, Murad and Ibrahim Bey and their followers, and the leading shaykhs, who locked themselves up in al-Azhar in protest against oppression by the emirs. The agreement vindicates the supremacy of the shaykhs, as Murad and Ibrahim

In support of Muhammad 'Ali 1805

have to promise to revoke new unjust impositions, to send grain to the Holy Cities and various other matters. The reconciliation implies that the shaykhs have forced the emirs to comply.

Taken together, the 199 necrologies of volume II amount to nearly two-thirds of the text (166 out of 273 pages): shaykhs, emirs and others, in this order.

Volume III cover the period from 1798 to the end of 1220/1805. The volume is introduced with a short summary of the history of these years: things seemed to have happened faster and to have brought more important, disastrous and destructive changes than ever before. But to the author this was only what Egypt deserved: if the people of Egypt had acted rightly, God would not have let it happen ('yet thy Lord would never destroy the cities unjustly, while as yet their people were putting things right' (Qur'an 11:117)). To the author, the calamities of 1798–1805 seem to have been self-inflicted.

The text is arranged by years, each divided by months, followed by necrologies (except for 1217/1802–3). The 54 necrologies amount to one-tenth of the text (38 out of 357 pages).

The last entries of the regular text of volume III, in the month of Safar 1220 (May 1805), describe how the shaykhs depose the Ottoman governor Ahmad Pasha and appoint Muhammad 'Ali as the new governor of Egypt. This is confirmed by the government in Istanbul in July 1805 (III, 336). Before the author turns to his usual yearly conclusions (this time a lamentation on the depreciation of the currency) and necrologies, he describes the magnificent parade of the new governor through the streets of Cairo. The last notes make it clear that the text of the first three volumes was written in 1806 and that the author plans to continue his account with a fourth volume, starting with events in 1221. He is apparently writing in a hopeful mood, seeing signs of a new future with better conditions, fewer anxieties and better cooperation among the people of Egypt.

From this brief outline it appears that the annalistic framework developed in the MS Mudda and MS Mazhar – dated entries in chronological order, divided by months and years and with a summary of miscellaneous events at the end of the year, followed by a section of necrologies – is retained whenever the author's material enables him to use it. In the first volume his material rarely allows it, in the second he attains this level only in 1200–3, while in the third he has enough information to carry on the story at the same level of detail from the point where the MS Mazhar stops until the end. In fact, the first and second volumes seem to be more a collection of necrologies than a continuous history.

It seems as if his periodization of the years from 1688 to 1805 and his division of the chronicle into parts and volumes have been arranged to highlight events in the relationship between the shaykhs and the rulers where the rulers should abide by the advice of the 'ulama and their leading shaykhs. It also seems that by rulers the author means the actual rulers of Ottoman Egypt. Although the reigns of two sultans and the terms of office of some Ottoman governors are used as part of the chronological framework, the major divisions are made with the actual rulers of Egypt in mind. The first volume ends with the death of Muhammad Abu al-Dhahab, who listened to and respected the 'ulama; the second when the shaykhs force the two emirs Murad and Ibrahim to abide by the existing agreements; and the third when the shaykhs take it into their hands to depose a useless governor and appoint a new one, who seems to have the right attitude to secure peace and justice by listening to the shaykhs. The author's final, optimistic note on the future seems to indicate a trust in this new governor, i.e. Muhammad 'Ali's ability to listen to the advice of the right people.

The fact that this note has not been deleted when preparing the text for the integration of the fourth volume, with its heated attacks on Muhammad 'Ali's rule, indicates that this feature and, by implication, the general theory of government in the introduction (which will be discussed below) belong to the three-volume edition of 1805. Seen in this light, and still keeping the possibility open that this may be the result of later changes, the third version of al-Jabarti's work, the MS Aja'ib of 1805/6, seems to represent a new stage in his political thinking, a new political programme in which the shaykhs should act as the ultimate arbiters of the Muslim community and its secular rulers, and the material has been arranged or changed to fit this programme.

This would explain that although the subjects of the necrologies include people other than shaykhs and emirs, these two groups constitute the bulk of the material, and that the shaykhs are invariably mentioned first, emirs second.

The opening paragraphs of the first two volumes, listing the people in power, clearly have the function of summing up, for the benefit of the reader, the rulers whose actions will be the subject of the following story. This is borne out by the opening of the first volume (I, 24), which lists the members of the two factions, the Faqariyya and the Qasimiyya, in accordance with the explanation in the preceding introduction, while the opening of the second volume starts with the sultan and proceeds to list the governors and the emirs.[13] As we saw, this feature was deleted in the MS Mazhar to make room for the preface and introduction. It now turns up as the opening paragraphs of the first two volumes, rather than the third, where it originally belonged. Instead, in this volume the author stresses the extraordinary nature of events to be related. This suggests that he sees the developments from 1798 to 1805 as having taken place inside the political framework suggested by the opening of the second volume, but in such a way that it more or less destroyed, or at least thoroughly changed, this framework.

When turning the MS Mazhar into part of his new work, the MS Aja'ib, the author does not seem to have touched the basic structure and compositional features taken over from the preceding manuscript, the MS Mazhar. Only at three points does he seem to have decided that more radical measures were needed.[14]

In the first place, he decided to delete his comments on the French proclamation. This radically altered the composition of this part of the text, in the process lending the proclamation a thoroughly new meaning. Right from the start, this section in the MS Mudda was aimed at introducing the French invaders to the reader. The comments on the proclamation were meant to show that the French were not what they pretended to be. Now, the deletion of the commentary on the proclamation leaves the reader of the MS Aja'ib with no alternative but to accept the proclamation, and the French intentions contained in it, at face value. It is hard not to believe that this was what the author intended. The change would be in line with the features already noted in connection with the division into volumes and parts. The author wants the reader to see the French as rulers who, because of their intention to act as virtual Muslims, would be acceptable to the Muslim community.

Second, the deletion of the story of Muhammad Kurayyim and its removal, together with that of Salih Bey, to a new section of necrologies seems to serve two purposes: first, to remove to a less conspicuous place an item which in the MS Mazhar was used as an example of French tyranny and revenge; second, to serve as balancing role in this new section. Although the author had the text of the MS Mudda and its quite different account of Muhammad Kurayyim in front of him, he did not find it necessary to change the presentation of this individual at all. The reason could be that he needed a person of this character in the composition of the necrologies, in order to make his point in this part of his narrative.

Third, the inclusion of the Arabic translation of the French documents on the assassination of General Kléber, which covers thirty printed pages (III, 117–34), is perhaps one of the most conspicuous changes made in the MS Mazhar when it was reused for the MS

Aja'ib. As we have seen, al-Jabarti usually did not hesitate to quote French documents. But in the MS Mazhar he merely mentioned that the French had distributed leaflets on the case of the murder of General Kléber in three languages, in which they discussed the events and its particulars. He states that he was going to ignore the text in the MS Aja'ib, because of its length and poor style, but changed his mind, because he had 'observed that many people were eager to peruse the leaflets because they contained an account of the event and of the trial; which was indicative of the legal investigation and court procedure of the French who hold reason supreme, and do not profess any religion' (III, 116–17).

In the following comment al-Jabarti elaborates on this statement. Apparently he himself was one of those perusing the leaflets, in order to find an explanation for the (to him astonishing) fact that, although they caught the murderer red-handed, the French took the trouble to go through the regular legal procedures in accordance with the laws of the French Republic. In the end the murderer and his accomplices were sentenced and executed, but the legal procedures meant that the calligrapher Mustafa Efendi al-Bursali, who had been arrested as a suspected accomplice, was released. This, al-Jabarti notes, 'is quite different from what we saw later of the deeds of the riff-raff of soldiers claiming to be Muslims and fighters of the Holy War who killed people and destroyed human lives merely to satisfy their animal passions, as will be reported below' (III, 117).

This suggests that the decision to include this document in the narrative constitutes more than a mere service to readers interested in the strange and unpredictable results of the French adherence to reason and their refusal to follow any religion. The 'riff-raff of soldiers' no doubt refers to the Ottoman army, who entered Cairo after the French had left in the summer 1801. Even though they professed to be Muslims and fighters of the Holy War, these soldiers proved unable to restrain their animal passions. This alludes to the words of the introduction (I, 7) on the need for a strong ruler, dispensing justice according to the *shari'a*. So the text on the trial of the murderer of General Kléber is included to point out that in spite of (or perhaps even thanks to?) their adherence to reason, the infidel French have been able to act with the wisdom and balance of judgement required of the rulers of human society, according to his general theory of government.[15]

---

[1] 'Abd al-Rahman al-Jabarti, *Aja'ib al-athar fi' l-tarajim wa' l-akhbar*, 4 vols., Bulaq Press edition, Cairo 1879–80; *'Abd al-Raman al-Jabarti's History of Egypt*, 3

In support of Muhammad 'Ali 1805

vols., ed. and trans. Thomas Philipp and Moshe Perlman, Stuttgart 1994.

2 Moreh, 'Introduction', pp. 4–5.

3 MS Aja'ib, III, 357.

4 Moreh, 'Introduction', p. 5, n. 21. Moreh ('al-Jabarti's Method') does not comment on this important note, which precludes the possibility that the MS Aj. Cam was used as the autograph for vol. IV. In his introduction to the forthcoming critical edition of the MS Aja'ib, which professor S. Moreh has kindly made awaiably to me, he states that vol. IV of the Bulaq edition was copied from another manuscript, MS Aj.Ber.9490, in the Staatsbibliotek zu Berlin.

5 MSS Aj.BN and BM.The existence of a manuscript in Dar al-Kutub, Cairo, containing only vol. III, indicates that vols. I–III came about in two stages: vol. III (a revision of the MS Mazhar) before 1805; and a three-volume edition, including additions in vol. III, in 1805–6. The character of the manuscript in Dar al-Kutub suggests that it was copied by a scribe, perhaps for circulation: see Moreh, 'al-Jabarti's Method', pp. 350, 354.

6 MSS Aj.BN and BM. See Moreh, 'Introduction', pp. 5, 6.

7 Moreh, 'Introduction', p. 18. and note 4 above.

8 MS Aja'ib, IV, 319.

9 Moreh, 'Introduction', p. 18.

10 Ibid., p. 14.

11 Morch ('al-Jabarti's Method') seems to have been able to identify the manuscripts in the collection of Dar al-Kutub, as those used by the Bulaq Press for the Arabic edition. Moreh notes that these manuscripts (and by implication the Bulaq edition and its translation) are inaccurate in certain places. But unfortunately he still has not explored the circumstances of the integration of the fourth volume.

12 A good place to start would be the comment in III, 284, blaming Muhammad 'Ali for most of the disastrous developments in Egypt, after the French evacuation in 1801. This comment, judging from the context and the favourable comments on Muhammad 'Ali in other parts of the text, has all the appearance of a later addition.

13 The resemblance between these opening paragraphs and the opening paragraph of the MS Mudda is evident, and as such they corroborate the evaluation of this feature in the analysis of the MS Mudda.

14 A fourth could be said to be the inclusion of a letter from al-Sadat to the representative of the Ottoman government, 'Uthman, the Khatkhuda, in which al-Sadat condemns the conduct of the Ottomans during the siege of Cairo in 1800 in the strongest possible terms: III, 103.

15 Moreh sees this as one of the few oblique references in the MS Aja'ib to the existence of the MS Mazhar. See Moreh, 'Introduction', p. 2, n. 7.

23 The preface and introduction

When al-Jabarti set about writing a preface and an introduction to his new version some time between 1801 and 1805 he had the MS Mazhar in front of him. The passages 'he who reads them will learn a lesson – only men possessed of minds remember' (I, 2) and 'I hope that whoever reads it – whatever mistakes he may find in it' (I, 3) are taken directly from the preface of the MS Mazhar, while many passages from the historical survey of the introduction in this MS turn up in the corresponding sections in the introduction of the MS Aja'ib. This suggests that the preface and introduction of the MS Mazhar served as a basis for the new version. An analysis of the preface and introduction in the two versions corroborates this. Although the new preface, and to a lesser degree the new introduction, has been thoroughly enlarged and changed, it still follows the same plan:

The preface and introduction to the MS Mazhar can be summarized under eight headings:

1. Invocation
2. An attempt to interpret historical events in Egypt: the arrival of the vizier as the fulfilment of God's word (pp. 1–13)[1]
3. How the work came into being (pp. 13–14)
4. A note on his use of al-'Attar as a source (p. 14)
5. The title and the reason for it (p. 14)
6. Reflections on the nature of man and the implications thereof for the laws and government of human society (pp. 15–16)
7. The history of the world and of Egypt from Adam to the Ottomans (pp. 16–23)
8. Reflections on the rule of the Ottomans (pp. 23–6)

The preface and introduction of the MS Aja'ib can be summarized under nine headings:

- Invocation (= Mazhar 1)
- The content of the work, how the work came into being and its aim (I, 2) (= Mazhar 3)
- The title and the reasons for it (I, 2–3) (= Mazhar 5)
- The purpose of history (I, 3)
- How the Islamic chronology came about (I, 3–4)
- Reflections on the writing of history and the relation of the present work to this (I, 4–6)
- The author's denial of serving any prominent person (I, 6–7)

- Reflections on the nature of man and the implications thereof for the laws and government of human society (I, 7–14) (= Mazhar 6)
- The history of the world and of Egypt from Adam until the year 1689, i.e. the beginning of the twelfth century AH (I, 14–23) (= Mazhar 7)

From this summary it will be seen that although the author of the MS Aja'ib touches on many other topics and deletes some of those in the MS Mazhar, he still discusses them in the same sequence. In connection with the verbal agreement of the passages both in the beginning and in the end, this should be sufficient to prove that the author used the preface and introduction of the MS Mazhar as the basis of his new version. This suggests that the preface and introduction of the MS Aja'ib represent not just a new preface and introduction but, by implication, the author's comment on what he wrote in 1801. In the following the preface and introduction of the MS Aja'ib will be interpreted in this light.

Invocation

After the standard invocation the author praises God's all-embracing powers to create, to destroy and to resurrect and bear witness to the uniqueness of God and to his servant and messenger to all human beings, Muhammad. In the MS Mazhar the invocation had a much more specific content, praising God for favouring God's cause and the Ottoman dynasty and the Prophet Muhammad, who was divinely assisted in establishing the true religion by war.

The author no longer marvels at the ability of God to favour the cause of the true religion through the Ottoman dynasty, but stresses his power to change everything, his generosity in avoiding disasters and in making people understand what is really going on. The author clearly wants to present events in a new perspective, suggesting that his interpretation of events in the MS Mazhar was unsatisfactory.

The content of the work, how the work came into being and its aim

In line with this he has deleted his former interpretation of events (= Mazhar 2), which saw the arrival of the Ottoman army as the fulfilment of God's word, and now presents himself as the 'humble' 'Abd

In support of Muhammad 'Ali 1805

al-Rahman ibn Hasan al-Hanafi, who has assembled 'some pages' (!). He then proceeds to list the contents and their arrangement in a 'well-arranged chronological order' and to state the purpose of the work, which, just as in the MS Mazhar, is to enable the reader to learn a lesson from past calamities, be consoled by them and remember them. To al-Jabarti the task of recording the past has a practical purpose. The lessons gleaned from the past should be remembered and used in the evaluation of the present and the future. As we have seen, this has been his attitude all along, from the MS Mudda. Al-Jabarti sees himself and his work as a contribution to contemporary thinking.

The title and the reasons for it

The author does not see fit to name his friend al-'Attar as a source in the new preface, and has deleted this passage (= Mazhar 4). The reason for this is not hard to guess: as noted above, al-'Attar was the source of some of the poetry which acclaimed the Ottomans and the vizier. It has been suggested that he served as al-Jabarti's inspiration for his interpretation of events. Now that this interpretation (and much of the corresponding poetry) has been discarded,[2] there is no reason to retain his name in this prominent place. But al-'Attar is still remembered in the following section, where the author lists the people whose lives should be the subject of history: prophets, saints, scholars, wise men, poets, kings and sultans. As we shall see, this list, and especially the sequence, constituton the core of al-Jabarti's political thinking in the MS Aja'ib. But it is only here that poets are mentioned (significantly, after the wise men, but before the kings and sultans!) as a worthy subject of history.

   In line with the new perspectives suggested in the invocation and by the following deletions, the author now stresses the unusual and varied nature of events and formulates the new title accordingly: 'Remarkable Remnants of Lives and Events', in direct contrast to the finger-pointing, not to say hopeful, title of the MS Mazhar: 'A Clear View of the Sanctifying (Will of God) in the Departure of French Rule'.

The purpose of history

This section constitutes an elaboration of the two previous sections, stating in more general terms the subject and purpose of history and stressing history as not only an opportunity to warn the wise of those situations in which former nations have vanished, but also as a guide

Reflections on the nature of man and the implications thereof
for the laws and government of human society

In the MS Mazhar the author proceeded to state his theory of government, which was fairly simple and straightforward: As man needs to associate with his own kind, but finds it difficult to agree with other people, God has established the *shari'a* as a law to join together all human actions in one path. But it is necessary that there be a man of power and strength to direct people to these laws. If not, man would sink to the level of 'roaming cattle and grazing livestock'.

In the MS Aja'ib this is still the basis of his thoughts. But, against the background of the changes made in this section of his introduction, we may infer that he has now found it necessary to elaborate on two points in this theory: the nature of the *shari'a* and of the ruler, the *khalifa*. The essence of the first is twofold: knowledge and justice. Justice is the consequence of knowledge of the things that lie midway (between extremes), and this is expressed in the religious law as the straight path. As for the second, the ruler (the *khalifa*) is the man to whom God grants a portion of his justice and makes a cause and means for the communication of the flow of his grace, the point being that it is only when God grants him this that he is able to dispense justice.

Having made this clear, the author finds it necessary to supply a supplementary note on the five categories of human beings who dispense justice: prophets; 'ulama; kings and rulers; people who observe justice in their dealings and settle their crimes with equity; and, finally, those who exercise governance over themselves. From the space he affords to each category it is evident that the crucial ones are the 'ulama, the rulers and those who exercise governance over themselves.

The author apparently felt a need for such clarification, and the logical interpretation would be that events since 1801 have made it necessary to develop his thinking on the government of a Muslim community in detail. In the difficult days of the autumn of 1801 it did not seem necessary or opportune to enlarge on these matters. A Muslim ruler such as the Ottoman vizier would know and accept these things as a matter of course. Now, in 1805, it has become imperative to state them openly:

The 'ulama represent the source of knowledge of the Divine law, which, as already stated, is the necessary prerequisite for dispensing justice. The rulers are the practical guardians of justice and equity among people and subjects. As such it is imperative that the ruler knows the *shari'a* of Islam, what is permitted and prohibited in it. But every human being, i.e. not only 'ulama and rulers, but everybody, man being God's vicar on earth, should try to purify his soul. Without command of his own body and soul, man is unable to govern other men. Al-Jabarti presents this as a choice between man's spiritual and physical powers. Only those who devote their energy to developing the first by learning, speech and understanding are worthy of being God's vicars on earth.

It is important to note that to al-Jabarti these basic tenets constitute a general theory, which applies to every ruler, be he Muslim or non-Muslim (I, 9: 'Whether the state be Muslim or non-Muslim, the foundation and pillars of the realm, the stability and framework of the nation, are justice and equity'). This, of course, is the natural outcome of his realizing that not even the Muslim government of the Ottomans could be trusted to perform its duties of justice and equity. Nor does he have much faith in the ability of the 'ulama of his own time. He notes that some scholars have shown a deplorable love of honours and riches, leadership and position, and have shown envy and malice. But this deterioration of affairs should not afflict anyone. To al-Jabarti, the right people, the true guides of mankind, do exist, but they are hidden in obscurity: 'Divine Providence and wisdom keep their state unrevealed'! Al-Jabarti still cherishes the arguments put forward in the MS Mudda on the role of the shaykhs. The ideal remains the venerable shaykhs al-Masiri of Alexandria and al-Sadat, who stayed unattached to the French.

Al-Jabarti does not take the crucial step of commenting on the relationship between the 'ulama and the ruler. After three years of French rule and several more diwans, of one of which he himself was a member, it is remarkable that his theory of government does not include a word on this feature. But this, of course, is an impossibility. As long as he considers it a necessary prerequisite for the shaykhs, the sources of knowledge for the ruler, to live in obscurity in order to retain their freedom of independent counsel, such a feature is unthinkable. Instead, he adds a piece of counsel for the welfare of the people containing an analysis of what leads to bad government ('the reasons for the destructions of kings'). With many references to authorities on these matters, he pleads for everybody to stick to his duties in accordance with 'intelligent, selected indications from the composition of behaviour for the instruction of kings, which exposes the proper qualifications'.

But he is fully aware that this point is crucial: How then, are these people made to act in the right way? To al-Jabarti the answer does not lie in the establishment of a system of checks and balances or in the formalization of the relationship between the ruler and his advisers. Obviously, his experience in the diwans has not impressed him in the least. As he sees it, it is a question of an original, innate good disposition. The right personal qualities cannot be acquired through training and discipline, if the person is not attracted to them by his original nature. But the person who combines virtues with vices may attain a noble character by exercising his rational self and seeking the right company. So to al-Jabarti good government is a question of personal qualities. But he is not deterministic: in certain circumstances the personal qualities can be acquired. And for this reason these reflections on the nature of man and the prerequisites of good government take on the form of warning, advice and prayer.

The target of this advice is not indicated. The author, apparently, has no specific person or group in mind. The MS Aja'ib seems to be directed at the general, and by necessity, educated public.

The history of the world and of Egypt from Adam
until the year 1689 (the beginning of the twelfth century AH)

After having stated his theory of government, the author is now ready to begin his 'comprehensive history'. What follows is in all essentials the historical perspective developed in the MS Mazhar, from Adam to the Ottomans. The story has been enlarged and given more precision and detail. Notes on buildings erected by the different rulers in Cairo have been added, but the general trend and the evaluation of these rulers have been changed only slightly. His heroes are still Salah al-Din of the Ayyubid dynasty and the Ottoman sultans Selim I and Süleyman I. But the Mamluk sultans al-Muzaffar Qutuz, Baybars and al-Nasir have now been added to the list, while the Ottomans' ability to rule the Islamic community is restricted to the outset of their reign. The author repeats, from the MS Mazhar, what this implies. The rightly guided Muslim ruler should be able to

- guard the territory and frontiers of the state;
- uphold the performance of the Islamic rites and the *sunna* of Muhammad;
- honour the 'ulama and religious leaders;
- support the maintenance of the two Holy Cities;
- uphold the rules and principles of justice by observing Islamic law and practices.

Al-Jabarti notes that when Selim I returned to his own country, he took the Abbasid caliph with him. This, al-Jabarti points out, meant

In support of Muhammad 'Ali 1805

the end of the caliphate and the swearing of an oath of fealty (I, 20). To al-Jabarti, who has faithfully recorded the way in which the Mamluk sultans had presented themselves as servants of this shadow caliph in order to legitimize their rule, the Ottoman sultan apparently did not succeed in continuing this tradition.[5]

But after Süleyman I, his son Selim II assumed the sultanate. Apparently this was where things went wrong. By way of explanation, al-Jabarti relates an anecdote on this sultan, the point of which seems to be that the acceptance of bribery by governors and administrators dealt a damaging blow to the Ottoman dynasty, exactly because the sultan took advice from the wrong person. To al-Jabarti this fatal development is a cause of severe grief, but as he adds, 'the present state of affairs [i.e. in the Ottoman Empire] is not something unknown, so that one has to speak openly about it' (I, 21). Things were already going wrong for the Ottoman dynasty at this time, but the author sees no reason to enlarge upon it.

In the MS Mazhar the author was ready to state that the Ottoman dynasty, alone among the dynasties of the world, had been exempted from heresy and decay. Since their conquest, Egypt had been protected from evildoers and infidels. The French invasion was seen as an act of fate, which did not blemish the fame of the Ottomans, in so far as the final victory was theirs. This statement has been deleted in the MS Aja'ib. The victory over the French has apparently failed to live up to its promise, and the author now sees the Ottoman dynasty as just another string of rulers, subject to the temptations and pitfalls of power. But as they are still, at least nominally, the sovereigns of Egypt, he restrains his comments.

Instead, he develops another theme, new in the MS Aja'ib, but more important now that he has decided to tell the history of Egypt in the twelfth century AH, and has discarded the Ottomans as the heroes of the story. The all-embracing split which opened up 'among the troops of Egypt' after the Ottoman conquest, between the Faqariyya and Qasimiyya factions, was 'a heathenish custom and devilish innovation, one which sowed the seeds of duplicity among them and established discord in their midst'. As for the origins of the split, he wavers between seeing it as a measure taken by Sultan Selim to secure Ottoman power in Egypt by keeping the Egyptian emirs divided among themselves, and an indigenous development, born out of the innate feeling of competition among the emirs.

Because of the space the author affords to this feature, it is reasonable to suppose that to him the split constitutes the main reason for the calamities of Egypt ('How many villages were laid waste, brave men slain, homes destroyed, palaces burned, free women taken captive and noble men vanquished because of it?'). But he does not feel sure enough on this point to commit to naming either the Ottomans or the emirs as the villains of his tale, and leaves the matter for the reader to ponder.[6]

So we may conclude that the preface and introduction of the MS Aja'ib are based on the preface and introduction of the MS Mazhar, and their contents are best interpreted as the author's comment on what he wrote in 1801. The author has left his hopeful vision of the victorious Ottomans as the final solution to the problems and calamities of Egypt. They, too, have proved to be at the mercy of the temptations and pitfalls of power. Instead, the author has developed and clarified his simple and straightforward ideas of what is required to rule a Muslim country into an elaborate theory of government, its goals and prerequisites. The essential goal of the *shari'a* is now clearly defined as justice, a balanced way between extremes. To follow the *shari'a* is the task of the ruler. In order to perform his duties, he has to listen to the 'ulama, who are the source of knowledge of what this entails in practice. But this does not imply that the ruler should set up consultative bodies, like the diwans of the French. This would, and has, led to corruption of the 'ulama and their shaykhs. The 'ulama should concentrate on acquiring knowledge and stay out of the spotlight. It is the task and duty of the ruler to seek them out and acquire the knowledge he needs. To al-Jabarti good government is a question of how the ruler selects his spiritual advisers. As such it rests on the personal qualities of the ruler, which means that ultimately it is a question of God making him 'a cause and means for the communication of the flow of his grace'. In the following sketch of historical developments from the beginning to 1688 this theory is used to judge the record of the different rulers. The sultans of the Ottoman dynasty fell from grace in this respect after Süleyman I, by accepting bribes from governors and administrators, but the author has not made up his mind whether the split among the Egyptian emirs into two competing factions should be attributed to the Ottomans or to indigenous causes.

To al-Jabarti, this is a general theory. It is valid whether the rulers are Muslim or non-Muslim. It follows that to him even the French might qualify as rulers, if they show themselves to have the necessary grace of God to select the right advisers (i.e. in Muslim countries the shaykhs of the 'ulama) who can guide them in dispensing justice. Consequently, their actions should be evaluated on their merits, and not on the basis of the crude and simple pattern of infidels versus the true believers. As we have seen, this is probably what made him

In support of Muhammad 'Ali 1805

delete his comments on the French proclamation and to include the full text published by the French, on the investigation of the murder of General Kléber.

Basically, this clarification in al-Jabarti's political outlook constitutes a reversion to the ideas developed and propounded in the MS Mudda. The shaykhs of the 'ulama should stay out of formal attachments to the ruler and limit themselves to keeping communication open. But in contrast to both the MS Mudda and the MS Mazhar he stresses the importance of the shaykhs staying free of all sorts of honours and influence because of the corruption they entail.

In the part of MS Aja'ib covered by the MS Mudda he does not revert to his attacks on al-Sharqawi and the leading shaykhs. But it is significant that he does not make any attempt either to resurrect al-Sadat to his position as the venerable shaykh whose gentle nature brings about the necessary compromise in a quiet and unspectacular way. The author's theory on the position of the shaykhs in the Muslim community seems to have hardened into an unshakable demand for humility, seclusion and obscurity – a view, which, incidentally, coincides with the remarkable modesty of the author in the preface.

---

[1] For the sake of precision, I use the pagination of Philipp's translation of at this point.

[2] This seems to fit with the fact that al-Attar is already noted that Egypt early in 1802, only to return in 1815.

[3] See Creselius, Ahmad Shalabi ibn 'Abd al-Ghani and Ahmad Katkuda Azaban al- Damurdashi: Two sources for al-Jabarti's Aja'ib al-Athar fi'l-Tarajim wa'l-Akhbar, in Creselius (ed.) *Eighteenth Century Egypt*, p. 89-102 ff.

[4] Moreh, 'al-Jabarti's Method', p. 357, notes this point.

[5] As noted above, it has been suggested that the Ottoman government put this story in circulation in the late eighteenth century to strengthen their ideological position. If this is so, al-Jabarti obviously does not wish to follow this lead.

[6] I am much indebted to P.M. Holt (Bulletin of the School of Oriental and African Studies, 1962, vol.25, p. 38-51, Holt, P.M., al-Jabarti's Introdduction to the History of Ottoman Egypt) for pointing out to me the possibilities of a literary analysis of al-Jabarti's chronicles. The interpretation of al-Jabarti's account of the origins of the split between the emirs of Ottoman Egypt presented here corroborates Holt's interpretation, except for one point: It seems to me that Holt misses the final point, that by leaving the two accounts of this split side by side (one based on popular legends and

one based on information derived from the Damurdashi group of popular chronicles, composed by soldiers), al-Jabarti leaves it to the reader to decide whether this was an indigenous development or a split created and kept alive by the Ottoman sultans in order to prevent Egypt from regaining its freedom as a sovereign state.

24 From the MS Mazhar to the MS Aja'ib

The third volume of the MS Aja'ib starts out in 1798 with the parts of the text of the MS Mazhar that covered the events dealt with in the MS Mudda.[1] It opens with an invocation, noting the year 1213, and an opening paragraph which seems to introduce the whole of volume III: 'This was the first year of the fierce fights.' As noted above, the author saw developments from 1798 to 1805 as having taken place inside the political framework suggested by the opening of the second volume, but in such a way that it more or less destroyed – or at least thoroughly changed – this framework.

When working on his new version, the author used the MS Mazhar as the basis of this part of his narrative. But he also consulted his earlier version, the MS Mudda. This is attested in numerous additions where passages from the MS Mudda have been reinserted, in part or in full.[2] But it is equally plain that the author did not intend to revert to the line of argument on which the MS Mudda was based. The additions from the MS Mudda are only reinserted where they seem to serve his argument in the new version, the MS Aja'ib. Clear examples of the author having made such a choice are furnished by the central passage in the incident of the cockades and the position of the shaykh al-Sadat,[3] by the wording of the letters from the shaykhs to the people of Cairo and Egypt[4] and, especially, by the fact that he leaves out the information that the French had actually translated the Qur'an.[5] These instances are important because they strongly indicate that the deletions and additions in the MS Aja'ib constitute a conscious effort on the part of the author to convince the reader of the truth of his new line of argument.

However, changes affecting the position of the 'ulama and their leading shaykhs are few. As a consequence, the shaykhs are presented in much the same way as in the MS Mazhar, only acting and intervening when absolutely necessary, and generally dragging their feet when called upon to cooperate with the new rulers. Names are only mentioned when it cannot be avoided. Although the author must have been aware of the discrepancy between this picture and that presented in the MS Mudda, he evidently saw no reason to remedy it in the MS Aja'ib, except in a few but significant cases.

The appointment of the shaykhs to the first Diwan, is now depicted as the result of negotiation and the Diwan is no longer seen as a cover for criminal acts. Al-Bakri is back as the organizer of the celebration of the Inundation of the Nile, and al-Sadat again agrees to wear the cockade, but in such a way that the demands of the *shari'a* are respected. The shaykhs are again allowed to condemn the insurrection openly. This seems to point to the author allowing the shaykhs to play a more independent role in events, actively representing and protecting the *shari'a*.[6]

The changes in the MS Aja'ib do not significantly affect the position of the emirs. They are still cast as the main culprits. If anything, the changes indicate a return to the caustic attack of the MS Mudda: The French advance is no longer described as meeting any resistance; according to the MS Mazhar they were met by Murad Bey at Rahmaniyya! And the *mamluks* appointed by the French are in this account from the old (*mamluk*) houses, and not as tyrannical as the others![7]

The fact that Egypt is the sultan's land is still stressed, but small changes indicate that the Ottomans are no longer seen as the saviours of Egypt: the message to Istanbul is again seen as hopelessly futile, and the Albanian soldiers from the Ottoman army are no longer presented as heroes.[8]

It seems as if the author has attempted to present a more balanced picture of the non-Muslim groups. The critical remarks about the behaviour of Yacub have been reduced, and the fact that both the Copts' and the Syrian Christians' houses were in fact plundered by the mob during the insurrection has been reinserted. But the general animosity of the author against this group has been retained. It seems as if he is of the opinion that much of the blame for the trouble caused by the French measures should be placed on these people. But Malti the Copt, a leading Christian member of the Court of Cases set up by the French is no longer 'cursed'.[9]

The people of Cairo are no longer presented as part of the Muslim community, but, as in the MS Mudda, as a separate group of doubtful nature. Those who accept the French are the judicious ones, and in accepting defeat they completely forget how Muslims ought to behave in battle. As a consequence, the unity of the shaykhs and the people is no longer stressed, although the idea of a common cause, and the willingness to support it, is retained, and they no longer express joy at the French defeat or see the collapse of the arch in Azbakiyya as a good omen. In general, the author is of the opinion that the people should stop meddling in affairs that are not their business![10]

The position of the beduin and *fellahin* has not been touched. They still represent an unruly, treacherous element, and a threat to the people of the city.

As already noted, the majority of the changes in the text from the MS Mazhar to the MS Aja'ib are minor corrections, which tend to remove or reduce the impression conveyed in the MS Mazhar of

258   In support of Muhammad 'Ali 1805

the French as the implacable and unacceptable enemies of the Muslim community. But the fact that this is done without altering the basic text of the MS Mazhar, except in the case of the comment on the proclamation and the story of Muhammad Kurayyim, conveys the impression that at this stage the author wants to present the French as hard, but not tyrannical, rulers. His comments on the reason for sending soldiers to al-Azhar after the insurrection and the suggestion of a link between the killing of Dupuy and the execution of the shaykhs signal that the author wants to strike this delicate balance.[11] It should be borne in mind,when trying to summarize the picture presented of the French in the MS Aja'ib, that the change in the author's attitude to the French from the MS Mazhar to the MS Aja'ib is only a partial reversal to the attitude of the MS Mudda.

Following the lead made by the deletion of the comment on the proclamation, indicating an acceptance of the intentions of the French as stated in this document, the author no longer condemns them as cursed and infidels,[12] although he still entertains open dislike for some of them.[13] The idea of French 'ruses' has been completely discarded.[14] Open condemnation of their actions as 'falsehoods and lies' is avoided.[15] They are no longer presented as enemies of religion, who have killed their sultan and strayed from the path of other nations.[16] Actually, they intend to set up a diwan with the shaykhs as members, to enforce the *shari'a* and take pains to communicate with the dignitaries in Arabic[17], which is no longer repulsive, but simply a case of their lacking sufficient knowledge of this language.[18] The author does not hide his disapproval of their checking behaviour in al-Azhar, but they are no longer condemned as obscene people, nor are they accused of killing people they meet in the *riwaq*s of the mosque.[19]

Consequently, the entry of the French into Cairo is presented as the arrival of a group of harmless tourists, who generally try to pay for services rendered. They act effectively to stop the plunder, their measures to improve the sanitary standards of the city are generally seen as reasonable, and it is stressed that those who assist them in their search of the houses do so voluntarily.[20]

The most conspicuous feature of the author's new attitude to the French in the MS Aja'ib is the emphasis he puts on the many practical and technical innovations they bring along, and their scientific attitude. This was already present in the MS Mudda, and although much of it was suppressed in the MS Mazhar, even this version added some new items of this nature (e.g. a note on the windmills). But in the MS Aja'ib the author does not limit himself to reinserting the deleted passages on this subject, but adds a whole string of new examples (on the restaurants, the music, the wheelbarrows and the soldiers' provisions).[21] In the case of the windmills, a comment ('in wondrous fashion') is added, while in the description of the Institute he not only adds new instances of the scientific, artistic and mechanical activity of the French, but stresses their wish to impart their knowledge to everybody. The author strongly appreciates this and is fully aware that the French ability to solve practical problems is based on this scientific attitude.[22] This feature is so prominent in the picture presented by the author in the MS Aja'ib that it must be seen not only as an expression of the author's (and that of his patron and other shaykhs'?) personal interest in these matters, but as an integral part of the new image he wants to convey of the French masters. He is obviously at pains to present this scientific attitude as one of those qualities that make the French acceptable as rulers of a Muslim country like Egypt. A positive attitude to scientific and practical innovations is more than just an interesting feature of the French behaviour, but something that should be accepted and promoted by any ruler!

In line with this more positive picture of the French invaders, the author seems to relax his view of the unity and cohesiveness of the Muslim community, so conspicuous in the MS Mazhar, while the actions and attitudes of other participants get a more judicious evaluation. The confrontation between the infidels and the Muslim community in the MS Mazhar has disappeared. The idea of a common cause and the willingness to support it among the different groups are still there. But the defence of Egypt is presented as a national, not a religious task,[23] and one which is no longer the sole concern of the Muslims: even the Greeks take part in Murad Bey's army, and the emirs have become Egyptian emirs.[24]

So, to sum up: the changes in the composition and content of the MS Aja'ib in the part of the MS Mazhar that dealt with the content of the MS Mudda signify a new attitude to the French invaders. They are now presented as people whose intention of acting as Muslims should be taken seriously. It is suggested that, having realized their duty to enforce the *shari'a*, they would actually be acceptable as rulers of a Muslim country. The position of the shaykhs as the qualified advisers of such rulers was already present in the MS Mazhar, but has been slightly improved by stressing their attention to observing the limitations both for the ruler and the people.

This indicates that between the writing of the MS Mazhar and the MS Aja'ib, the author's position on the issue of how the shaykhs should cooperate with the ruler has shifted once again. The ruler should respect the *shari'a* as the foundation of society and listen to those – the 'ulama and their leading shaykhs – who are able to tell him what it demands.. This, as we noted, was the main theme of the MS Mazhar and there the author expected the Ottomans to fit this role, and took pains to make the shaykhs appear exceptionally well suited for the job of advisers to the ruler. In the MS Aja'ib the intentions and actions of the French are presented in such a way that they, too, would qualify as rulers. The author seems to have come to the conclusion that the crucial test of a ruler in a Muslim country like Egypt is not whether the ruler is Muslim. What matters is his respect for the *shari'a* and his ability to listen to the people who are able to advise him on this matter: the 'ulama and their leading shaykhs.

However, this conclusion has been reached on the basis of an analysis of the changes in the tiny portion of the MS Aja'ib which dealt with the text of the MS Mudda. It must necessarily be tentative. Nevertheless, it strongly supports trends found in other elements of the MS Aja'ib of 1805, such as the division into volumes and the new preface and introduction.

---

[1] References will be to the pagination of the Bulaq edition, used in the English translation.

[2] III, 3, 7, 8, 15, 17, 19, 20, 24, 25, 30, 34, 34–5.

[3] III, 16–17.

[4] III, 30, 31.

[5] III, 34. When the author expanded the description of the Institute by reinserting the material from the MS Mudda, he left out the note about the Qur'an being translated into French. The note is situated in the middle of the text he decided to include, and could not be missed. The fact that he decided to discard this piece of inconvenient information can only be explained by a wish to promote a positive appreciation of French rule.

[6] III, 11, 13, 17, 30.

[7] III, 4.

[8] III, 3, 8.

[9] III, 15, 25, 16, 13, 24.

[10] III, 4, 9, 6, 32, 15.

[11] III, 29.

[12] III, 12, 19, 20, 24, 26, 30, 62.

[13] Especially Barthelemy and Bonaparte, see III, 37.

[14] III, 4, 12, 38.

[15] III, 21, 38.

[16] III, 21, 17.

[17] III, 19.

[18] III, 10, 19, 20.

[19] III, 26.

[20] III, 11, 13, 32,13, 19, 24, 32,13.

[21] III, 12, 15, 33, 38.

[22] III, 33, 34-5, 38.

[23] The importance of the common prayers in the al-Azhar is no longer stressed (III, 6).

[24] III, 4, 20.

25   Al-Sharqawi and al-Sadat in the MS Aja'ib in 1805

Al-Sharqawi was apparently still alive when volume I and the necrology of al-Kurdi were written, and the author is full of praise for his commentary on one of the works of al-Kurdi,[1] but apart from this, the author clearly did not think highly of his leadership.[2] Al-Sharqawi is mentioned mostly in his capacity as a leader. Only rarely does he come through as an individual person in the narrative. He is shown as rejecting the cockade and as protecting a merchant, but (only?) because of the family ties between them.[3] The honours bestowed upon him by the French are less than those bestowed on al-Sadat. But he confronts the Copts when they become too impertinent.[4] Al-Sharqawi praises Murad Bey,[5] conforms with the popular cult of al-Badawi in Tanta, and the author takes some pleasure in noting how he loses the post as superintendent of al-Azhar. This incident suggests that the rivalry between al-Sharqawi and al-Sadat, between the Husayni shrine and the al-Azhar, still existed at the time of writing. Al-Sharqawi takes part in the deposition of the Ottoman pasha in 1805, but is clearly not considered a leading spirit in this move.[6]

Al-Sadat, too, was apparently still alive when the necrology of al-Zabidi in volume I was written.[7] The impression conveyed of al-Sadat in this necrology is of a person highly thought of by the author, who continues to chronicle his actions and personal situation. Al-Sadat is highly praised as a leader of the family, and of the (sufi) order, and as a scholar, and quite a few poems in his praise are quoted.[8] Some remarks suggest a direct relationship between al-Sadat and the author: he is presented as 'our master'. Some of his students studied with the author's father; his circle comprised Shafi'i shaykhs and the shaykh of the Maghribi *riwaq* at al-Azhar. Teaching took place at his base, the Husayni shrine.[9] He is presented as an important figure during the French occupation, who complies with French demands, but takes care to respect the *shari'a* and to protect members of the Muslim community and speaks out against French hypocrisy.[10] However, after the (second) siege of Cairo in 1800 the French looked upon him as an enemy and the author follows his troubles closely.[11] His relationship with the Ottoman vizier Yusuf Zia Pasha is presented as cordial.[12] Apparently he had no significant part in the action to depose the pasha. The author confines himself to noting, regularly and apparently as an important event, al-Sadat's celebration of the *mawlid* of Husayn. He does note,

lished by the French, the *Courier de l'Égypte*, shows no significant affinity to al-Jabarti's text. This paper, though, seems to be based on the French *ordres du jour* and these, or perhaps a summary of these in Arabic, made by al-Khashshab, may have provided al-Jabarti with his information. Still, I have not come across any references to such material.

But some of al-Khashshab's writings have survived. In the *Description de l'Égypte*[4] Delaporte published a short description of the *mamluk* emirs during the time of the Ottomans. In his introduction Delaporte says: 'J'ai guidé dans mon récit par la tradition de témoins oculaires et par une petite histoire que le cheikh Isma'il-Khashshab, secrétaire du Diwan du Kaire, mon professeur, en traça d'après ma demande. Ce petit manuscrit, que j'ai apporté avec moi d'Égypte, se trouve actuellement à la Bibliothèque du Roi.' The manuscript is still in the Bibliothèque Nationale in Paris (MS Arabe 1858). According to Gran the text in the *Description de l'Egypte* is a nearly verbatim rendering of this manuscript.[5] If this is correct, al-Khashshab has supplied Delaporte with a summary of the history of the emirs from 1707 until the late 1790s. The text supplied by Delaporte appears to be a very matter-of-fact narrative of the exploits of the better-known Egyptian emirs in the eighteenth century.[6]

The existence of such a summary before 1801, when Delaporte left for France, indicates that al-Jabarti's friends were taking an interest in, and actually having a try at, recording the history of Egypt some time before the composition of the MS Mazhar (which does not touch on the subject of the history of Egypt before 1798 in detail) and well before the MS Aja'ib came into existence. On the basis of Delaporte there does not seem to be any indication that al-Jabarti used this manuscript (or a copy of it) for volumes I–II of the MS Aja'ib. A more thorough investigation of the Arabic text may well turn up some evidence in this direction.[7] But al-Khashshab's manuscript should be investigated further, not only to look for any discrepancies between the translation of Delaporte and the text of al-Khashshab, but, more importantly, to compare the evaluation of each of the emirs with the evaluation of al-Jabarti.

Another short piece by al-Khashshab exists in the Bibliothèque Nationale, *Khulasat ma yurad min akhbar al-amir Murad* ('Extract of what was mentioned in the history of the emir Murad'), published by Hamza A. Badr and Daniel Crecelius.[8] This manuscript allows us to push the argument a bit further. A notation in French on the first page states that it is the autograph copy of the archivist of the French Diwan in Cairo, which is sufficient to identify the author as Isma'il al Khashshab. The catalogue number in the Bibliothèque Nationale suggests a close affinity to the text of Delaporte. This is borne out by the fact that the wording is almost the same in several places. The text is an extract, probably of the text related by Delaporte mentioned above, and what we get is a most cursory account of the career of Murad Bey. The manuscript states that it was finished on 1 June 1801. Like the manuscript of Delaporte, it testifies to the fact that al-Jabarti's friends were able to – and indeed did – deliver to the French a summary of the career of Murad Bey, one of the major contemporary figures in Egypt, six weeks after his death on 12 April 1801. As such, it suggests that some of the information included in the first two volumes of the MS Aja'ib was already present before the MS Mazhar was finished. This is strengthened by another point. The only place in the manuscript where al-Khashshab becomes more specific concerns the confrontation between the emirs and the shaykhs in November 1794 which, as we noted above, forms the end of volume II of the MS Aja'ib. There is a strong affinity between the texts of al-Khashshab and al-Jabarti, especially when it comes to the final verdict on the incident[9] – so strong that they must either have a common source, or have been copying each other directly. Against this background it is interesting to notice that the final verdict of al-Khashshab on Murad is quite different from that of al Jabarti. According to al-Khashshab, Murad was a broad-minded and generous emir, but 'leadership is not without oppression'![10]

On this evidence it would be fair to conclude that al-Khashshab was more than just a friend of al-Jabarti. Some sort of practical literary cooperation existed between the two, and between them and the French scientists. But the exact nature and ramifications of this are difficult to ascertain without more evidence than that provided by the texts of al-Khashshab preserved in the Bibliothèque Nationale.

---

[1] IV, 238.

[2] IV, 238–9.

[3] Ayalon first pointed out the importance of al-Khashshab and the existence of his manuscript in the Bibliothèque Nationale: Ayalon, 'al-Jabarti and his Background', p. 243.

[4] Commission des Monuments d'Egypte, *Description d l'Egypte ou recueil des observations et des recherches qui ont eté faites en Egypte pendant l'expédition de l'armée française, publié par les ordres de sa Majesté l'empereur Napoleon le Grand*, Paris 1809–22, vol. II, part I, pp. 165—84, M. Delaporte, Troizieme Dynastie, Mamlouk Beiks ou Ghozzez.

[5] I am indebted to Peter Gran for having made me aware of this connection.

[6] Pieterberg, 'Formation', p. 283 and Hathaway, *The Politics of Households*, p. 28 both see the *Tadkhira* of al-Khashshab as a highly inaccurate narrative which shows how the behavioural patterns of the elite were perceived in the late eighteenth century. As a source for events in the eighteenth century it is of no real value. But as Pieterberg points out, it is of great interest as a source for how the elite was conceived by people from the outside in the late eighteenth century. But to me the fact that it was probably written for the benefit of the French complicates these possibilities in this last respect.

[7] Holt, Al-Jabarti's Introduction etc. 1962, p. 40, mentions a recension of al-Ishagi's chronicle in the Bibliothèque Nationale(MS Arabe 1854) and finds reason to believe that al-Jabarti used this recension, which is anonymous and lacks a title. To me the interesting point would be whether this manuscript ended up in the Bibliothèque Nationale in the same way as al-Khashshab's text, i.e. through Delaporte, as suggested by the library accession numbers. If this is so, it would suggest that al-Jabarti was already working on the MS Aja'ib before the French left in 1801.

[8] Ismai'l al-Khashshab, *A Short Manuscript History of the Mamluk Amir Murad Bey: Khulasat ma yurad min akhbar al-amir Murad*, ed. and trans. Hamza A. Badr and Daniel Crecelius, Cairo 1992. The manuscript: Bibliothèque Nationale, MS Arabe 1859.

[9] Al-Khashshab, *Khulasa*, p. 35: 'This revolt subsided on its fourth day and the markets opened, but after only about 30 days the situation returned to what it had been before'; MS Aja'ib, II, 258: 'The markets were opened and the situation settled down as such for about a month. Then everything which was mentioned returned and even more.'

[10] Al-Khashshab, *Khulasa*, p. 39.

27 In support of Muhammad 'Ali in 1805

The first three volumes of the MS Aja'ib should be seen as representing the author's views in 1805–6. The survey made above indicates that the changes made in these volumes when incorporating them into the following four-volume edition were rather superficial.

The investigation of these three volumes has shown that there is sufficient reason to believe that when he set out to turn the MS Mazhar into the three-volume edition some time between 1801 and 1805, the author's purpose was to present his arguments, based on the evidence given by the history of man from the earliest times, for a specific theory of Islamic government. The evidence further indicates a connection between this three-volume version of the MS Aja'ib of 1805–6 and the shaykhs of the 'ulama promoting and legitimizing Muhammad 'Ali as Ottoman governor of Egypt. To al-Jabarti the raising of Muhammad 'Ali to the governorship in 1805 in close cooperation with the leading shaykhs of the 'ulama in Cairo seems to constitute a new beginning after the turbulent events of the years following the surrender of the French in 1801.

The analysis of the changes in the composition and content in the part of the MS Aja'ib suggests a change in attitude to the French invaders. They were now presented as people whose intention of acting as virtual Muslims should be taken seriously. In the new version of his chronicle they would actually qualify as rulers of a Muslim country, because they had realized their duty to enforce the *shari'a*. Notes on the many practical, technical and scientific innovations of the French were restored from the MS Mudda, and even amplified. It has been argued that this feature should be seen not only as an expression of the author's and other shaykhs' personal interests in these matters, but as an integral part of the new picture the author wanted to convey of the French masters. He is obviously at pains to present this scientific attitude as one of the aspects that make the French acceptable as rulers of a Muslim country such as Egypt: a positive attitude to practical and scientific innovations is more than just an interesting feature of French behaviour, but something that should be accepted by any ruler. The inclusion of the report on the trial of the murderer of General Kléber should probably also be seen in this light.

The position of the shaykhs as the qualified advisers of a legitimate ruler was already present in the MS Mazhar. It is slightly improved in the MS Aja'ib by emphasizing their attention to marking the limits both of the ruler and the people. The author seems to want the shaykhs to play a more independent role in events, actively representing and protecting the *shari'a*.

This seems to indicate that between the writing of the MS Mudda and the MS Aja'ib, the author's position on the issue of how the shaykhs should cooperate with the ruler had been clarified: the ruler should respect the *shari'a* as the foundation of society and listen to those who are able to tell him what it prescribes: the 'ulama and their leading shaykhs. This, as we saw, was the main theme of the MS Mazhar: In the MS Mazhar the author expected the Ottomans to fill this role, and took pains to make the shaykhs appear exceptionally well suited for the job of advisers to the ruler. In the MS Aja'ib the intentions and actions of the French are presented in such a way that they, too, would qualify as rulers. The author seems to have come to the conclusion that the crucial test of a ruler in a Muslim country like Egypt is no longer whether the ruler is Muslim or not. What matters is whether he respects the *shari'a* and listens to the people who are able to advise him on this matter.

The preface and introduction corroborates this. They present a fully developed theory of government: In order to uphold the *shari'a*, the essence of which is equity and justice, the ruler, whether Muslim or non-Muslim, should listen to the 'ulama. But this did not imply that he should set up consultative bodies like the French diwans. This would only lead to corruption of the shaykhs of the 'ulama. The 'ulama should concentrate on acquiring knowledge and if possible stay out of the political spotlight. It is for the ruler not only to seek them out, but to seek out the right ones when he needs them. Good government is a question of the personal qualities of the ruler.

The material al-Jabarti had at his disposal when he set out to write his interpretation of the history of mankind in the introduction to the MS Aja'ib in 1805 barely allowed him to realize this grandiose scheme. The greater part of volumes I and II consists of necrologies. However, he seems to have made good use of what he had. In presenting the necrologies he invariably starts with the shaykhs. The periodization reflected in the division into parts and volumes as well as in the opening paragraphs of each volume obviously seeks to exemplify and vindicate his view of the proper relationship between the ruler and the 'ulama.

Against this background it is interesting to note that the author seems to have retained his animosity towards al-Sharqawi and a correspondingly close relationship with and sympathy for the shaykh al-Sadat, as we have noticed in his earlier versions. The fact that in the MS Aja'ib of 1805–6 he has taken pains to include a letter from al-Sadat to the representative of the Ottoman government, 'Uthman the Katkhuda, in which the conduct of the Ottomans during the siege of Cairo in 1800 is condemned in the strongest possible terms, testifies to the author's care to present al-Sadat as a shaykh conforming with the general trend of the MS Aja'ib. The fact that al-Sadat does not seem to have taken a leading part in the political developments after the return of the Ottomans in 1801 may be seen in the same light.

The relationship between shaykh al-Sadat and the author still seems to be close. Unfortunately, it has not been possible to describe the exact nature of this relationship, except that the author considers him his 'master'. The term obviously implies some sort of patronage. We do get an idea,however, that a circle, a *salon*, existed around al-Sadat, and that the author – or at least his friend al-Khashshab – belonged to this circle. The affinity found between the text of al-Jabarti and the writings left by al-Khashshab show that the history of the Egyptian emirs in the eighteenth century was a topic not only being discussed but actually being put into writing well before the departure of the French.

V

THE FINAL YEARS,
1806–21

28 Volume IV of the MS Aja'ib

The fourth volume of the MS Aja'ib represents the author's continuation of his work on the history of Egypt after the release of the
three-volume edition. As noted above, the differences between the
three-volume edition of 1806 (represented by MSS Aj.BN and BM)
and the Bulaq edition suggest that this continuation also entailed
a revision of the first three volumes. A comparison between these
two editions would reveal the nature of such a revision and by implication provide us with a key to the interpretation of the fourth
volume. However, such a comparison has not been attempted here.
As noted above, this revision does not seem to have been very thorough, and the following survey of the fourth volume may give us
some idea of when, how and why the fourth volume was written
and of the nature of the changes the author made in the first three
volumes in order to make them continue smoothly into the fourth
volume.

Volume IV starts with an opening paragraph on the astronomical specifics of the year 1221, noting that they signified 'the
stability of the present ruler's dynasty and of hardships for the subjects', but the following Qur'anic quotation ('Judgment belongs to
God, the All-High, the All-Great')[1] suggests that the author wants to
leave the final verdict on events to others. The following text is arranged according to the established annalistic framework, with dated
entries divided by months and years, each year followed by a section
of necrologies. From the year 1223/1808–9 the author resumes his
habit of summing up miscellaneous events of the year. This continues
to the year 1230/1814–15. At this point there seems to be a break.
The following year (1231/1815–16) starts with a note on who was in
power in Egypt, very much like the opening paragraphs of volumes
I and II. The list highlights the fact that Muhammad 'Ali Pasha was
'ruler and master' of Egypt, Jeddah, Mecca, Medina and the Hijaz,
and proceeds to list the incumbents of various governmental offices.
This pattern is repeated in the following three years (1232–4). In
1234/1818–19, the opening paragraph states that Mahmud II was
sultan in his capital Istanbul and Muhammad 'Ali Pasha his governor in Egypt, while the other officials were the same as those of the
previous year. In 1235 this opening paragraph disappears again, this
time for good. Apart from this feature the annalistic framework is retained. In 1234/1818–19 a short note ends the year and the necrologies disappear. The last year, 1236/1820–1, ends with a short note on
the most important events of the year.

The narrative of volume IV centres around the rise to power of Muhammad 'Ali Pasha, signified by the opening paragraph of 1231/1815–16. To the author, the gist of it seems to be that Muhammad 'Ali did not, as the author had expected, turn out to be a just ruler who abided by the advice of the shaykhs. In the beginning, while his power was still insecure, he exempted the revenues of the shaykhs from levies of taxes. This greatly enhanced their wealth and standing, but to al-Jabarti it also corrupted their moral integrity and made them an easy prey for Muhammad 'Ali when he felt sufficiently strong to do away with these privileges. This happened after the death of al-Alfi and the evacuation of the English from Alexandria. His encroachment on the established economic basis of the leading shaykhs made them unite in protest, but Muhammad 'Ali succeeded in splitting the shaykhs (apparently with the help of the old hands: al-Sadat, al-Sharqawi, al-Dawakhili and al-Fayyumi!), exiling his fiercest opponent, the *naqib al-ashraf*, 'Umar Efendi Makram, to Damietta.[2] It appears that al-Jabarti now believes that the shaykhs should have backed al-Alfi, the last emir with any potential as a leader. When eventually Muhammad 'Ali did away with the power of the emirs in the most brutal fashion, the author relates it without any comment.[3]

The mood of the author in volume IV is one of disappointment and disillusion, which may account for his caustic comments in the necrologies of the two leading shaykhs in his story, al-Sadat and al-Sharqawi (see below). The author seems to have realized that his vision of a Muslim society based on the *shari'a* and with the shaykhs as the checks on and ultimate arbiters of the secular ruler in the new age of change and technological innovation had failed. Muhammad 'Ali did not turn out to be the just ruler he expected, the leading shaykhs proved too weak and too easily corrupted. The shaykhs should have backed the only possible alternative, the emir al-Alfi. 'Umar Makram should not have stopped negotiating with al-Alfi and switched the loyalties of the shaykhs to Muhammad 'Ali. However, al-Alfi died and the 'ulama were allowed no hand in the restoration of Egypt after the devastation of war and civil strife in the following years.

This mood is most clearly expressed in the necrology of al-Alfi. Here the author presents quite a different version of how Muhammad 'Ali came to power as governor of Egypt. In volume III Muhammad 'Ali set about making plans for the deposition of the governor Ahmad Pasha, but the crucial appointment of Muhammad 'Ali as *qaim maqam* and later governor of Egypt was accomplished by the shaykhs, under the gallant and energetic leadership of the *naqib al-ashraf*, 'Umar Makram. Now, in the necrology of al-Alfi, Muhammad 'Ali's ascendancy is portrayed as caused by his own clever scheming,

The Final Years 1806-21

as he flattered 'Umar Makram into believing that he would be the right man for the shaykhs, while al-Alfi is presented as having all the right ideas concerning the ruler's duties.[4]

In the necrology of al-Alfi, al-Jabarti notes that 'what happened to the English and the amirs will be related below'. This implies that this part of the story had already taken place and that the necrology of al-Alfi was inserted in the text at a later date. Unfortunately the allusion to the emirs is too vague to determine how late, but the note itself is sufficient evidence to suggest that the author revised this part of the text and that he did so in a mood of general regret and disillusion.

Later on the author states that he gathered his material on a day-to-day basis, verified it and then put it in its right place in the revision.[5] It seems that he was able to adhere to this pattern until the end of 1230/1815–16. After this year he seems to have lost his grip, and the story slowly peters out. On this basis it would be logical to infer that the part of volume IV covered by 1221–1230 has been subjected to a revision, reflecting the author's new mood and that allusions to the plans of Muhammad 'Ali in volume III constitute (one of) the changes made in the preceding volumes on this occasion.

The fact that his friend Isma'il al-Khashshab died in the preceding year (1229/1814–15) could be the explanation for this shift in volume IV. Although the author denies having any knowledge of what happened to the historical writings of this very well-informed person,[6] there is little doubt that at the end of the French occupation a working relationship existed between al-Khashshab and al-Jabarti in connection with the history of the Egyptian emirs in the eighteenth century. It would be natural to assume that this relationship continued as long as their friendship, i.e. until the death of al-Khashshab in 1814. But things had apparently changed. The poet and grammarian Hasan al-'Attar became the successor of al-Shanawani as shaykh al-Azhar on his return to Cairo in 1815. The promotion of this old friend is only vaguely alluded to in al-Jabarti's fourth volume.[7]

Al-Jabarti used the death of important persons to state his opinion of their behaviour and personal character, and as an occasion to review past events. The necrologies of al-Sharqawi and al-Sadat are no exception.[8]

References to al-Sharqawi in volume IV indicate no change in the author's attitude to this shaykh. He is clearly presented as an example of one of the leading shaykhs 'who love honour and riches, leadership and position, and who show envy and malice', in contrast to his successor as shaykh al-Azhar, al-Shanawani, who is presented as one of the 'righteous – hidden under domes of obscurity'.[9] This picture of al-Sharqawi is reinforced by the few incidents in volume IV in which his attitude is presented in more detail: He could be pressured to forget his protests and to perform the prayers for a rise in the waters in the Nile with a threat of revoking his economic privileges. The mere suggestion of such a thing makes him choke with rage![10] Al-Jabarti suggests that a rivalry developed between al-Sharqawi and the other shaykhs, especially 'Umar Makram, and that Muhammad 'Ali took advantage of this – first to depose 'Umar Makram then to remove the tax privileges of the shaykhs.[11]

Al-Sharqawi died on 9 October 1812. His necrology is fairly short, and presents him as an upstart, who came from a poor, provincial background and systematically made his way to the top, mainly by his ability to mobilize his friends at the right moment and to use the rulers, including the French, to further his interests. 'The world was good to him and as his appetite for worldly things increased', al-Jabarti notes, 'his turban increased so in size and grandeur that it became proverbial'! Together, the author and al-Sharqawi attended the *dikhr*s and meetings of the master of the sufi order of the Khalwatiyya, Muhammad al-Kurdi, and al-Sharqawi taught at al-Jabarti's *riwaq* in al-Azhar. But this relationship between the two does not induce the author to take a more favourable view of al-Sharqawi. Al-Jabarti mentions his various theological works in the most cursory fashion and openly accuses him of copying his (i.e. the author's) biographies of the modern Shafi'i jurists. A history of Egypt which al-Sharqawi wrote on the arrival of Yusuf Pasha is characterized as short, extremely dry and full of mistakes (His praise of al-Sharqawi's commentary on al-Kurdi in volume I is obviously completely forgotten!). The author makes a point of demonstrating al-Sharqawi's lack of understanding and common decency by contrasting it with the personal qualities of the lady Tokay, the wife of Sultan al-Nasir Muhammad ibn Qalawun, whose mausoleum al-Sharqawi took over and converted into a mausoleum for himself. As a final token of his disgust with this enterprising upstart, al-Jabarti relates the story of the election of his successor as shaykh al-Azhar, Shaykh al-Shanawani, who not only behaved with the humility demanded by a real *'alim*, but even went into hiding when his name was brought forward as a candidate for this post. Al-Shanawani's rival was al-Mahdi, the secretary of the diwans under the French, but the backing of Muhammad 'Ali, who insisted on a person free of special interests, secured the election of al-Shanawani.

These instances seem to fit the author's general theory of government, presented in the introduction. The fact that Muhammad 'Ali backs the right candidate as the new shaykh al-Azhar is important, as it points to this necrology being part of the unrevised volume IV in which the author still had faith in Muhammad 'Ali.

It seems as if the author loses interest in al-Sadat. In volume IV he is only mentioned in his necrology in the year 1228/1813. On the other hand, his necrology is not only much longer than that of al-Sharqawi, but also more complicated, showing significant discrepancies and contradictions in the author's attitude to this shaykh.

The shaykh al-Sadat died on 21 March 1813. In his necrology he is introduced as 'a famous professor, a proficient scholar, a pre-eminent chief, uniquely venerable, a prodigy of his age, peerless in his epoch'[12]. The author supplies a long list of his education and connections with important scholars of his time. But the following account of his life tells a different story! He is presented as a very ambitious, proud, and high-handed man with a great talent for collecting riches and worldly goods, but also as exceedingly stingy, seeing 'tax bureaus as based on injustice, and everything they charged to him as an abomination'. When he got older his pride and vanity grew: 'No indeed; surely Man waxes insolent' (Qur'an 96:6).[13] But he spoke up against Hasan Pasha in 1786, and thus gained the respect of the emirs. This enabled him to take over the post of shaykh of the Husayni mosque, and after this he ruthlessly went after other similarly well-endowed institutions, intimidating and evicting less important but decent persons in the process. He is made responsible for the extension of the *mawlid* of Husayn from one to fifteen days and the deplorable innovations in this respect.[14] 'In summary,' the author concludes, 'Shams al-Din [al Sadat] turned things upside down and changed the natural order. Formerly, his family's home had been the seat of right guidance, of authority and faith, but it became something like the house of a police magistrate, to be feared for the slightest infraction.'[15] His relationship with the French was intimate and cordial. The author remembers visiting them in his company to look at their paintings, drawings and other curiosities. But in the aftermath of El Arish he committed an error, out of cupidity, and lost the trust of the French. The author notes a rumour that this happened on the instigation of Murad Bey, who wanted revenge for al-Sadat's criticism of his preparations for the defence of Egypt. He fell out of favour with the French, who imprisoned him several times. On the other hand, this treatment ensured him a favourable reception by the Ottomans. During the first years of Muhammad 'Ali's reign, his influence was overshadowed by that of 'Umar Makram, the *naqib al-ashraf*. However, after 'Umar Makram had been exiled to Damietta, al-Sadat succeeded in gaining his post as *naqib al-ashraf* as well. The author takes care to relate, with evident approval, how Muhammad 'Ali handled the situation after al-Sadat's

[1] IV, 40; 12.

[2] IV, 68, 93ff, 98.

[3] IV, 42, 127ff.

[4] III, 327, 329, IV 32, 41.

[5] IV, 124.

[6] IV, 239.

[7] In MS Aja'ib IV, 232 (in 1814–15) a poem by al-'Attar is introduced with the words 'his [i.e. the deceased treated in the necrology] best, most nearly perfect pupil, our master the learned, our friend the savant, now without peer in philosophy, whose advice is sought in literature, master of a marvellous style and of verses like flowers of spring, sheikh Hasan al-'Attar'. Moreh, 'al-Jabarti's Method', p. 357, notes that al-'Attar criticized al-Jabarti severely in his private copy of the MS Aja'ib in marginal notes on some of the biographies. Moreh (in: The Egyptian Scholar Hassan al-'Attar etc) explores these comments, but apparently they do not touch on the contents of the Aja'ib.

[8] IV, 160–5, 185–97.

[9] I, 8.

[10] IV, 80, 123.

[11] IV, 18, 19, 96, 98.

[12] IV, 185.

[13] IV, 187, 188.

[14] This in contrast to the story told in the MS Aja'ib III, 40ff.

[15] IV, 191.

[16] Ayalon, 'al-Jabarti and his Background', p. 229.

VI

IN SEARCH OF THE TRUE
POLITICAL POSITION
OF THE 'ULAMA

29 The purposes of al-Jabarti's chronicles

The four volumes of the MS Aja'ib in the Bulaq edition are the out-come of nearly twenty years of writing, rewriting and expanding of the original drafts of 1798. However, each of the intermediate ver-sions was written with a definite purpose. Each contains a clear mes-sage, which, with the exception of the one represented by volume IV of the MS Aja'ib, was intended to influence the current political situation in Egypt.

The first, represented by the MS Mudda, was found to be two drafts, termed the rough and the second draft, of a chronicle which had the nature of preliminary reports on the question of how the leading shaykhs of the 'ulama should handle their collaboration with the new French masters. They propounded the view that it was essential to pre-serve the unity of the Muslim community, and especially unity among the leading shaykhs of the 'ulama. It further intended to show that by accepting formal participation in the diwans set up by the French, al-Sharqawi and the other leading shaykhs had seriously weakened their bargaining position and, as a consequence, jeopardized the future of the Muslim community of Egypt. These shaykhs, it was argued, ought to have realized that the French could not be trusted to respect the religious foundations of this community. To the author the position taken by the shaykh al-Sadat – keeping clear of any formal ties with the new masters but keeping the lines of communication open – presented both the proper and the most intelligent way of preserving the influ-ence of the shaykhs and the well-being of the Muslim community.

The evidence suggests that the author had been inspired and, at least in the case of the second draft, probably authorized by the shaykh al-Sadat to write a history of Egypt during the first seven months of the French occupation. Muhammad Shams al-Din, shaykh al-Sadat and shaykh of the al-Husayni shrine, did not join the French diwans, but neither did he go into exile with the emirs, as the *naqib al-ashraf* 'Umar Makram did. Instead, he apparently chose an intermediate position, staying unattached to the rulers, but keeping the lines of communication open with the new masters. The two drafts of the MS Mudda attempt to vindicate the wisdom of this stand. For this reason, the audience, real or prospective, of both should be found among the 'ulama and their leading shaykhs. The fact that the corrections of the second draft tend to sharpen the arguments put forward in the first testifies to the existence of an ongoing debate among the 'ulama on how to act in the new situation created by the French occupation.

This debate among the 'ulama seems to have been sparked by the insurrection in Cairo in October 1798, most probably under the impact of the split among the shaykhs in this affair. The split afforded the Cairene mob the moral leadership it lacked. To the authors of the MS Mudda the insurrection was a fatal mistake, which killed a lot of people, desecrated the mosque of al-Azhar and destroyed parts of the city of Cairo. It also changed the situation of both the shaykhs and the French for the worse. The evidence of the text itself points to the first drafts, now lost, of the MS Mudda being written some time in October–November 1798, and the rough draft, i.e. the MS Mudda without additions and corrections, coming about in November 1798, the second draft not later than January 1799. The differences between the rough draft and the second draft indicate that al-Sadat and al-Jabarti were on the defensive. The advocates of a more formal collaboration with the French were getting the upper hand. The time of writing of the MS Mudda is confirmed by the evidence of the affinity between this text and the wording of the Ottoman *firman* of September 1798. Actually, the line taken in the MS Mudda closely followed the arguments of this *firman*. The stand taken by the author of the MS Mudda and his patron represent the point of view of the Ottoman government.

The next version of al-Jabarti's chronicle, the MS Mazhar, was finished in December 1801, in a completely different situation. The combined forces of the British expeditionary army and the Ottomans under the vizier Yusuf Zia Pasha had defeated the French. The MS Mazhar is supposed to have been presented to the Ottoman vizier some time in late 1801. The MS Mazhar seems to have been a memorandum to the returning Ottomans with the purpose of impressing upon them the task that lay before them after the evacuation of the French: to restore the safety and prosperity of the Muslim community of Egypt, by just rule on the basis of the *shari'a*. The idea behind this new and much expanded version was to demonstrate to the Ottoman sultan and his deputies that the leading shaykhs of the 'ulama supported them and that the shaykhs, and not the old partners, the emirs, were eminently suited as the future counsellors of Ottoman rule in Egypt. The shaykhs had proved their steadfastness as representatives of the Muslim community. Under the rule of Bonaparte and Kléber they had cooperated with the infidel French only when strictly necessary. On the other hand, when the French under Menou finally got around to understanding that a Muslim community like Egypt had to be ruled in close cooperation with the leaders of this community and on the basis of the precepts and laws contained in the *shari'a*, the shaykhs had proved able to control and direct things to the benefit of both. The MS Mazhar is a vindication of the necessity for the new Ottoman rulers to base their presence in Egypt on the advice and assistance of the leading shaykhs of the 'ulama. The MS Mazhar represents a conscious choice on the part of the author to back the Ottomans not from a position of weakness but from one of strength. In November 1801 the vizier had been defeated in his attempt to eliminate the emirs and would have been in need of support.

As the Ottomans were Muslims, the line of argument presented in the MS Mazhar has a close and logical affinity to the views propounded in the drafts of the MS Mudda on behalf of the shaykh al-Sadat and his intermediate position on the question of cooperation with the rulers, but with the important amplification that if the rulers confined themselves to backing the Muslim community and the *shari'a*, such cooperation might involve the 'ulama in a more formal role as the practical administrators of the policies of the ruler.

The shaykh al-Sadat still figured prominently, and favourably, in the narrative of the MS Mazhar, but his role as the author's spiritual mentor seems to have been shared with the poet and grammarian al-'Attar, to whom the idea of utilizing the MS Mudda drafts in a memorandum to the new rulers should probably be attributed. At least he seems to have supplied much of the poetry and literary expertise, and perhaps even the basic interpretation of events, of this version.

Judging from the praise lavished on the Ottoman vizier Yusuf Pasha in the preface and the deletion of the more vulgar items of information, the audience of this new version is generally assumed to be this vizier and his entourage in late 1801. It should be noted, however, that a similar situation existed in January 1800, after the convention of El Arish. It should be kept in mind that part of the MS Mazhar may have been written earlier, i.e. in late 1799 or early 1800, with the same purpose.

However, whether the MS Mazhar was handed over in 1800 or 1801, it is still difficult to see a relatively low-ranking shaykh such as al-Jabarti doing it on his own, and in 1800 his friend al-'Attar, too, did not seem to have had a standing in Cairene society which would have allowed him to represent any section of the 'ulama. Both seem to have been in need of patronage. For this reason al-Sadat should still be considered the patron of this new version of al-Jabarti's chronicle.

The fact that the author of the MS Mazhar made a serious effort to present the 'ulama as a united group indicates that the shaykh al-Sadat and his associates now found it opportune to play down or completely forget the debates of 1798–9 on the political position of the shaykhs of the 'ulama. Whether this picture of unity among the 'ulama was the genuine outcome of this debate from 1799–1801 within the 'ulama group, or just an attempt to gloss over any difference of opinion in the difficult situation presented by the arrival of the Ottomans, we do not know. However, the existence of another memorandum to the vizier by the opponent of al-Sadat within the 'ulama, al-Sharqawi, and the continuing animosity in the MS Mazhar towards this shaykh suggest that no agreement had been reached and that the split still existed. Each group apparently tried to present itself as the worthy representatives of a united group of 'ulama. But the stress put on unity in the MS Mazhar may also stem from the fact that the return of the Ottomans also entailed the return from exile of important leaders among the Muslim community, especially the *naqib al-ashraf*, 'Umar Makram. Presenting the actual state of affairs, laying open the differences which had existed and perhaps still existed in 1801 on how to handle the task of mediating between the rulers and the people of Egypt, would have made it easy for the Ottomans and others to get around the leading shaykhs.

The years after 1801 did not bring peace to Egypt. On the contrary, they witnessed a long and desperate fight for power between the Ottoman governors, the Ottoman army in Egypt and its Albanian troops under Tahir Pasha and Muhammad 'Ali, the emirs and the British expeditionary force supporting the interests of the emirs. Al-Jabarti or his patron now decided to transform his history of the French occupation into a new and very much expanded version, the MS Aja'ib. The existence of some pieces of text on the history of the emirs in the eighteenth century from the hand of his friend al-Khashshab and the evidence of affinity between these texts and the MS Aja'ib suggest that such work – or at least the idea of seeing things in a longer perspective – had already taken shape in the circle around al-Sadat in early 1801.

However, to state the purpose of the MS Aja'ib presents some difficulties. The printed version, the Bulaq edition, actually represents at least two stages in the author's work: the first three volumes, published in 1805–6; and the fourth volume, the integration of which may have entailed some changes and additions to the first three volumes.

There is sufficient reason to believe that when the author set out to turn the MS Mazhar into the three-volume edition some time between 1801 and 1805, his purpose was to present his arguments, based on the evidence of the history of man from the earliest times,

In search of the true Political Position of the 'Ulama

for a specific theory of Islamic government. The composition of the first two volumes seems to have been arranged according to this theory. The fact that the final pages of volume III are devoted to the description of how the shaykhs of the 'ulama took an active and important part in, and legitimized the appointment of, Muhammad 'Ali as Ottoman governor of Egypt in 1805, indicates the purpose of the MS Aja'ib of 1805. The intention seems to be to impress upon the reader that a ruler should rely on the 'ulama for advice and counsel, and also that the shaykhs should stay out of the political spotlight to avoid the corruption this invariably entails. The author pins his hopes on Muhammad 'Ali as a ruler who will be able to follow these precepts, and the purpose of the MS Aja'ib in the 1805 version was to furnish the 'ulama and its leading shaykhs – and perhaps Muhammad 'Ali himself and his entourage – with the necessary arguments to sustain their position. Like the MS Mazhar, the MS Aja'ib was intended for educated readers, but while the MS Mazhar was directed at the Ottoman vizier and his entourage, the MS Aja'ib seems to be meant for Egyptians – not for the local ruling elite, Muhammad 'Ali and his entourage (who would need a translation into Turkish), but those who remained of the emirs and, especially, the Egyptian 'ulama.

The shaykh al-Sadat still figures prominently and favourably in the narrative, a fact which suggests that this shaykh was meant to furnish an example of how a leading shaykh of the 'ulama ought to act. This would suggest that the author was still working under his patronage.

The preliminary survey of the arrangement of the material and the author's attitudes in volume IV suggests that this volume should be seen as two fairly distinct parts, one covering the period from 1221/1806–7 to 1230/1814–15, the other covering that from 1231/1815–16 to the end, i.e. 1236/1820–1. As promised at the end of volume III, the author set out to write a fourth volume arranged according to the already established pattern. It is suggested that the original version of this part of the text of volume IV followed the general trend outlined in volumes I–III, presenting Muhammad 'Ali as the just ruler, listening to the advice and counsel of the right shaykhs, and that the shaykh al-Sadat was cast in the role of the supreme example of such a shaykh. By implication this version of volume IV must have been written more or less continuously in the years after 1806, which would indicate some sort of draft. The evidence suggests that such a draft was revised in 1230/1814–15 under the influence of the author's general disillusionment with the new ruler, Muhammad 'Ali. The opening paragraph on the astronomical signs indicating 'stability of the ruler's dynasty and hardships for his subjects' may be interpreted as an allusion to Muhammad 'Ali, and as such it would signify a summary of the author's new attitude to events at this date. This revision of the text in 1230 probably entailed the insertion of the very favourable necrology on the emir al-Alfi and a very critical appraisal of the life of the shaykh al-Sadat. The revision may also have entailed some changes to the first three volumes. This may account for some of the discrepancies in the author's attitude to Muhammad 'Ali in the last part of volume III.

In 1230/1814–15, having revised his draft for the fourth volume (and having made some changes in its foundation, the first three volumes from 1805), the author seems to have carried on working on the fourth volume, but now in a quite different mood. The opening paragraph for the year 1231/1815–16 suggests a new beginning, a new political framework, with Muhammad 'Ali as the 'ruler and master' of Egypt. But the yearly repetition of this feature, the steady decline in the level of information and the disappearance of necrologies suggest that this second part represents an unfinished continuation, which the author never got around to revising.

However, the fourth volume was probably never put in circulation and used to influence current affairs in Egypt. Nevertheless, the authorities knew of its existence and tried to lay their hands on it because of its very critical attitude to Muhammad 'Ali. Apparently, the attitude of al-Jabarti seems to have been shared by others.

It is evident that in one way or another the purposes of al-Jabarti's chronicles involved the 'ulama and their leading shaykhs. The chronicles of al-Jabarti represent a more or less continuous search for the true position of the 'ulama in the shifting political landscape of Egypt in the decades around 1800. The two MS Mudda drafts tried to persuade some of these shaykhs to change the way they collaborated with the French. The MS Mazhar supported the new Ottoman governor and attempted to convince him of the necessity of taking the shaykhs into his confidence. The first version of the MS Aja'ib (1805–6) furnished the shaykhs of the 'ulama and any others who cared to listen with a fully reasoned theory of government and the historical evidence to support it, while at the same time pointing to Muhammad 'Ali as the new legitimate ruler. The MS Aja'ib of 1805–6 constitutes a fully-fledged political programme for the future government of Egypt. Only the fourth volume seems to fall outside this pattern, as the sad epilogue of a man who has seen all his hopes and ideas coming to nothing.

The different versions of al-Jabarti's historical works attest to the fact that throughout this period he was actively and continuously trying to influence developments in Egypt on behalf of his patron, the shaykh al-Sadat. But they also show that in this respect he was sorely disappointed. His ideas and hopes met only scant response. His patron, the good-natured al-Sadat of the MS Mudda, turned into a stingy old man, and as time was running out and he revised his draft in 1230 al-Jabarti did not look to the future, but to the past, finding his last hero, the emir al-Alfi, among those already dead.

30 The shifting opinions and values of the chronicles

The shifting opinions and values expressed in the chronicles of al-Jabarti should be evaluated in the light of the purposes with which they were written. As these purposes represent attempts to define the true position of the 'ulama at various times in the political turmoil of Egypt following the French invasion in 1798, the opinions and values connected with the 'ulama and its leading shaykhs would obviously constitute the basic point of view of the chronicles.

THE 'ULAMA AND THEIR LEADING SHAYKHS

The analysis reveals a fair consistency in the basic tenets of al-Jabarti's thinking on the position of the 'ulama. From the first drafts in 1798 he propounds the opinion that the 'ulama constitute the pivotal centre of the Muslim community, and that the ideal *'alim* should concentrate on acquiring knowledge and living by its guidance. If and when the Muslim community or its rulers need them, they should be readily accessible for consultation and advice. However, they should keep clear of any formal attachment, as this would only lead to corruption of their thinking and counsel. This is what the MS Mudda tried to tell the 'ulama and their leading shaykhs. The MS Mazhar tried to persuade the new Ottoman rulers that the Egyptian 'ulama were their obvious future partners because they had proved themselves able to adhere to these principles. The MS Aja'ib of 1805 tried to persuade its readers among the Egyptian ruling elite and the 'ulama of the truth of this programme by providing both a reasoned theory and the necessary historical and biographical evidence to support it.

The consistency of these opinions on the duties of the members of his own class, the 'ulama, suggests that they represent part of the fundamental values of the author – or at least those of his patron, al-Sadat. But the changing events of the time made him shift his emphasis.

In the drafts of the MS Mudda the focus is clearly on the pitfalls of accepting a formal attachment to the ruler. Al-Sharqawi and the group of leading shaykhs agreed to work for the French on their diwans, and found themselves becoming mere tools in the hands of foreigners. At the critical point they did not have the necessary cohesion as a group to prevent a split in the ranks of the 'ulama, which had furnished the mob with the leadership it lacked. Maintaining the

emirs and the Ottomans – presented a serious problem. On one hand, they represented tradition and as such commanded the respect and veneration due to all traditional rulers. On the other, they were seen as the cause of much of the trouble in Egypt, as in the case of the emirs, or the representatives of a central power with dubious intentions, as in the case of the Ottomans.

In the MS Mudda the emirs are cast as the main culprits, together with the French. They have lost their ability to defend the country and have been squandering the riches of the country in their petty power games. Only the nostalgia of the ageing al-Jabarti turns the emirs – or at least one of them, al-Alfi – into worthy representatives of the ideal ruler.

The Ottomans do not figure largely in the MS Mudda. They are acknowledged as the formal masters of Egypt, the pasha's part in the defence of Cairo is duly noted and the style of their letters highly praised – but, significantly, not quoted! In the debate between the leading shaykhs on how to handle the French challenge, the representatives of the central government in Istanbul do not appear to be of any consequence, but this attitude toward the Ottoman government can be explained by the fact that the MS Mudda actually represents the central government's point of view, expressed by people who chose to act as its clients. Neither the Ottoman government's *firman* nor the political situation in Cairo in the autumn of 1798 suggested a more clear-cut pro-Ottoman stand. The author and his patron had to tread carefully.

In the MS Mazhar the situation and the purpose are more or less the opposite. Now the author and his patron are consciously and openly backing the Ottomans. A show of affection and trust in the sovereign and his representative, the vizier, and a more judicious and balanced judgement of the local emirs seems to be appropriate, to prove the suitability of the 'ulama for this task. Like the Ottoman sultan and his vizier, the emirs represent the traditional Muslim leaders, and as such should command at least some respect. Accordingly, the dynasty and the vizier receive positive treatment in the preface and introduction. One of the main themes of the Ottoman *firman* of 1798, that of the French ruses, is incorporated and substantiated. Letters from the vizier are quoted, while the vicious personal attacks on the conduct of Murad and Ibrahim Bey are deleted or moved to the necrologies. It is interesting to note that a more moderate opinion of Murad Bey can be detected from June 1801 in the writings of al-Khashshab, a friend of al-Jabarti's and another client of al-Sadat.

The 'ulama seem to have held back in the quickly shifting political situation after 1801, until in 1805 they finally decided to throw in their lot with Muhammad 'Ali against the emirs and the incumbent Ottoman governor. The changes made in the part of the MS Aja'ib that covers the MS Mudda do, as would be expected in this new situation, indicate a change in the author's evaluation both of the Ottomans and the emirs. As for the Ottomans, the fact that Egypt is the territory of the sultan is still stressed, but for obvious reasons they are no longer presented as the saviours of Egypt. Actually the author is now prepared to evaluate the record of the Ottoman dynasty in a more realistic way. As for the emirs, the changes suggest a reversal of the caustic attacks in the MS Mudda. Apparently, the author's purpose in the MS Aja'ib did not consider the traditional rulers of Egypt important enough to merit a reappraisal of their actions before and during the initial phases of the French occupation. In the description of events in the following years the military exploits and political manoeuvres of the emirs continue to be faithfully recorded, but with a conspicuous lack of enthusiasm. The author simply seems to have lost interest.

This should be seen in contrast to the view propounded in the continuation in volume IV. The author's dislike of the new governor, Muhammad 'Ali, made him see the emirs in a more positive light, especially al-Alfi, whose premature death he deplores. The pronouncements of al-Alfi, quoted in his necrology, show us a man with the views and opinions that fit the ideal ruler in the preface and introduction perfectly. But this does not seem to affect the position of the Ottomans in the mind of the author. Again, this should most probably be attributed to the nostalgia of the ageing author. By 1815, the emirs had long since been eliminated as a political force in Egypt.

THE FRENCH

While the power and influence of the emirs had been seriously weakened, if not fatally broken, by the French invasion in 1798, the French were very much in charge during the three years of occupation. The description of their actions is the core of the text of the chronicles of al-Jabarti. But the analysis of the composition and comments of the different versions has clearly demonstrated that differences in the way they are presented stem from the difference in the purposes of the texts.

In the two drafts of the MS Mudda the author and his patron are at pains to persuade the leading shaykhs of the 'ulama, the group around al-Sharqawi, that they have taken the wrong path when they accepted a formal attachment to the French. The French were trying to lure them into their fold in order to pacify them and control their power and influence over the Muslim community of Egypt. The leading shaykhs ought to have seen this if they had interpreted the behaviour of the French correctly. Accordingly, this behaviour is described in the most drastic terms: in his comments on the French proclamation the author insists on showing that, far from being Muslims, or people basing their actions on the firm principles of reason, the French simply did not have any principles at all. And as if this is not enough, pieces of background on the stupidities and atrocities of the revolution in France are supplied. Examples of their disgusting behaviour are freely distributed throughout the text. However, as the drafts of the MS Mudda are part of a debate on how to cooperate with these people, the author also has to demonstrate that the relationship between the Muslim community and the French is an open one, with the possibility of a compromise, if the leading shaykhs could handle the situation correctly. Accordingly, the French are shown to be hesitant to suppress the insurrection in October 1798, while their scientific endeavours in the Institute are handled as curiosities.

In 1801, when the MS Mazhar was written, the French were gone and this debate was no longer relevant. Now it was only necessary to present the French in more conventional Muslim terms, as cursed infidels who tried to set up stratagems, which fooled nobody in the Muslim community. Accordingly, the comments on the proclamation were revised, but not changed; the examples of the more disgusting habits of the French, including their work at the Institute, were deleted; and the suppression of the revolt in October was shown to be instant and brutal. Only when the French, under Menou, undertook to establish a diwan consisting entirely of Muslims, and agreed to rule the country on Muslim terms, are they treated with some respect.

In the Aja'ib of 1805–6 the French occupation was a thing of the past, and the author and his patron had other things on their minds. They were now trying to convince the 'ulama and their leading shaykhs of the truth of a theory of government which saw the 'ulama as the ultimate arbiters of Muslim society and made them responsible for the maintenance of the *shari'a*. To sustain this argument, the French were now presented as people whose stated intention of acting as if they were Muslims should be taken seriously. In the MS Aja'ib of 1805, they are actually portrayed as legitimate rulers, as long as they stuck to their duty to be the enforcers of the *shari'a*. The argument further entailed a reappraisal of their many practical, technical and scientific innovations. These aspects of French behaviour were no longer seen as mere curiosities, but something that should be accepted by any ruler.

For natural reasons, the French do not figure as more than mere names in the necrologies of volume IV. They had ceased to be as a power with serious ambitions in the eastern Mediterranean, and their occupation of Egypt was now nearly fifteen years previously. Since then there had been so many other events of equal moment that the author had no need to enlarge upon their actions when evaluating the lives of his contemporaries. The French occupation had been reduced to a distant episode in the recent history of Egypt. The occupation had become 'the time of the French'.

The relation between the purposes and the opinions and values of the chronicles of al-Jabarti implies a fairly consistent basic outlook on the part of the author and his patron, the shaykh al-Sadat, on the duties of the 'ulama. The basic ideal seems to be the humble 'alim, living in seclusion and in accordance with the tenets and precepts of his faith, as the ultimate arbiter of Muslim society. However, the way this ideal is put into practice depends on the circumstances. Leaving seclusion will always pose a serious danger to the morals of the 'ulama, and especially their leading shaykhs. This outlook does not imply a similar consistency in the opinion of other participants, not even of rivals among the leading 'ulama. The author's opinions of the actions and merits of both these and of the traditional rulers, the emirs and the Ottomans, as well as the new masters, the French, may vary according to circumstance. The author and his patron seem to have kept an open mind on these people. What really seems to matter is the position they afford the 'ulama in society. The chronicles represent a search for the true political position of the 'ulama. As the focus of this search shifts, so does the evaluation of the rulers, both the traditional and the new.

31 The chronicles of al-Jabarti as sources for the history of Egypt in the eighteenth and nineteenth centuries

The shifting opinions and values of the chronicles imply that the information they provide can be used only in the light of their purposes and the point of focus these purposes entails. The author is prepared not only to change his comments but also to select his facts to further these purposes. A few examples may illustrate this point.

Al-Jabarti's favourable comments in the MS Mudda on the French army's ability to operate with cohesion and precision are obviously presented as background, and as part of his argument, in his heated condemnation of the personal qualities of the emirs and their *mamluks* as the people primarily responsible for the defence of Egypt. Western historians, steeped in the successes of the French armies during the Revolutionary and Napoleonic wars, have tended to see this as an indication that even an Egyptian *'alim* was able to perceive the French military supcriority. But in doing so they overlook the fact that this statement is mainly intended to vilify the real culprits in al-Jabarti's narrative of the battle: the emirs. The emirs, Murad and Ibrahim, have fared badly in the history of Egypt because of this, in spite of the fact that their actions, i.e. retreat to the south and cast in order to wear out the enemy, seem both sensible and in complete accordance with Egyptian experience in the centuries before 1798. Even the emirs' lack of united leadership and central command, noted by historians as their main weakness (although, significantly, not by al-Jabarti!) turn out to be an advantage in this crisis, forcing the French to divide their attention and military resources. Seen in this perspective, the battle of Imbaba, the famous battle of the Pyramids to the French, takes on the aspect of a token, mock battle, set up by the two emirs for the benefit of the people in Cairo and, perhaps, Istanbul and as a measure to gain time for setting up the real defences in the south and east with the help of beduin tribes and Ottoman forces. For the narrator of MS Mudda, the thought of defending Egypt in this way and with the help of the treacherous beduin tribes was clearly not opportune. Al-Jabarti himself may have been more understanding, but for the sake of the argument he is constructing in the MS Mudda, he cannot allow his narrator to express such thoughts.

This point should encompass even the small, insignificant items of information in al-Jabarti's text. The MS Mudda, although not such a mine of information on the everyday life of Egyptians as the MS Mazhar and MS Aja'ib, does contain information on such seemingly insignificant things as the prices of specific goods,[1] so valuable to the social history of the city of Cairo. Such items should be treated with caution, considering the fact that the thorough dislocation of the community, in the face of the French challenge constitutes a part of al-Jabarti's argument.

But the real point of this argument would be that the attitudes to the French expressed in the MS Mudda cannot be used as an indication of attitudes to Western thought and technology in the Muslim community in Egypt around 1800. They are part of a debate on a much more important issue: the question of who should be the intermediaries between the sultan in far-away Istanbul and the people, and as such the real rulers of Egypt, in the power vacuum which was opening up after the retreat of the emirs. The merits, or lack of merits, of Western thought, organization and technology were not the issue, but the means by which opponents in the new struggle for power in Cairo tried to obtain the most influential position. The attitudes to Western ideas were twisted to serve this purpose. Consequently, the heated rejection (or the opposite) of such Western innovations expressed in the chronicles should not be taken as a rejection in principle (although they may be expressed as such). They would change when the real issue had been clarified, without great difficulty to the consciences of the people involved.

The real value of the MS Mudda as a source for the history of Egypt seems to be that it attests to the fact that an 'alim connected with al-Azhar, some time in late 1798 or early 1799, felt the urgent need to communicate, at length and in detail, clear warnings to the leading shaykhs of the 'ulama. Collaboration and disunity posed grave dangers to their duties as mediators between the rulers and the people in order to protect the Muslim community in the crisis created by the French invasion. The MS Mudda is a contribution to a heated debate in the Muslim community of Cairo in the autumn of 1798 on how to handle the challenge posed by the French invasion. It is as a source for this debate that the MS Mudda becomes important.

The MS Mazhar does not figure prominently as a source for the history of Egypt during the French occupation. The fact that Moreh saw it as an attempt on the part of the author to clear his name in the eyes of the Ottomans has not favoured the use of this text. The supposedly apologetic nature and the staunchly Muslim stand of this version has not appealed to historians of the period. The MS Aja'ib version has been preferred.[2]

This position is untenable. In the first place, the MS Mazhar should be acknowledged as the primary source for the period from January 1799 to December 1801 among the chronicles of al-Jabarti. The changes made in the MS Mudda in order to make this text fit the MS Mazhar suggest that it is not a very reliable source. However, as the MS Aja'ib, as we have seen, relies on the MS Mazhar in much the same way as the MS Mazhar relies on the MS Mudda, the MS Aja'ib can never replace the MS Mazhar for the history of this period – or the MS Mudda for the preceding one, for that matter.

An example may illustrate this point. There is evidence of a great and general patriotic sentiment in Cairo on the eve of the battle of Imbaba in both the MSS Mazhar and Aja'ib. In the MS Mudda there is no recollection on the part of the author of such things. Working on the MS Mudda several months later, he only remembered the confusion and lack of proper leadership.[3] If the story of the events in Cairo on the eve of the battle should be written on the basis of al-Jabarti's story alone and in strict accordance with a methodological evaluation of his material, the conclusion would be that there was no trace of patriotic fervour in Cairo, just general confusion!

However, although very much influenced by the purpose of its author, the MS Mazhar is still a valuable source for understanding the views and opinions in Cairo at the time of writing, i.e. December 1801. The MS Mazhar testifies to the fact that al-Jabarti had a dream of unity, of seeing the Muslim community rise to the challenge in unity, faith and unselfish sacrifice. In December 1798 in the MS Mudda he lamented the lack of unity and courage in the Egyptian army at the battle of Imbaba. But the dream remained, and was strong enough to make him replace fact with fiction, when he set out to support the Ottomans in 1801. He wanted to present his new masters with a series of armed encounters between the French and the Muslim community of Cairo, in which the Muslims, although losing all of them, showed exactly this unity and faith: the battle of Imbaba already mentioned; the insurrection in October 1798 (in which he deleted all comments on the lack of unity); and finally the siege of Cairo after the failure of the convention of El Arish in March and April 1800.

As for this last incident, the MS Mazhar is the primary source. It is not possible to prove that this, too, has been tampered with to fit it into the author's idea of unity. But al-Jabarti's way of presenting the story is suggestive: after the initial confusion, everybody seems prepared to join the defence of the city: the common people,[4] the emirs 'Uthman Khatkhuda, Hasan Bey al-Jiddawi, Muhammad Bey al-Alfi, the merchants and affluent people under the leadership of Ahmad al-Mahruqi all played their part.[5] To al-Jabarti most of the deplorable incidents in the city, the looting and unlawful killings, originated with a certain Maghribi. Murad Bey remained calm and peaceful in the mountains, waiting for new developments.[6] This state of affairs continued until the situation became untenable and an armistice was arranged. To al-Jabarti this was the sensible thing to do. But to his disgust, the above-mentioned Maghribi stirred up the people against the shaykhs, accusing them of weakness, and the armistice came to nothing. Instead the French stormed, looted and burned Bulaq. At last, after '37 days filled with battles, anxiety, upheaval, dissolution, agitation, destruction of houses, disasters, killing of people, plundering of possessions, the dominion of the wicked and degradation of the noble— especially the things the French afterwards inflicted on the people'[7] the siege came to an end. The story resembles earlier incidents (the insurrection in October 1798) in concentrating the blame on certain named individuals, in this case the Maghribi (and on the French, of course), while stressing the good behaviour of the members of the local Muslim community, especially the leaders of society. The MS Mazhar should be used as the primary source for these events, but only with great care and keeping in mind that the author was prepared to change his story to make it fit his agenda, which was to emphasize Muslim unity.

However, these arguments – and the very existence of the MS Mazhar – prove that such dreams of unity, faith and sacrifice (and a willingness to find convenient culprits) were current in the circles in which al-Jabarti moved in Cairo, the 'ulama and their shaykhs, on the eve of the French occupation. Used in this way, it is apparent that the MS Mazhar could be a most valuable source, providing insights into political ideals and values current among the Egyptian 'ulama at the beginning of the nineteenth century.

But it is important to remember that we have no way of determining how important this idea of unity was in 1801, or whether its importance changed with time. We only know that the ideals and values propounded in the MS Mazhar were not the only ones. It is only natural to suppose that the debate suggested by the existence of the MS Mudda went on and developed, with shifting frontiers and focus. But it would be natural, too, to see the idea of Muslim unity propounded in the MS Mazhar as a result of the situation in 1801: the country was being liberated by outside forces, Muslim and British, but even if the Ottoman forces could be seen as natural allies, there would be an urge to assert the importance of the local contribution to the outcome. There would be a strong motive to see the armed encounters during the occupation as more decisive and important than they were, and conducted in a spirit of more unity and faith than was

In search of the true Political Position of the 'Ulama

actually the case. No doubt such a view of past events would constitute an important part of a political platform for the leading shaykhs
in the new situation created by the French evacuation.

The MS Aja'ib has been the version most favoured by scholars
working on the history of Egypt in the eighteenth and nineteenth centuries. The exact chronology of its annalistic framework, its wealth of
detail and generally balanced evaluation of the French have tempted
many to see it as al-Jabarti's *chronique sincère* and use it as a basis for the
reconstruction of the complicated situation in Egypt in these years.
However, even though conclusions concerning the possibilities of the
MS Aja'ib as a source for the history of Egypt can only be provisional,
some important points should be stressed.

First, although the MS Aja'ib covers the history of Egypt from
1689 to 1821, only the part covering the years from 1801, when the
MS Mazhar comes to an end, to 1821 should be acknowledged as a
primary source. This does not exclude the use of some of the information on events during the French occupation changed or added
in the MS Aja'ib. But such material should be carefully sifted in the
light of the general purpose of the MS Aja'ib. An example may illustrate this point. In volume III a string of new details are added to the
picture of the French settling in Cairo in 1798.[8] These details appear
seven years after they were supposed to have happened, and one of
them, the appointment of the shaykhs as the result of negotiation, is
so obviously in line with the picture of general harmony which the
author is now trying to convey that it cannot be trusted.

As for the material presented in volumes I and II, from 1689
to 1798, it is now considered to be mainly secondary to other sources, the nature of which is slowly but surely being revealed. It seems
that in spite of his profession to the contrary, al-Jabarti had access
to and used most of the existing histories for this period. It does
seem, though, that for the period after the 1750s when the so-called
Damudashi group of chronicles comes to an end, he had to manage
on his own or with material, which has not yet been identified. The
very uneven character of volume II, only occasionally expanding into
something that can be termed a coherent narrative, suggests that if it
existed, such material had the nature of reports.

The exception to this, of course, would be the necrologies,
which he added to those of Murtada al-Zabidi. These would include
those of his father and Ahmad al-Khalil al-Shami, Murtada himself,
Muradi and the emirs Humam b. Yusuf al-Hawwari and Hasan Bey
Ridwan. But this material should be used with care. The author has
some very pronounced and emphatic views on the duties of the 'ulama and of the emirs, and as suggested, necrologies of the more im-

portant of these tend to take on the role of examples, illustrating and supporting the author's general ideas. The necrology of the author's father Hasan may serve as a case in point: the learned scholar, always ready to teach or serve, but only when asked to do so and never to promote his own fortunes.

The purpose of the MS Aja'ib outlined on the basis of this analysis, on the other hand, suggests that the three-volume edition of 1805–6 would be an important (and rewarding!) source for the situation of the 'ulama group at this crucial moment in the history of Egypt. It seems to suggest that at this stage, the discussions on the duties of the 'ulama, glimpses of which have already been provided by the MS Mudda and the MS Mazhar, had produced a general theory of Islamic government, with the necessary historical background to support it. This theory included a very liberal and open-minded stance on the practical and scientific innovations of the West and even envisaged the possibility of a non-Muslim ruler, as long as the 'ulama were taken into his confidence and consulted.

---

[1] Pp. 48, 58, 76.

[2] Raymond, 'Egyptiens et Français au Caire', p.155 seems to acknowledge the fact that the MS Mazhar is the primary source for the period from January 1799 to December 1801, but generally prefers the *texte finale* of al-Jabarti, i.e. the MS Aja'ib, especially when it is confirmed by French sources (see pp. 156, 157 and *passim*).

[3] MS Mazhar, p. 44; MS Aja'ib III, 6; MS Mudda, p. 49. Raymond quotes the MS Aja'ib.

[4] MS Mazhar p. 247: 'All the inhabitants of Cairo began to be day and night either in the alleys – those were the ones who could not fight – or at the outskirts, behind the barricades – those were the brave ones who could do battle. Nobody slept at home except the sick, the cowards, and fearful people.'

[5] MS Mazhar, p. 247, *passim*.

[6] MS Mazhar, pp. 249, 451.

[7] MS Mazhar, p. 268.

[8] III, 11–13 (section 4).

32 The character of the debates in Cairo in the years around 1800

Egypt around 1800 was a country without printing presses, and public debates would leave only few traces. However, for the history of Egypt – and for the entire Muslim world for that matter – the character of debates among the intellectual elite, the 'ulama, in these years of change and turmoil would be quite important. The real value of the chronicles of al-Jabarti lies in the fact that they allow the reader a first-hand insight into the shifting focus of the debates and discussions among the 'ulama of Cairo in the decades around 1800.

The chronicles allow us to study the debates and discussions in Cairo in four periods of time: in the autumn and winter of 1798; in late 1801; in 1805; and around 1815. On the basis of the analysis presented above only the first and, to a certain degree, the second can be described in some detail. A more thorough study of the texts of the MS Mazhar and the MS Aja'ib, and especially of the autographs of the author of these two versions, with their many additions and corrections, would probably provide more detailed information on the last two periods.

The chronicles testify to the fact that such debates actually took place. This may sound trivial, but the fact that it is possible to prove that the 'ulama were actually engaged in a debate, involving the status and duties of the religious and intellectual leaders and its repercussions on political life of Egypt, is important for the evaluation of the contributions of this group to the history of the Middle East. It suggests that the 'ulama did not simply try to pursue their basic economic and social interests, but were fully aware of the repercussions of such activity on their ideals. Like all human beings they seem to have been able to adapt ideologically to shifting political situations. The fact that such accommodation sparked off a heated debate, and that this debate did not significantly shake their basic position on the duties of the 'ulama – at least among the participants whose views we know – shows that they were men of some morals, actively and sincerely committed to the future of Muslim society.

It should be kept in mind, however, that the information provided by the chronicles of al-Jabarti only allows us to study these debates during short periods of time and on specific, though important, topics and from one side only, although this last point is moderated by the fact that the argument of one side allows us to study, at least to a certain degree, the argument of the other. However, the existence and character of this other side have been corroborated by the interpretation of the last two pages of al-Sharqawi's short chronicle. However, the chronicles of al-Jabarti do not allow us to see what was discussed before or between the different versions, and we can see only with some difficulty how they relate to the general intellectual situation of the period.

THE AUTUMN AND WINTER OF 1798

The analysis suggested that a heated debate was going on in the Muslim community of Cairo in the autumn and winter of 1798 as to how 'ulama and their leading shaykhs should handle the challenge posed by the French invasion. The main opponents seem to have been al-Sharqawi, the shaykh al-Azhar since 1793, who apparently favoured closer cooperation with the French, and Shams al-Din Muhammad, shaykh al-Sadat and shaykh of the al-Husayn mosque. From the treatment afforded other leading shaykhs in the texts, it seems fair to assume that the group around al-Sharqawi had the greater following among the leading 'ulama. But the evidence indicates that this group contained a variety of opinions on the main issue, and for this reason was more difficult to handle under the tensions and stresses created by the French actions and demands. Al-Mahdi, the secretary of the French diwans is generally treated with reverence and respect, while the shaykh al-Bakri seems to be taken to task for giving in too easily to French demands and accepting the post of *naqib al-ashraf* in the absence of 'Umar Makram. Although these differences may stem from the intention of the MS Mudda to lure away some of the members of this group, they do indicate differences in attitude. Some of these people were obviously more prepared than others to accommodate the French.

Outside these groups we have the 'ulama, who squarely rejected any sort of collaboration with the enemy. One group, under the leadership of the *naqib al-ashraf*, 'Umar Makram, chose to go into exile in Syria with Ibrahim Bey after the battle of Imbaba. Other shaykhs decided to stay in Cairo such as Badr al-Maqdisi and an unknown number of those executed by the French for complicity in the insurrection in October 1798. They seem to have bided their time, joining the fight against the French at the first opportunity.

The picture that emerges from the pages of the various drafts of the MS Mudda seems to be a familiar one. On one hand, we have the 'realists' (al-Sharqawi), who agree to cooperate, probably with vary-

In search of the true Political Position of the 'Ulama

ing degrees of enthusiasm (al-Mahdi, al-Bakri). On the other, we see the 'activists', who reject any cooperation with the invaders, divided into a group of *exilès* ('Umar Makram) and what could conveniently be termed the 'home front' (Badr al-Maqdisi). In this scheme of things the shaykh al-Sadat (and al-Jabarti) would represent a stand somewhere between the realists of the main body of leading shaykhs and the home-front activists. What made al-Sadat choose this position is never explained. We know that the French wanted him to become a member of their diwan, but somehow it did not happen. Instead, General Bonaparte seems to have made sure that he was consulted. Al-Sadat seems to have agreed to and accepted this informal arrangement.[1]

The Ottoman *firman* of September 1798 suggests that the Ottomans were very much part of the debates and discussions which took place in Cairo among the 'ulama in the autumn and winter of 1798. The *firman* seems to have been known to the author of the MS Mudda and his patron, and to have provided them with their main line of argument against the position of the realists of al-Sharqawi. The position of al-Sadat and al-Jabarti, staying clear of both the realists and the activists, should therefore be seen, not as an attempt to formulate an alternative to the realist position, but as a stand that followed the lead taken by the Ottoman government in Istanbul. Seen in this light, the position of al-Sadat and al-Jabarti may conveniently be termed 'loyalist'!

The first draft of the MS Mudda seems to have come into existence to defend this loyalist stand. We may assume that Al-Jabarti was asked to do the job by his patron because of his knowledge of the finer points of 'ulama tradition, based on his reputation as a biographer of former, eminent shaykhs. From the difference between the treatment of the realists and that of the activists we may infer that only the former was taken seriously. The first draft was probably written to meet the reproaches of the realists towards al-Sadat for trying to have the best of both worlds.

We are only able to speculate on the details of these reproaches, but judging from the fact that the first draft stresses the idealistic nature of the position of al-Sadat, it would be sensible to infer that al-Sadat had been accused of trying to protect his interests by asking a higher price for his cooperation. The episode of the shaykhs (i.e. al-Sharqawi and his realists) asking for their missing salaries is therefore taking tit for tat!

But why was this defence put into writing? The evidence indicates that al-Jabarti was fully aware of the dangers of such a thing, and was very careful in the handling of names in his draft. Unfortunately, the lack of solid knowledge of the role of the written word in the intellectual milieu in Cairo in the years around 1800 prevents us from having any definite ideas of how the author (and his mentor) expected their ideas to be transmitted, discussed and (hopefully) accepted. We do not know whether the draft of the MS Mudda was written for publication, and – even more seriously – we cannot know with any degree of certainty what publication actually implied in a society without printing presses. But from the nature of the additions which make up the second draft of the MS Mudda it is possible to infer that it was put into some sort of circulation, either through copies distributed to the right people or simply by being read aloud in 'ulama circles. The fact that al-Jabarti used it when he turned the MS Mazhar into the MS Aja'ib shows that the original autograph was still in his possession in 1805.

The short text provided by al-Sharqawi at the end of his history of Egypt must be treated with caution because of the discrepancy between its accepted date (late 1801) and the contents, which suggest a much earlier one. Further study into the full text is needed to clear up this difficulty. But taken as it stands the text is important, as it allows us to see the arguments of the realists directly. As such it enables us to confirm what was suggested by the interpretation of the MS Mudda versions: al Sharqawi and his group actually saw it as their duty to collaborate with the French in order to protect the people of Egypt. This position collapsed when the French did not keep their side of the bargain. But al-Sharqawi saw no reason to hide the fact that to him and his followers the French attitude and beliefs had made such a position quite feasible.

It was suggested that the last two pages of al-Sharqawi's text came into being as an apology for the position of the realists. The most straightforward answer to the question of why the MS Mudda came into being seems to be that the followers of al-Sadat, having chosen to follow the lead taken by the Ottoman government, wished to refute the arguments put forward by the realists. If this were so, it would also help us to get an idea of how these debates were conducted. Obviously some sort of written documentation was considered necessary. But the scarcity of copies would mean that the author would have to rely on his text being read by a few, key people, who would then relate it to others, first and foremost to the common 'ulama of Cairo and the clients of other leading shaykhs.

The timing may be significant, too. The evidence strongly suggests that the first drafts of the MS Mudda (and perhaps the text of al-Sharqawi, too) were written against the background of the insurrection in October 1798. This had crushed whatever influence the 'activist home front' had commanded, at least for the time being. In the MS Mudda it is more than intimated that the *exilès*, Ibrahim Bey and the 'ulama based in Gaza, had a hand in the insurrection. If this was so, their position, too, had been seriously damaged. This left the realists and al-Sadat. However, the realists had also been weakened by the insurrection, which had shown that they did not command a sufficiently strong position among the 'ulama, or the people for that matter, to prevent it. This would be the right moment for the group around al-Sadat – and for the Ottoman government he had chosen to side with – to make an attempt to get the upper hand in order to widen their basis of influence. The MS Mudda would represent al-Sadat's wish to go on record with a statement to the effect that the realists had taken the wrong path. The French were not to be trusted, at least not to such a degree that formal cooperation was possible.

The second draft of the MS Mudda should be seen as a reply, on behalf of al-Sadat and the loyalists, to open or implied criticism of the picture painted in the rough draft. This interpretation allows us to see which way the frontiers of the debate were moving. The additions indicate that the position of al-Sadat is on the defensive. His idealistic position has been questioned. It has apparently been hinted that he did not remain aloof out of any desire to save the traditional position of the 'ulama, but simply because he was too timid to risk a more open stand. The attitudes towards the future of the old rulers, the emirs, and towards the old rivals as advisers to the rulers, the Copts, seem to become more specific and definite. The new and more clear-cut position on the responsibility of the emirs suggests that the opposition, Shaykh al-Sharqawi and his realists, were on the verge of engaging in a debate on how Egypt should be ruled and defended in the future. The debate was obviously developing along familiar lines, as everybody now knew what ought to have been done, but it is nevertheless important as an indication of the mounting ambitions of the realists.

LATE 1801

We do not know what became of this debate after January 1799. But in late 1801, nearly two years later, al-Jabarti produced a new version, the MS Mazhar, with the assistance of the poet al-'Attar but probably still under the patronage of al-Sadat, this time with the purpose of supporting the returning Ottomans. In this version the 'ulama were presented as a united group of activists. The position of the leading shaykhs of the realist group towards the French was explained as a case of *force majeure*. They simply had to agree to join the diwans, and did their best to slow down or obstruct French initiatives.

This newfound unity among the 'ulama may have been the eventual outcome of the debate of 1798. But the most reasonable explanation seems to be that al-Sadat, as the loyal Ottoman subject, wanted to present himself as the obvious choice as leading adviser and supporter of the Ottomans at a time when they were under heavy pressure from the British to leave the emirs in charge of the province of Egypt. The Ottoman *firman* of 1798 seems to have provided the author with one of the main themes of the MS Mazhar. The traditionalism and safe conservatism of this memorandum to the returning Ottomans appear to have been provided by the Ottomans themselves, and this is corroborated by one of the other main themes of the MS Mazhar: the change in al-Sadat's position towards the French. In the summer of 1799 al-Sadat had clashed with Bonaparte on the question of how to treat the son of the Ottoman *qadi*. In 1800, after the second siege of Cairo, al-Sadat fell out with the French, and General Kléber and was severely punished on several occasions. This transformed al-Sadat into one of the 'activists', and in the MS Mazhar he is presented as one of the more conspicuous victims of French oppression. But in contradistinction to the 'realists', around al-Sharqawi, his hands were clean. The fact that the MS Mazhar attempts to include al-Sharqawi and the realists as activists at heart can hardly be explained by anything other than a wish to present a united front to the returning Ottomans, and perhaps the returning Egyptian *exilès*. There was, as we shall see, good reason for such a move. The reinstated *naqib al-ashraf*, 'Umar Makram, soon returned as the undisputed leader of the 'ulama.

Seen in this light the MS Mazhar, reflects ideas and conventions expected of the 'ulama by their eminent sovereign rather than the outcome of a continuation of their debate from 1798. Still, it is interesting to note that the author selects the picture of a fervently religious Muslim community united under the leadership of faithful 'ulama as the line of argument most fitting to convince the Ottomans of the usefulness of the latter as the proper advisers of the ruler. The idea of Muslim unity was apparently considered not only a traditional – and safe – way of ingratiating oneself with the ruler, but a powerful political platform from which to support the Ottoman government and to neutralize potential rivals, such as the returning Egyptian emirs and leading 'ulama and the former realists of al-Sharqawi (who, judging from the treatment they get, are not trusted any more than before).

The poetry of al-'Attar and others, included in the text, points to the existence of a patriotic fervour among the Egyptian subjects of the sultan of the Ottoman Empire. Considering the scorn with which the author treated such ideas in the MS Mudda, there seems to be no doubt that the activist position has gained in prestige and political usefulness.

Unfortunately it is not possible to date the text of the *Maqamat* of Hasan al-'Attar accurately, except for the fact that it clearly belongs to the period of the French occupation. Even so, it constitutes an important source of information for our understanding of the psychological situation of intellectuals on the fringe of upper class Cairo at this time. Al-'Attar's connection with al-Jabarti suggests that the ideas and arguments propounded in the chronicles of the latter were produced under the same conditions of patronage.

As clients of al-Sadat, al-'Attar and al-Jabarti reacted in different ways to the breach between their patron and the French masters. Al-'Attar fled to Upper Egypt, while al-Jabarti stayed and eventually became a member of the French Diwan under Menou, when relations between the French and the 'ulama became more relaxed. In the light of the tie between al-Sadat and al-Jabarti, corroborated by the MS Mazhar, it is difficult not to see this promotion of al-Jabarti as an attempt by the new French administration, no doubt approved by al-Sadat, to create a link between this important figure and the French.

That such links existed between the French and the clients of al-Sadat is borne out by the existence of the texts of al-Khashshab, preserved in the Bibliothèque Nationale in Paris, and used by Delaporte in the *Description de l'Egypte*. But they also suggest that al-Jabarti and his friends were taking an interest in, and were actually having a try at the recording of, the history of Egypt in the eighteenth century up to June 1801, and that this work somehow entered the next stage in the development of the chronicle, the MS Aja'ib volumes I–III. They also suggest that the evaluation of the behaviour of the emirs was being discussed at this time. At least it appears that al-Khashshab had a different and more positive opinion of Murad Bey than al-Jabarti had expressed in the MS Mudda. This would explain the more judicious and subdued way in which the emirs are presented in the MS Mazhar. However, the reason behind this new interest in the traditional rulers of Egypt is difficult to ascertain. Murad Bey died as an ally of the French, and perhaps the French were only collecting material to support this volte-face. On the other hand, the fact that this material ended up in the hands of the French and was used by them does not necessarily mean that they initiated it.

In 1805 al-Jabarti finished the three-volume edition of the MS Aja'ib. The existence of a number of copies proves that this version was put into circulation. The scope of the present analysis does not allow a more precise description of the frontiers of the debate and discussions among the 'ulama at this point, but it does provide some ideas as to where they had been going since 1801 and where they stood in 1805.

In the three-volume version of the MS Aja'ib of 1805–6, most of the elements of composition were found to be a development and refinement of elements that had come into existence in the MS Mazhar. Apparently the author and his patron considered such amplification to be necessary, and the obvious interpretation would be that it answered the ideological needs of the 'ulama at a time when they were promoting and legitimizing Muhammad 'Ali as Ottoman governor of Egypt. At this crucial moment in the history of the 'ulama in Ottoman Egypt, the author, apparently still under the patronage of the shaykh al-Sadat, wanted to impress upon his prospective audience among the 'ulama both the eminence of their position in Muslim society and their duty to live in seclusion: No formal cooperation between the ruler and the 'ulama was visualized; it was for the ruler to seek out his advisers.

The expansion of the preface and introduction and the insertion of the numerous necrologies seem to serve this purpose, and the sheer magnitude of this material testifies to its importance in the eyes of the author. Actually, even if he had some of the material lying ready from the time he when he was working with the biographies of former 'ulama for al-Zabidi and al-Muradi, he must have started work on it soon after finishing the MS Mazhar. Seen in this perspective, the MS Aja'ib takes on the aspect of an elaboration on the theme of the MS Mazhar, spelling out more directly exactly why the 'ulama qualified as advisers to the ruler. But the impressive amount of work put into this feature also suggests that the idea of the 'ulama being second in importance only to the Prophet, raised high above the rulers, but having no formal place in the workings of government, was a difficult position to maintain. It must have seemed much too idealistic by leaving too much to the personal qualities of the ruler and precluding all thoughts of formal ties between them. It must have been debated and discussed. It seems equally evident that it must have met with some opposition, if not downright rejection.

The ideas presented at such length in the MS Aja'ib bear the imprint of al-Sadat. Actually, they more than echo the ideas put forward in the MS Mudda. The way al-Sadat is treated suggests that he was seen as the prime example of the proper behaviour of a leading shaykh. The opposition seems to have remained centred on al-Sharqawi, who is still treated with disdain. The difference in the treatment of this shaykh and the much more positive and respectful description of the *naqib al-ashraf*, 'Umar Makram, the chief supporter of Muhammad 'Ali among the leaders of the religious establishment, indicates that the energetic – if not to say activist – 'Umar Makram was the real protagonist of the ideas put forward in the MS Aja'ib under the patronage of al-Sadat. The fact that the author's evaluation of 'Umar Makram changes drastically and for the worse after his fall from power and influence (which as we noted, was brought about with the help of al-Sharqawi and his realist friends from the days of the French!) suggests that the author and his patron were pinning their hopes on the policy of this leading shaykh in promoting Muhammad 'Ali to power in Egypt, but had difficulties in persuading the realists around al-Sharqawi of the wisdom of this move.

The author's care to stress that the crucial test of a person's ability to rule a Muslim country lay in their willingness to accept the *shari'a* as the basic framework for his actions should be seen in this context. Such a position would go some way to meet the objection that the representative of the legitimate ruler, the Ottoman governor, was still in residence in the Citadel in Cairo. However, the author wanted to make an additional point, equally important in the light of what was to come in the years ahead. His wish to elaborate on and praise the many practical and scientific innovations of the French suggests that this feature was now seen as something positive, which any ruler should put his mind to.

The eminent position of the 'ulama did not entail a rejection of such practical and scientific innovations. On the contrary, a positive attitude to these matters should be accepted by any ruler, and, we may infer, by his advisers, the 'ulama. The reinsertion and amplification of items on these matters in connection with the description of the French behaviour in the MS Aja'ib strongly indicates that in the debate in 1805 on the true political position of the 'ulama, technical innovations and scientific pursuits did not constitute a matter of dispute among the 'ulama, at least not to such a degree that it would prevent al-Jabarti's main point from being accepted.

AROUND 1815

The tentative interpretation of the compositional structure and general mood of the comments of the author of the fourth volume of the MS Aja'ib suggested that the ageing al-Jabarti set about to revise his notes for the fourth volume in 1815 in a mood of general regret. He had come to see that he had helped to back the wrong person ten years earlier. Muhammad 'Ali had secured his power in Egypt, and had brought the country peace and prosperity. But he had proved himself to be a dangerous threat to the position of the 'ulama. The *naqib al-ashraf*, 'Umar Makram, had gambled and lost. Muhammad 'Ali did show the expected veneration for the 'ulama, and did seem to be able to seek out the right ones. But his harsh taxation, and especially the economic consequences of the new property rights in the cadastre of 1814, seemed to the author to threaten everybody, including the 'ulama.

However, this was the opinion of the aged al-Jabarti, seemingly writing with no other purpose than to continue the work that must have taken most of his time for the last twenty years. His patron and his friends, as well as his enemies, had died. The ideal propounded in the MS Aja'ib of the humble *'alim* living and writing in seclusion had come true. By 1815 al-Jabarti had probably ceased to be part of whatever debates were going on among the 'ulama. From the attempt of the authorities to buy all existing copies of his work because of its critical attitude towards the founder of the dynasty, we know that the contents of the fourth volume of the MS Aja'ib were known in Cairo and so must have been put into some sort of circulation, and that it probably mirrored the animosity of many 'ulama, presumably mainly of the older generation, toward the sweeping reforms of Muhammad 'Ali. We do not know, however, whether it was circulated before or after the author's death and in what circumstances. For this reason the fourth volume is only of limited value as a key to our understanding of how the debates among the 'ulama and their leading shaykhs had progressed in the years since their fatal decision to back Muhammad 'Ali in 1805.

The chronicles of al-Jabarti may be difficult to use as sources for the history of Egypt in the turbulent decades around 1800. However, they do afford us some first-hand evidence as to what these events meant to the 'ulama and their leading shaykhs in Cairo. Used in this way, they make the representatives of this important part of the Muslim community in Ottoman Egypt come very much alive as human beings; they seriously tried to influence the momentous events that took place in front of them, and engaged in heated debates about their own part in them. A more thorough study of the MS Aja'ib than the one supplied by the scope of the present analysis would no doubt furnish many more details on these debates, especially in 1805 and 1815.

¹ It is interesting to note that the French, or at least the editor of the *Courier de l'Égypte* (no. 15, 20th Brumaire, VII), see the activists as 'ulama who felt excluded from power and influence: 'la plupart de ces sheikhs se sont engagés dans la révolte [in October 1798] par haine pour ceaus de leurs confrères, que la général en chef a promus aux emploi public'.

33   The political position of the 'ulama in Egypt in the eighteenth and nineteenth centuries

Seen from a longer perspective, the debates among the 'ulama that can be deduced from the chronicles of al-Jabarti constitute an important and significant aspect of the position of the 'ulama in Ottoman Egypt around 1800. However, it is important to keep this position in proportion. From the chronicle of Nicolas Turc it appears that al-Jabarti's contemporaries did not ascribe to the 'ulama the same crucial political position as he did. His chronicles focus on the 'ulama, and are meant to influence or highlight the attitudes and actions of this group; he arranges his material and selects his facts and comments to support this aim.

The 'ulama were important to the Ottoman government and the emirs. In the decentralized Ottoman Empire the influence of the central government was maintained by a policy of divide and rule, supporting groups to counterbalance other groups, creating ties of clientage and patronage while weakening or breaking the alliances favoured by local *a'yan* and their households. The emirs of Ottoman Egypt, especially the masters of what remained of the Qazdagli household, operated along the same lines, sometimes as in the turbulent 1780s in fierce competition with the central government, at other times in uneasy cooperation.

Both parties cultivated the 'ulama. During the eighteenth century the central government took care to pose as the protector of the religious institutions, and made sure that this was made known by concrete, material expression such as bestowing favours on eminent 'ulama and institutions in the capital and in the provinces of the empire. Special ties were established with key figures such as the shaykhs al-Sadat and al Bakri, leaders of other sufi orders and individual 'ulama, such as shaykh Hasan al-Jabarti, the author's father; al-Hifni, the Khalwati *khalifa* and shaykh al Azhar; and Murtada al-Zabidi, the author's early master. The changing Ottoman governors in Egypt supported this policy, but also, like Muhammad 'Ali, worked to further their own political careers. Many emirs made a show of their religious fervour, inviting shaykhs of the 'ulama to their mansions for readings and discussions, and favouring them with gifts and positions. The French, very much accustomed to the importance of the ideological and religious dimension of the political game, made a point of allowing the 'ulama a significant position in the new political framework of their prospective protectorate in Egypt.

The late eighteenth and early nineteenth centuries could thus easily be regarded as the heyday of the 'ulama in Ottoman Egypt, a time when competing powers vied for their loyalty and backing. But caution is necessary. The 'ulama were not free to assume the role of unprincipled operators collecting favours from whatever quarter they were offered. There were limits. Favours had to be repaid. The 'ulama, and especially their shaykhs, would be expected to take sides. The Ottoman government may have expected the shaykhs al-Sadat and al-Bakri to back Hasan Pasha in 1786, but only al-Bakri did so, and had to pay for it when the faction supported by the Ottomans collapsed in 1791. In the late eighteenth century the 'ulama had been co-opted into the leading households of the emirs of Egypt and in 1786 al-Sadat appears to have stuck to this trend and supported the Qazdagli emirs in small but significant ways. In 1798 the same thing seems to have happened. The shaykh al-Bakri again backed the wrong party by supporting the French and once more had to pay the price when the French left, while al-Sadat followed the lead taken by the Ottoman government and held back until the situation was sufficiently clarified. This made him the target of the wrath of General Kléber, but later allowed him some influence under the more moderate Menou through his client, al-Jabarti. This policy stood him in good stead when the Ottomans returned. But the French evacuation also brought back the emirs, and an entirely new player on the political scene: the British. Again he seemed to have tried to hold back until 'Umar Makram made his move to support Muhammad 'Ali as governor of Ottoman Egypt. At last, in 1809, this policy seemed to have paid off. 'Umar Makram was deposed and al-Sadat installed as *naqib al-ashraf*.

The importance of the chronicles of al-Jabarti lies in the fact that they supply a new aspect to this, the picture of al-Sadat as a cynical political operator, which the old and disillusioned al-Jabarti presents in his necrology of al-Sadat from 1813. The existence of the first three versions of the chronicle shows that al-Sadat actually had a reason, or at least wanted to make clear to his fellow 'ulama that his policy of cautious restraint could be defended on religious grounds. The ideal *'alim* should live in seclusion in accordance with the tenets of his faith. He should avoid formal ties with worldly powers, but be accessible for consultation by those who sought his advice. This was not a revolutionary idea. Actually it represented the old, venerated and traditional ideal of the 'ulama. Al-Sadat was advocating a very conservative, safe and un-'activist' line. It also made him a 'loyalist', advocating the restraint required by the Ottomans, and it would be easy to put this down as a consequence of his ties with the central government. The consistency of this point of view throughout the different versions, however, suggests that it represents something more. It suggests that al-Sadat was sincerely convinced of the necessity to stick to well-established ideas in order to protect the Muslim community in times of danger and crisis.

He seems to have had some difficulty in making his contemporaries see his point, as would any wealthy and influential person advocating a policy of humility and restraint on the part of others. The heated arguments, especially in the MS Mudda, and the writings of al-Sharqawi point to the existence of another view among the 'ulama, who saw the possibility of making a distinction between matters affecting the *shari'a* and those that did not. But al-Sadat surely had a case. Past experience showed that such restraint would serve the interest of the 'ulama in the long run. A policy of detachment and seclusion would enable the 'ulama to avoid such distinctions, which would always contain an element of subjectivity and for this reason were bound to foster disagreement. Detachment and seclusion would make it easier to keep the 'ulama together as a group. Unity among them on such matters would deprive the rulers of the veneer of legitimacy they needed to establish more permanent institutions of government and would curb their ambitions. Their need for revenue would decrease. Life would become easier and – this would surely be a major point – the ability of the believers to live in accordance with the demands of their faith would be greatly enhanced. In the eyes of al-Sadat and al-Jabarti the true political position of the 'ulama in the turbulent and highly competitive political environment of Ottoman Egypt should be one of restraint and neutrality.

The consistency of this point of view in the writings of al-Jabarti is impressive. The emphasis would vary from one version to the next. The situation at hand would make him focus on different aspects and arguments. In 1798 it would be the dangers of formal attachments; in 1801 the necessity and advantages of unity; and in 1805 the nature and policy of a ruler, acceptable to the 'ulama. But at each point the basic issue was the unattached position of the 'ulama. The consistency of this issue speaks for its sincerity.

A position of seclusion and humility would not be without dangers. It would place the 'ulama on the periphery of the political milieu, and would not only deprive them of influence on specific issues, such as taxation and protection of friends and clients, it would also make it impossible for them to influence the major issues of a society whose institutions were crumbling. The rulers might be able to manage on their own without the active support and legitimacy provided by the 'ulama. The policy of Muhammad 'Ali towards them, while officially accepting their eminent position as arbiters of Muslim society, clearly tended to neutralize them as an independent political power by incorporating the religious institutions into the new state machinery. And the leading shaykhs of the 'ulama especially would be in danger of severe punishments if they held aloof. In the eyes of the ruler such detachment would invariably be interpreted as opposition and treated accordingly, as al-Sadat was to realize under Bonaparte and Kléber.

A position of seclusion and detachment should not be confused with submission. It would demand a well-developed self-respect on the part of the 'ulama. Hence the eminent position afforded to them and the conspicuous awareness of the role played by the personal qualities of the ruler in the MS Aja'ib. In the light of later developments it is important to note that this position did not imply opposition to the practical and scientific innovations presented by the French. On the contrary, the ruler – at least in 1805 – was expected to put such innovations to good use.

In contradistinction to Iran, where the political circumstances and the Shi'ite tradition of *ijtihad* (independent judgement) favoured more active participation of the 'ulama,[1] the policy of restraint and seclusion advocated by al-Sadat in the chronicles of al-Jabarti seems to have been adopted by succeeding generations of 'ulama in Egypt. To historians of the Modernization mould this has been seen as a serious problem. To these historians one of the major themes in the history of the 'ulama in the nineteenth century is their failure to respond actively and innovatively to repercussions of the changes in Egyptian society, especially from 1809 to 1816, when Muhammad 'Ali clamped down on the rights and privileges of the leading 'ulama, and during the period of reform, especially of al-Azhar, starting in 1872 and continuing until 1961, but centred around the seminal contribution of Muhammad 'Abduh from 1895 to his death in 1905.

To the Modernizers the responses of the 'ulama to the situation created by the French occupation have been characteristic of their response to the changes in Egyptian society to the present. To these historians the 'ulama never ceased to view the French occupation as more than a political crisis, failing to appreciate its ideological or scientific aspects. The earliest and most consistent responses to the challenges to their well-entrenched system of belief and practice were political in nature because the challenge itself was viewed by the 'ulama as political, not cultural and ideological. They elevated and legitimized Muhammad 'Ali as the new governor of Egypt, but made sure that this was not presented as a challenge to Ottoman authority and that he did not forget that he owed his position to their support. In doing so they were only defending the old equilibrium and their own positions and the enormous expansion of their social influence and rapidly acquired wealth. Restraints on their open diversion of *waqf* revenues entrusted to their administration were also removed. These and other privileges were expanded by Muhammad 'Ali. For their part, the 'ulama showed themselves eager to participate in the Pasha's government.[2]

However, according to this school of thought, the 'ulama were an unequal match in the struggle with Muhammad 'Ali, a struggle that rested on the precarious position of each of the parties and the availability of alternative candidates whom the 'ulama could choose to support rather than on the strength of any influence inherent in their own position. Once Muhammad 'Ali had deposed all his rivals and decided to curtail their privileges, influence and wealth, the 'ulama were quickly brought to heel. The revolutionary aspect of his reign consisted in his willingness to depart from traditional patterns and concepts of government. The most dramatic and far-reaching consequence of his new programmes was the dissolution of the partnership between the 'ulama and the ruling elite. After initially ignoring their criticism and repudiating intervention in his affairs, the new Pasha gradually moved to a total rejection of their traditional attitudes and the ideas they continued to represent and propagate.[3] He came to rely on foreigners to initiate and supervise his modernizing programmes. Members of the former intellectual class who could not adapt to the new conditions were totally disregarded. The 'ulama were virtually ignored. For this reason they could not play the role of their counterparts in Istanbul, where the Ottoman 'ulama helped formulate and implement the innovative programmes of their sultans. Though the leading 'ulama and their middle-class compatriots in the corps of 'ulama were generally able to maintain their economic positions throughout the nineteenth century, their political influence in government affairs had effectively been destroyed.[4]

From the 1830s to the 1870s the 'ulama, as a group, failed to preserve their influence, which was based on their socio-economic and cultural–spiritual status. Their status declined, both in relation to its former position and to that of other social groups. The 'ulama of Egypt were a deeply rooted indigenous group which sprang from, and lived among, the native Arabic-speaking population. Their spiritual and religious authority was founded on tradition and, in addition to this, based on the existence of 'ulama families. This situation was not seriously affected in the years of Modernization and Westernization that followed. However, the fact that it was based on continuity and tradition, not factors of power lodged in the new structures and values, meant that the influence of the 'ulama gradually declined, not only because they lost much of their economic position, especially as large land owners, but also because of their unwillingness to fashion the new reality according to their concepts and values. They ceased to constitute a prominent factor in the state machinery and among the intelligentsia and lacked the initiative to integrate into the new educational structure, thus isolating themselves from the centres of reform.[5]

They continued to exert a negative influence, by establishing limits beyond which reform could not be pushed. For most of the nineteenth century the government and the 'ulama were able to maintain a precarious truce, each respecting the special competence of the other within clearly defined limits. However, as the century progressed, the truce was broken and the reformers began to criticize the 'ulama and to demand readjustments from them. When the 'ulama finally had to come to grips with reform, it was imposed upon them in spite of their constant criticism and opposition.[6]

The law of 1872 normally held to be the beginning of modernization of al-Azhar had only modest repercussions. The true beginnings of reorganization and modernization of al-Azhar took place in the 1890s with the efforts of Muhammad 'Abduh. The reforms at the beginning of the twentieth century were responsible for the emergence of the shaykh al-Azhar as the recognized head of all 'ulama in Egypt and of al-Azhar as the centre of all Islamic education in Egypt. The laws of 1908 and 1911 that became the foundation for al-Azhar's future development were imposed upon the 'ulama, and their reactions were violent. The conservative shaykhs maintained a virtual monopoly over the position of shaykh al-Azhar between 1899 and 1927 and used the considerable powers which the reformers had attached to this office to block attempts at further reform. A minor reform of the al-Azhar was promulgated between 1930 and 1936. Only in 1961, in the wake of the 1952 demise of the monarchy, were more sweeping reforms instituted.[7]

Since the 1980s this representation of the history of the 'ulama has been modified. As the idea of Modernization as an unavoidable force has faded, scholars have tended to view the response of the 'ulama in a broader context. The movement towards the incorporation of Islam within the sphere of the state countered the movement towards secularization. Islam had to be controlled – not only for its own sake, but also because the question of legitimacy of the government had arisen, especially after the establishment of the

In search of the true Political Position of the 'Ulama

British protectorate in 1882. The attempts at reform of al-Azhar are now seen as part of the Egyptian state's ambition to gain control of all aspects of life. It included other initiatives, such as the inauguration of the administration of the state mufti in 1895 and a reorganization of the leadership of the shaykh al-Bakri over the sufi orders in the same year. Towards the end of the nineteenth century a new and more politicized official Islam was emerging. This new, political Islam took different forms according to political circumstances, but they were all new, a construction by younger generations living in urbanized mass societies and not a survival of medieval Islamic forms. The debate on Islamic theology inaugurated by the Salafi movement was part of this, as were oppositional Islamic movements such as the Muslim Brotherhood. The stage was set for a contest between the state and various opposing forces in a common public discourse, supported by the revolutionary transformation created by the mass media: printed books, journals and newspapers. In spite of restrictions and shortcomings, the press contributed to the formation of ideological positions and the introduction of an atmosphere of pluralism in Egyptian public life. An Islamic press arose in Egypt as it did elsewhere, and many of the editors were Azhari scholars. To them printing and the press provided a pulpit and an audience among the literate elite which they could never have reached without it. The fact that opposition forces were driven underground did not effectively remove them from the political field.[8]

The implication of this interpretation would be that the opposition, withdrawal and obstructionism of the 'ulama, as presented by the historians focusing on the challenges of Modernization, should be seen as relevant and intelligent, if perhaps not very successful, parts of this new contest, rather than as the rearguard action of representatives of Medieval Islam. In the late nineteenth century the 'ulama, the cultural brokers of Muslim society, were reacting and adapting to a weak government trying to co-opt the religious establishment in order to strengthen its hand vis-à-vis the foreign occupying power and a general nationalist sentiment. They responded by a combination of disengagement, restraint and an appeal to the traditional values and status of the 'ulama.

The analysis of the chronicles of al-Jabarti suggests that this revisionist interpretation of the position of the 'ulama in the late nineteenth century would apply to the 'ulama of the late eighteenth and early nineteenth centuries as well. In the introduction it was argued that the idea of a 'golden age of the 'ulama' in the decades around 1800 should at least be modified. Even if the interest of the leading shaykhs of the 'ulama in worldly affairs in this period does reflect reality, it might be seen as the natural reaction of men in charge of large institutions, whose income was being eroded by mounting inflation and political turmoil. The analysis has shown that the extravagant wealth and political influence attributed to the 'ulama in these years in the chronicles constitute part of the argument presented by al Jabarti, to whom such wealth and influence on the part of the 'ulama constituted the gravest danger to their long-term position and that of the Muslim community. Considering the readiness of al-Jabarti to select his facts to fit his arguments, the notion of a 'golden age of the 'ulama' seems difficult to uphold without more evidence.

What seems to emerge is a picture of leading 'ulama deeply engaged in a search for the true political position of their group in a period when ambitious and partly foreign but weak regimes were competing for the favour of the religious community to gain the legitimacy that the 'ulama could provide. In this debate there were no final answers, only different options, each charged with obvious dangers. In this difficult situation the chronicles of al-Jabarti propagate a policy of restraint and detachment, over and above the 'realists' headed by the shaykh al-Azhar, who tried to accommodate the rulers by agreeing to sit on their diwans in order to trade the legitimacy this would provide for concessions that would leave essential aspects of Muslim society untouched. Both agreed that the 'activist' attitude posed an even graver danger, and tried to contain it. As the political situation clarified and Muhammad 'Ali consolidated his power this debate lost its relevance. Tradition, based on accumulated experience, prescribed an attitude of submission and accommodation to the ruler who was able to uphold law and order. The new generation of leading shaykhs would assume this role without difficulty.

This interpretation of the situation of the 'ulama in the decades around 1800 would support the even more radical revisionist view of Timothy Mitchell. To Mitchell the inaction of the 'ulama, at least in the first half of the nineteenth century, did not stem from an inability to see the implications of the reforms, but the opposite: that the reforms did not seriously touch on the Islamic character of Egyptian society. According to this point of view, the 'ulama, for example, did not cling to an outdated and inefficient education system, but one that actually worked. Trying to get behind the screen of Modernization, Mitchell has discovered an education system free of coercion, without curricula, plans, classrooms or timetables, since students should not necessarily learn the same things in the same order and at the same speed. This interpretation has been criticized for being too rosy, at least when it comes to the situation in al-Azhar at the time of 'Abduh in the late nineteenth century. But as this criticism is based on information furnished by 'Abduh, who represents exactly those who would be unable to see the old order as a sensible system, Mitchell still seems to have a point: The benefits of the old system have become imperceptible to succeeding generations because of the gradual and unnoticed change of perspective following in the wake of colonialism.[9]

Seen from this perspective, the apparent passivity of the 'ulama during most of the nineteenth century may turn out to have been founded on sound reason. Why change a system that worked to the satisfaction of all those involved? The Egyptian 'ulama did not withdraw and obstruct the Modernization process. They did not because the system in which they operated actually functioned, and because Modernization did not touch its essential elements. The years of crisis and political turmoil around 1800 forced them to reconsider the political position of the 'ulama, all the time being perfectly aware that what they said and did was part of and contributed to a long-standing discourse on their role in the protection and propagation of Islam. When the crisis subsided the debate disappeared, not because they did not perceive the challenge posed by the reforms of Muhammad 'Ali, but because the challenges of these reforms did not as yet touch on what to them would be the basic issue: man's sense of dependence on God. Only when the social and cultural consequences of the scientific revolution in the late nineteenth century seemed to question this principle did leading 'ulama attempt to meet the challenge, but by no means all; and those who still favoured a position of restraint and detachment could do so by pointing to the fact that here, at the beginning of the twenty-first century, when the scientific revolution seems to be losing the battle to solve the problems of man's existence, the restraint and detachment of the 'alim would seem to have regained some of its traditional value.

[1] After the collapse of the Safavid Empire in 1722 a sharp dispute developed among the Shi'i 'ulama on the possibility of the indivdual's excising independent judgement in matters of law. This confrontation was won by the usuli faction, who maintained the need for mujtahids (i.e. those exercising independent judgement) in view of what they saw as inevitable conflicts in interpretation. The victory assured the independence of the Shi'i 'ulama in Iran from the political authority of the ruler. Under the new, but relatively weak, Qajar dynasty (1779–1925) the Iranian 'ulama secured a large measure of financial independence. The usuli jurists introduced a novel interpretation of a part of the religious tax of khoms, known as 'the share of the Imam'. An instance of cooperation between the 'ulama and the state

during the first Perso-Russian war (1811–13) enabled the Shi'i 'ulama to secure the tacit consent of the government of their right to collect it. The independence of the 'ulama from the Iranian government was further enhanced by the fact that the leading 'ulama resided in the Shi'ite holy cities of Iraq, which were under Ottoman rule. Later, in the nineteenth century, Qajar autocracy and tyrannical behaviour led the Shi'i 'ulama to engage in agitation against the dynasty. See Akhavi, *Religion and Politics in Contemporary Iran*, pp. 11, 14–15, and Said Amir Arjomand, *The Turban and the Crown*, New York 1988, p. 14.

[2] Crecelius, 'Nonideological Responses', pp. 179ff.

[3] Ibid., p. 180.

[4] Ibid., p. 181; De Jong, Turuq and Turuq-linked Institutions in Nineteenth Century Egypt p.12, 20, 31; MS Aja'ib, IV, 164.

[5] Shaked, 'Biographies of the 'Ulama', pp. 73 ff.

[6] Crecelius, 'Nonideological Responses', p. 187.

[7] Ibid., p. 200; Wolf-Dieter Lemke, *Mahmud Saltut (1893–1963) und die Reform des Azhar*, Frankfurt 1980, p. 242.

[8] Skovgaard-Petersen, *Defining Islam*, pp. 28, 46, 50, 55. Reinhard Schulze identifies three sources of this new politicized Islam in the nineteenth century: the *ancien regime*'s need for legitimization, supported by the 'ulama and sufi orders; the need on the part of members of the new European-trained elite of officers etc. for a political ideology; and more traditional Islamic opposition movements supported by 'ulama and sufi orders. Schulze suggests that at least the last has roots in the eighteenth century. R.Schulze, ,Die Politisierung des Islam im 19.Jahrhundert', *Die Welt des Islams* 22 (1982 [1984]), pp. 103ff.

[9] T. Mitchell, *Colonizing Egypt*, Cambridge 1988, p. 82 ; Skovgaard-Petersen, *Defining Islam*, pp. 47–8.

In search of the true Political Position of the 'Ulama

Choueiri, Youssef M., *Modern Arab Historiography, Historical Discourse and the Nation-State*, rev. edn., London 2003

Commission des Monuments d'Egypte, *Description de l'Egypte ou recueil des observations et des recherches qui ont eté faites en Egypte pendant l'expédition de l'armée française, publié par les ordres de Sa Majesté l'empereur Napoleon le Grand, état moderne*, vol II, Paris 1809–22

Cottart, N. (ed.), *La Transmission du savoir en Islam (VIIIe–XVIIIe siècle)*, London 1983

Crabbs, Jack A., *The Writing of History in Nineteenth Century Egypt*, Cairo 1984

Crecelius, D., 'Ahmad Shalabi ibn 'Abd al-Ghani and Ahmad Katkhuda 'Azaban al-Damurdashi: Two Sources for al-Jabarti's *'Aja' ib al-athar fi' l-tarajim wa'l akhbar'*, in Crecelius (ed.), *Eighteenth-Century Egypt*, pp. 89–102

Crecelius, D. (ed.), *Eighteenth-Century Egypt: The Arabic Manuscript Sources*, Los Angeles 1990

Crecelius, D., 'The Emergence of the Shaykh al-Azhar as the Pre-eminent Religious Leader in Egypt', in Assabgui et al. (eds.), *Colloque internationale*, pp. 109–23

Crecelius, D., 'The Mamluk Beylicate of Egypt in the Last Decades before its Destruction by Muhammad 'Ali Pasha in 1811', in Philipp and Haarmann (eds.), *The Mamluks*, pp. 128–49

Crecelius, D., 'Nonideological Responses of the Egyptian Ulama to Modernization', in Keddie (ed.), *Scholars, Saints and Sufis*, pp. 167–210

Crecelius, D., *The Roots of Modern Egypt: A Study in the Regimes of Ali Bey al-Kabir and Muhammad Bey al-Dhahab*, Chicago 1981

Crecelius, D., 'Russia's Relations with the Mamluk Beys of Egypt in the Late Eighteenth Century', in Farhad Kazemi (ed.), *A Way Prepared, Essays in Honour of Bayley Vinder*, New York 1988, pp. 56–67

Cuno, K., *The Pasha's Peasants: Land, Society, and Economy in Lower Egypt, 1740–1858*, Cambridge 1992

In search of the true Political Position of the 'Ulama

Cuoq, J., 'Jabarti, Chroniqueur de l'expédition française d'Egypte, 1798–1800', *Revue de l'Institut des Belles Lettres Arabes* (1978): 91–105

Daly, M.W. (ed.), *The Cambridge History of Egypt*, vol. II, Cambridge 1998

al-Damurdashi, Ahmad, *al-Damurdashi's Chronicle of Egypt:*1688–1755, ed. and trans. Daniel Crecelius and Abd al-Wahhab Bakr, Leiden 1991

de Jong, Frederick, 'Mustafa Kamal al-Din al-Bakri (1688–1749), Revival and Reform in the Khalwatiyya Tradition?', in Levtzion and Voll (eds.), *Renewal and Reform*, pp. 117–32

de Jong, F., *Turuq and Turuq-Linked Institutions in Nineteenth-Century Egypt*, Leiden 1978

Delanou, Gilbert, *Moralistes et politiques musulmans dans l'Egypte du XIXe siècle (*1798–1882*)*, Lille 1978 and 1980

Dodge, B., *al-Azhar. A Millennium of Muslim Learning*, Washington, DC 1961

Dykstra, Darrell, 'The French Occupation of Egypt, 1798–1801', in Daly (ed.), *The Cambridge History of Egypt*, pp. 113–38

Eisenstein, Elisabeth, *The Printing Press as an Agent of Change*, vols. I–II, Cambridge 1979

Enayat, Hamid, *Modern Islamic Political Thought*, Austin 1982

The Encyclopedia of Islam, vol. X, Leiden 2000

Fahey, R.S.O. and B. Radtke, 'Neo Sufism Reconsidered', *Der Islam* (1993): 52–87

Fahmy, Khaled, *All the Pasha's Men*, Cambridge 1997

Fahmy, Khaled, 'The Era of Muhammad 'Ali Pasha 1805–1848', in Daly (ed.), *The Cambridge History of Egypt*, pp. 139–79

Faroqhi, S., Halil Inalik, and D.Quataert (eds.), *Economic and Social History of the Ottoman Empire*, vols. I–II, Cambridge 1994

Findley, Carter V., *Ottoman Civil Officialdom. A Social History*, Princeton 1988

Fleischer, Cornell H., *Bureaucrat and Intellectual in the Ottoman Empire: The Historian Mastafa 'Ali (1541–1600)*, Princeton 1986

Floor, Willem, 'The Revolutionary Character of the Iranian 'Ulama: Wishful Thinking or Reality?' *IJMES* 12, 4 (1980): 501–24

Gaffney, Patrick D, 'Authority and the Mosque in Upper Egypt: The Islamic Preacher as Image and Actor', in Roff (ed.), *Islam and the Political Economy of Meaning*, pp. 199–225

Geaffroy, E., *Le Soufisme en Egypte et en Syrie sous les derniers mamelouks et les premiers ottomans*, Damascus 1995

Gibb, H.A.R. (ed.), *Whither Islam?* London 1932

Gibb, H.A.R. and Harold Bowen, *Islamic Society and the West*, vol. I, parts 1–2, London 1950–7

Gilbert, E.J., 'Institutionalization of Muslim Scholarship and Professionalization of the 'Ulama' in Medieval Damascus', *SI* 52 (1980): 105–34

Glassé, Cyril, *The Concise Encyclopedia of Islam*, San Francisco 1989

Gocek, F.M., *East Encounters West*, Oxford 1987

Goody, Jack, *The Logic of Writing and the Organization of Society*, Cambridge 1986

Gormann, Anthony, *Historians, State and Politics in Twentieth Century Egypt, Contesting the Nation*, London 2003

Gran, Peter, *Islamic Roots of Capitalism: Egypt, 1760–1840*, Austin 1979 (reviewed by G. Baer in *JESHO* 25 (1982), pp. 217 ff., and by F. de Jong in the *IJMES s* 14 (1982), pp. 381–99)

Green, A.H., *The Tunisian 'Ulama 1873–1915: Social Structure and Response to Ideological Currents*, Leiden 1978

Hanna, Nelly, 'Culture in Ottoman Egypt', in Daly (ed.), *The Cambridge History of Egypt*, pp. 87–112

Hathaway, J. '"Mamluk Households" and "Mamluk Factions" in Ottoman Egypt: A Reconsideration', in Philipp and Haarmann (eds.), *The Mamluks*, pp. 107–17

Hathaway, J., *The Politics of Households in Ottoman Egypt: The Rise of the Qazdağlis*, Cambridge 1997 (reviewed by D. Behrens-Abouseif in *BSOAS* (1998), pp. 342–3; by L. Peirce in the *American History Review* 104 (1999), pp. 286–87; and by M.A. Fay in *MEJ* 52 (1998), pp. 281–2)

Hathaway, J. 'Problems in the Periodization of Ottoman History: The Fifteenth through Eighteenth Centuries', *Turkish Studies Association Bulletin*, 20, 2 (1996): 25–31

Hathaway, J., 'Sultans, Pashas, *Taqwims*, and Mühimmes: A Reconsideration of Chronicle-Writing in Eighteenth-Century Egypt', in Crecelius (ed.), *Eighteenth-century Egypt*, pp. 51–78

Hay, Denis, *Annalists and Historians: Western Historiography from the Eighth to the Eighteenth Century*, London 1977

Heyd, Uriel, 'The Ottoman Ulema and Westernization in the Time of Selim III and Mahmud II' (1961), repr. in A. Hourani et al. (eds.), *The Modern Middle East: A Reader*, London 1993, pp. 29–59

Heyworth-Dunne, J., *An Introduction to the History of Education in Modern Egypt*, London 1938; repr. 1968

Holt, P.M., *Egypt and the Fertile Crescent 1516–1922. A Political History*, London 1966

Holt, P.M. 'al-Jabarti's Introduction to the History of Ottoman Egypt', *Bulletin of the School of Oriental and African Studies* 25 (1962): 38–51

Holt, P.M., 'Literary Offerings: A Genre of Courtly Literature', in Philipp and Haarmann (eds.), *The Mamluks*, pp. 3–16

Holt, P.M. (ed.), *Political and Social Change in Modern Egypt: Historical Studies from the Ottoman Conquest to the United Arab Republic*, London 1968

Hourani, Albert, *Arab Thought in the Liberal Age*, 2nd edn., Cambridge 1983 [1962]

Howard, D.A., 'Ottoman Historiography and the Literature of "Decline" of the Sixteenth and Seventeenth Centuries', *JAH* 22 (1988): 52–77

Itzkowitz, Norman, 'Eighteenth-Century Ottoman Realities', *SI* 16 (1962): 73–94

Itzkowitz, Norman, 'Men and Ideas in the Eighteenth-Century Ottoman Empire', in Naff and Owen (eds.), *Studies*, pp. 15–26

al-Jabarti, 'Abd al-Rahman, *'Abd al-Rahman al-Jabarti's History of Egypt*, ed. and trans. T. Philipp, M. Perlman et al., 3 vols., Stuttgart 1994

al-Jabarti, 'Abd al-Rahman, *Aja'ib al-athar fi'l-tarajim wa'l-akhbar*, 4 vols., Bulaq 1879–80

al-Jabarti, 'Abd-al-Rahman, *Journal d'un notable du Caire durant l'expédition française 1798–1801*, trans. and annotated by Joseph Cuoq, Paris 1979 (reviewed in *Revue d l'Institut des Belles Lettres Arabes* 43, 145 (1980/1))

al-Jabarti, 'Abd al-Rahman, *Mazhar al-taqdis bidhihab dawlat al-faransis*, ed. H. Gawhari and U. al-Dasuqi, Cairo 1969

al-Jabarti, Abd ar-Rahman, *Mazar at-taqdis bi-dhahab daulat al-faransis*, trans. and annotated Thomas Philipp, Cambridge MA, 1983 (unpublished manus)

al-Jabarti, 'Abd al-Rahman, *Ta'rikh muddat al-faransis/Chronicle of the First Seven Months of the French Occupation of Egypt*, ed. and trans. S. Moreh, Leiden 1975

Kabrda, J., *Quelques firman concernant les relations franco-turques lors de l'expédition de Bonaparte en Egypte*, Paris 1947

Keddie, N.R. (ed.), *Scholars, Saints and Sufis*, Los Angeles, Berkeley 1972

Kepel, Gilles and Yann Richard (eds.), *Intellectuels et militants de l'Islam contemporain*, Paris 1990

al-Khashshab, Isma'il, *A Short Manuscript History of the Mamluk Amir Murad Bey: Khulasat ma yurad min akhbar al-amir Murad*, ed. and trans. Hamza 'Abd al-'Aziz Badr and Daniel Crecelius, Cairo 1992

Kondrup, Johnny, *Levned og Tolkninger, Studier i Nordisk Selvbiografi*, Odense 1982

Kunt, I. Metin, *The Sultan's Servants: The Transformation of Ottoman Provincial Government*, 1550–1650, New York 1983

Lagrou, Pieter, 'Victims of Genocide and National Memory: Belgium, France and the Netherlands 1945–65', *Past and Present* 154 (1997): 181–222

Lambton, A.K.S., *State and Government in Medieval Islam. An Introduction to the Study of Islamic Political Theory: The Jurists*, Oxford 1981

Lapidus, I.M., 'Muslim Cities and Islamic Societies', in I.M. Lapidus (ed.), *Middle Eastern Cities*, Berkeley 1969, pp. 47–79

Laurens, Henri, *L'Expédition française de l'Egypte: Bonaparte et l'Islam: le choc des cultures*, Paris 1989

Lemke, Wolf-Dieter, *Mahmud Shaltut (1893–1963) und die Reform des Azhar*, Frankfurt 1980

Levtzion, Nehemia and John O. Voll (eds.), *Eighteenth Century Renewal and Reform in Islam*, New York 1987

Lewis, B., *The Middle East and the West*, Bloomington 1965

Lison, Marcus, 'Selbstverständnis, Gruppenidentität und informelle Macht der 'ulama in Ägypten Ende des 18./Aufgang des 19. Jahrhunderts aufgrund einer Analyse der gelehrten Biographien des Abd al-Rahman al-Jabarti', unpublished MA thesis, Erlangen University

Livingstone, J.W., 'Shaykh al-Bakri and Bonaparte', *SI* 80 (1994): 125–43

Mallat, Chibli, *Shi'i Thought from the South of Lebanon*, Oxford 1988

Marlow, L. *Hierarchy and Egalitarianism in Islamic Thought*, Cambridge 1997

Marsot, Afaf Lutfi al-Sayyid, 'The Beginnings of Modernization among the Rectors of al-Azhar', in Polk and Chambers (eds.), *Beginnings*, pp. 267–80

Marsot, Afaf Lutfi al-Sayyid, 'A Comparative Study of 'Abd al-Rahman al-Jabarti and Niqula al-Turk', in Crecelius (ed.), *Eighteenth-Century Egypt*, pp. 115–26

Marsot, Afaf Lutfi al-Sayyid, *Egypt in the Reign of Muhammad 'Ali*, Cambridge 1984

Marsot, Afaf Lutfi al-Sayyid, 'The Role of the Ulama in Egypt during the Early Nineteenth Century', in Holt (ed.), *Political and Social Change*, pp. 264–80

Marsot, Afaf Lutfi al-Sayyid, 'A Socio-economic Sketch of the Ulama in the Eighteenth Century', in Assabgui et al. (eds.), *Colloque*, pp. 313–20

Marsot, Afaf Lutfi al-Sayyid, 'The 'Ulama' of Cairo in the Eighteenth and Nineteenth Century', in Keddie (ed.), *Scholars, Saints and Sufis*, pp. 149–65

Marsot, Afaf Lutfi al-Sayyid, 'The Wealth of the Ulama in Late Eighteenth-Century Cairo', in Naff and Owen (eds.), *Studies*, pp. 205–16

Martin, A., *Histoire scientifique de l'expédition française en Egypte*, Paris 1815

Martin, B.G., 'A Short History of the Khalwati Order of Dervishes', in Keddie (ed.), *Scholars, Saints and Sufis*, pp. 275–305

Messick, Brinckly, *The Calligraphic State*, Los Angeles 1993

Mitchell, T. *Colonizing Egypt*, Cambridge 1988

Mørch, Søren (ed.), *Danmarks Historie*, vol. X, Copenhagen 1992

Moreh, S., 'Introduction', in al-Jabarti, *al-Jabarti's Chronicle of the First Seven Months of the French Occupation of Egypt*, trans. S. Moreh, Leiden 1975, pp. 1–30

Moreh, S., 'al-Jabarti's Method of Composing his Chronicle', *JSAI* 25 (2001): 346–73

Moreh, S., 'Reputed Autographs of 'Abd al-Rahman al-Jabarti and Related Problems', *BSOAS* 28 (1965): 524–39

In search of the true Political Position of the 'Ulama

Moreh, S., The Egyptian Scholar Hassan al-'Attar (d.1834) and his Journey from Cairo to Izmir, in: *Expressions et representations litteraires de la Mediterranee: Iles et ports, XVIe-XX siecles, Actes du Colloque, Centre Culturel Europeen de Delphes, 5-6 Novembre* 1999, *p.* 19-32, 2002

Mottahedeh, Roy, *Loyalty and Leadership in an Early Islamic Society*, Princeton 1980

Naff, Thomas and Roger Owen (eds.), *Studies in Eighteenth Century Islamic History*, Carbondale and Edwardsville, IL 1977

al-Nahhal, Djalal H., *The Judicial Administration of Ottoman Egypt in the Seventeenth Century*, Minneapolis 1979

O'Fahey, R. S. and Radtke. B., 'Neo-Sufism Reconsidered', *Der Islam* (1993): 52–87

Olsen, Flemming, *Elements of Textual Analysis*, Copenhagen, 1986

Oxford Encyclopedia of the Modern Islamic World, vol. IV, Oxford 1995

Peters, Rudolph, 'Erneurungsbewegungen im Islam vom 18.bis zum 20.Jahrhundert und die Rolle des Islams in der neueren Geschichte', in Werner Ende and Udo Steinbach (eds.), *Der Islam in der Gegenwart*, Munich 1987, pp. 91–131

Peters, Rudolph, 'Religious Attitudes towards Modernization in the Ottoman Empire', *Die Welt des Islams* 26 (1986): 76–105

Philipp, Thomas, 'Class, Community and Arab Historiography', *IJMES* 16 (1984): 161–75

Philipp, Thomas, 'The French and the French Revolution in the Works of al-Jabarti', in Crecelius (ed.), *Eighteenth-Century Egypt*, pp. 127–40

Philipp, Thomas, 'Personal Loyalty and Political Power of the Mamluks in the Eighteenth Century', in Philipp and Haarmann (eds.), *The Mamluks*, pp. 118–27

Philipp, T. and U. Haarmann (eds.), *The Mamluks in Egyptian Politics and Society*, Cambridge 1998

Pieterberg, G., 'The Formation of an Ottoman Egyptian Elite in the Eighteenth Century', *IJMES* 22 (1990): 275–89

Polk, W.R. and R.L. Chambers (eds.), *Beginnings of Modernization in the Middle East*, Chicago 1968

Poonawala, Ismail K., 'The Evolution of al-Garbati's Historical Thinking as Reflected in the *Muzhir* and the *Aga'ib'*, *Arabica* 15 (1968): 270–88

Poulsen, Henning, 'Dansk Modstand og Tysk Politik', *Den jyske Historiker* 71 (1995): 7–18

Rahman, Fazlur, *Islam and Modernity: Transformation of an Intellectual Tradition*, Chicago 1982

Raymond, André, *Artisans et commerçants au Caire au XVIIIe siecle*, vols. I–II, Damascus 1973–4

Raymond, André, *Le Caire des Janissaries: l'apogée de la ville ottomane sous 'Abd al-Rahman Katkuda*, Paris 1995

Raymond, André, 'Egyptiens et Français au Caire, 1798–1801', *Institut Français d'Archeologie Orientale, Bibliothèque Générale* 18 (1998)

Raymond, André, 'Quartiers et mouvements populaires au Caire au XVIIIième siècle', in Holt (ed.), *Political and Social Change*

Reichmuth, Stefan, 'Notes on Murtada al-Zabidi's *Mu'jam* as a Source for al-Jabarti's History', *JSAI* 25 (2001): 374–83

Roff, W. (ed.), *Islam and the Political Economy of Meaning*, Los Angeles 1987

Rosenthal, Franz, *A History of Muslim Historiography*, Leiden 1968

Said, E.W., *Orientalism*, New York 1978

Schulze, Reinhard, 'Die Politisierung des Islam in 19. Jahrhundert', *Die Welt des Islams* 22 (1982 [1984]): 104–16

Shaked, Haim, 'The Biographies of the 'Ulama in Mubarak's *Khitat* as a Source for the History of the 'Ulama in Nineteenth Century Egypt', in Baer (ed.), *The 'Ulama in Modern History*

Shaw, S., *Between Old and New, the Ottoman Empire under Sultan Selim III,* 1789–1807, Cambridge, MA 1971

Shaw, S., *The Financial and Administrative Organization and Development of Ottoman Egypt,* Princeton 1962

Shaw, S., *History of the Ottoman Empire and Modern Turkey,* vol. I: *Empire of the Gazis: The Rise and Decline of the Ottoman Empire* 1280–1808, Cambridge 1976

Shaw, S., *Ottoman Egypt in the Age of the French Revolution,* Cambridge, MA 1964

Shaw, S., *Ottoman Egypt in the Eighteenth Century,* Cambridge, MA 1962

Shaw, S. and Ezel Kural Shaw, *History of the Ottoman Empire and Modern Turkey,* vol. II: *Reform, Revolution and Republic* 1808–1975, Cambridge 1977

Sicker, Martin, *The Islamic World in Decline,* London 2001

Skovgaard-Petersen, Jakob, *Defining Islam for the Egyptian State. Muftis and Fatwas of the Dar al Ifta,* Leiden 1997

Sonbol, Amira el-Azhary, *The New Mamluks, Egyptian Society and Modern Feudalism,* Syracuse 2000

Sorby, Karol, 'Decline of Mamluk Power in Egypt 1803–1804', *Asian and African Studies* (Bratislava) 23 (1989): 151–77

Sorby, Karol, 'Egypt – the Last Phase of Political Anarchy, 1804–1805', *Asian and African Studies* (Bratislava) 24 (1989): 151–77

Sorby, Karol, 'The Struggle between Great Britain and France to Influence the Character of Government in Egypt 1801–1803', *Asian and African Studies* (Bratislava) 22 (1986): 161–89

Stauth, G. and S. Zubaida (eds.), *Mass Culture, Popular Culture and Social Life in the Middle East,* Frankfurt 1987

Thomas, Lewis V., *A Study of Naima,* New York 1972

Turc, Nicolas, *Chronique d'Egypte* 1798–1804, ed. and trans. Gaston Wiet, Cairo 1950

Wiet, Gaston, see Turc, Nicolas

Winter, Michael, 'The *Ashraf* and *Niqabat al-ashraf* in Egypt in Ottoman and Modern Times', *Asian and African Studies* (journal of the Israel Oriental Society) 19, 1 (1985): 17–41

Winter, Michael, *Egyptian Society under Ottoman Rule* 1517–1798, London 1992

Winter, Michael, *Society and Religion in Early Ottoman Egypt: Studies in the Writings of Abd al-Wahhab al-Sha'rani*, New Brunswick 1982

Zebiri, Kate, *Mahmut Shaltut and Islamic Modernism*, Oxford 1993

Zelondek, Leon, 'The French Revolution in Arabic Literature in the Nineteenth Century', *The Muslim World* 57 (1967): 202–11

Zilfi, Madeline C., *The Politics of Piety. The Ottoman 'Ulema in the Post-Classical Age*, Minneapolis 1988

In search of the true Political Position of the 'Ulama

GLOSSARY

adab · (belles-lettres)

agha · (head of a regiment)

ahl al-bayt · (descendants of the Prophet's family)

aja'ib · (curious incidents)

akhbar · (story, political events)

akhlaq husna · (excellence, superiority, moral perfection)

'alim

amir al-hajj · (commander of the Pilgrimage)

'aqil · (reasonable, understanding, intelligent)

'ardhal · (report, petition)

ashraf · (sg. *sharaf*, claimants of descent from the Prophet and his
        Companions)

a'yan · (local grandees)

bash ikhtiyar · (chief officer of a regiment)

basmalla · (the traditional invocation at the beginning of a manuscript)

bas shagird · (chief clerk)

bayt · (household)

bey · (governor of a sub-province)

bid'a · (blameworthy innovation, heresy)

fadl · (kindliness, superiority, refinement, culture)

faqih · (pl. *fuqaha*; jurisprudent)

fellah · (pl. *fellahin*; peasant)

fiqh · (jurisprudence)

firman · (Ottoman imperial decree)

hadith · (traditions relating to the deeds and utterances of the Prophet as
        recounted by his Companions)

ijaza · (certificate of competence to teach a particular work)

ijtihad · (independent judgement)

iltizam · (tax-farm)

jihad · (Holy War)

jizya · (traditional head tax)

katib al-bahar · (secretary of the spice trade)

kapudan · (admiral)

khabar · (news; pl. *akhbar*. annals)

khalifa · (pl. *khulafa*; caliph, deputy, successor)

khalwa · (solitary retreat)

kharaj · (land tax)

khutba · (Friday sermon)

kiswa · (the covering of the Ka'ba)

INDEX III PLACE NAMES

In search of the true Political Position of the 'Ulama

.